Polemic cannot banish prejudice. Polite explanation backed up by convi

this book in a page

(in case the back-cover is covered by your library)

When two languages cross, they inevitably create misunderstanding. Japanese and English are *exceptionally* far removed, i.e., exotic, to each other. In "direct" translation they not only fail to convey the feeling of the original, but create prejudicial feelings with respect to the original language and those who speak it.

The inability of English to match the simple and unobtrusive honorific prefixes and postfixes of Japanese has resulted in the unnatural use of "honorable" (*"You make us most content/ oh honorable nourishment!"* B.B., 1905) and helped to create the Orientalized image of the Japanese. Likewise, the nature of Japanese syntax, which requires that subjects be stressed, leads Japanese to grossly overestimate the impact of the personal pronoun in English and this has helped to create the image of the egoistic and abrasive Westerner.

Orientalism is not vital to the self-identity of most Occidentals. That may be one reason why our scholars are able to discuss it so matter-of-factly. But, it is not so easy for the Japanese, whose very identity is the antithetical stereotype of the Westerner, to reappraise their *Occidentalism*. Neither is the prejudice (for *Occidentalism* is as biased as *Orientalism*) held by Japanese a matter of pathology or plot, as some Western writers would have it. Given the translations that Japanese constantly encounter, and their understandably mistaken ideas of what it means to speak English, it is perfectly normal for Japanese to feel as they do. Rather, it would be strange if they did *not* feel so!

Polemic cannot banish prejudice. Polite explanation backed up by convincing proof is needed. As the author notes in the text: *A bit of knowledge makes the East* East *and the West* West. *A bit more can put them back together again.*

Robin D. Gill is an American, who began to study Japanese as an adult and published his first seven books in that language while working as an acquisitions editor and translation checker of fine nonfiction for Japanese publishers. While his examples come from the languages he knows best, his argument has broad implications for translation, sociolinguistics and cross-cultural comparison. The essay should inform and entertain all who love words and ideas.

日本人の読者へ

以前から、拙著『英語はこんなにニッポン語』（ちくま文庫）、『反=日本人論』（工作舎）、『誤訳天国』（白水社）他を英語版でも出してみないか、というお話はあったのだが、本の内容は日本人向けで、そのまま英語にしたら、読者のなかに、かえって誤解ないし偏見の種を蒔きかねないと思い、お断りを続けてきた。その一方でこれらの本が代表する我が３０代の仕事を、いや人生を、家族を始め、日本語の世界に縁もゆかりもない母国の人々に紹介したい、という浅ましい心も棄てら れ ず 、 このほどようやく出版の運びとなった。むろん、内容は日本人向けの拙著とは、微妙に異なる。欧米人・英語を批判し、日本人・日本語の擁護する頻度が高くなっている。とは言っても、いつもの辛口毒舌乱調脱線に変わりはないので、小心者要注意！

OrientalismとOccidentalismについて、ひとこと。前者は、古くから東洋に対する西洋人の「偏見」としてよく知られている。現在では、あまたのOrientalismsが存在し、その中には、「東洋」への肯定的オリエンタリズムも多い（モンテーニュらの中国＝合理的政治、エマーソンらのインド＝汎神論、現代美術家の日本＝禅的審美観，など）。
それに対し、後者のOccidentalismは、さほど知られてはいない。かつて、「朝日新聞」の文化欄で、＜西洋への先入観「オキシデンタリズム」＞として、紹介したこともあるが、それは、日本人論（あるいは、イスラム人の自己像など）の裏返しであり、オリエンタリズムと同様に、否定的なものも肯定的なものも見受けられる。相手に対する良い先入観はかまわないが、悪い先入観ないし偏見はやはり困る。この指摘自体はべつに新しくはない。互いにエキゾチックな言語を持つ者のあいだでは、先入観が自然にもしくは必然的に生まれてしまうという仮定のもと、その先入観の発生過程をきちんと理解しなければ偏見を取り除くことも不可能だという実践的なアイディアと提言にこそ、拙論の新味があるのではないかと信じたい。

文化的相対論を口に唱えるにも、人には当然、好きと嫌いがある。それも大事だ。時には、＜年忘狂女に恋す酔心＞（子規）という無分別の喜びを味わうのもいい。だが、やはり分別や差異化もなくては、人間にとって、世界にとって責任あるしかも楽しい文化を創ることはできない。吾輩は、依然として象牙の塔の世界の外から、好きと嫌いを馬鹿にしてではなく、それを大切にしながら、偏見との戦いを続けたい。とは言っても、これ以上はできれば人に任せたい。文化論はもう十分である。言いたいことは全て言った。今は、俳句ばかりやりたい。夕べ、初蚊の羽風を愛しく聴いた。天狗よりも鼻の高い清少納言でさえ閉口させたものゆえ、アリガタヤ、アリガタヤと、独り笑いもした。そう。それが今のこころである。

満腹で朝待つ窓の蚊が何を　　敬愚

ORIENT
AL*ISM*
&
OCCIDENT
AL*ISM*

Is Mistranslating Culture Inevitable?

robin d. gill

道可道
非常道
paraverse press

This is the second book published by paraverse press,
home of truly creative nonfiction, which is to say,
nonfiction that is neither journalism, nor history,
nor how-I-overcame-this-or-that, nor narrative.
Our books will not help you get rich, healthy
or up-to-date. Whatever their subject,
they offer one thing always the same
yet different; and that is ideas,
*"food for thought,
all you can eat!"*

We hope the Library of Congress will help us catalog
someday but, meanwhile, how about this?
Publisher's Cataloging-in-Publication:

Orientalism and Occidentalism
– is the mistranslation of culture inevitable? –
by robin d. gill
(with indices of people cited and ideas)

ISBN# 0-9742618-2-3 (pbk)

1. **Identity – collective -- Japan**
2. **Orientalism -- Occidentalism**
3. **Intercultural communication – stereotypes**
4. **Translation theory – Japanese/English**
5. **Japanese – sociolinguistics**

A corrected 2nd printing (6/2004) of the
1st edition (1/04), printed by Lightning Source
in the United States and United Kingdom. Distributed
by Ingram at least. Amazon and other mail-order stores
should list it within two months of publication.
To learn more, please visit our website, or send a stamped
envelope to: **Paraverse Press / pmb #399 / 260 Crandon
blvd, suite 32 / Key Biscayne, FL 33149-1540**

歪

The atmosphere of the Pacific seems to possess the obnoxious power of throwing above the horizon on either side not only an inverted but a perverted image.

Nitobe Inazo – "The East and the West"
(*The Japanese Nation* (1912))

contents

preface

How an Essay Became a Book

I wrote the main body of this book in 1994, after a total of seventeen years in Japan, mostly spent as an acquisitions editor, translation checker, translator and writer.[1] Two of my seven published books (all written in Japanese) deal specifically with language. One, which might be translated as ENGLISH IS *SO* JAPANESE! (Chikuma Bunko: 1984/1989) is a comprehensive refutation of stereotypes held by Japanese concerning their own language and its antithetical mirror-image, English. The other, MISTRANSLATION PARADISE (Hakusuisha: 1989), shows how preconceptions about the West in general and English in particular are behind the extraordinary amount of mistranslation and bad translation found in Japan.

My original reason for writing the essay "*Orientalism and Occidentalism*" was to have *something* to show my family, for no one in it speaks Japanese – I myself only began to learn it as an adult – and to develop *a style* in English prior to attempting a book. At the same time, I entertained the possibility of producing a publishable article. This last was not to be. Being well-published in a foreign tongue apparently meant nothing to the New York establishment (My mother suggested the "*New Yorker,*" which didn't give me the time of day.) But everyone else I sent the manuscript to *loved it.* Northwest Writing Institute director Kim Stafford, whose nonfiction HAVING EVERYTHING RIGHT (1986) is one of the best books on *place* I have read, wrote:

> "You lead us through delicious nuances in the whole work of travel by the path of language into important mysteries." (letter 21 April, 1996)

James Carrier, head of the department of Anthropology, University of Durham and editor of a book on OCCIDENTALISM (Oxford U.P. 1995), wrote:

> "I found your manuscript both intriguing and closely related to my interests. It is a nice example of practical occidentalism that is also, given the visibility of things Japanese in the West, timely and useful. . . . With a bit of anthropological jargon at the front and back (and cutting down to 10,000 words or so) it is the sort of thing that should find a response from scholarly journals." (letter: 12 September, 1995)

Nothing ever came of this manuscript hopelessly lost somewhere between poetry and anthropology. I am a writer, not a salesman or an academic. Having no desire to waste time selling myself or exchanging good short words for ugly long ones, I put it aside and plunged into research of Edo era (17th and 18th century) haiku and senryu (witty and risqué people-oriented poems). This research continues today and is now my main interest and area of expertise. Indeed, my first book in English has turned out to be not this one but a 480 page monster with almost a thousand haiku about sea cucumber in the original Japanese, with an average of two translations each, for reasons that will be explained in this book.

Recently, I reread parts of *Orientalism & Occidentalism* in preparation for writing a more thorough book on the respectively exotic tongues of Japanese and English. Usually, I find rereading myself tedious at best. Not so for this essay! It was just *too* entertaining. I concluded that it would be a shame to use it like I usually use old material, as a junked car, for parts.

At the same time, I knew that specialists would find my argument insufficient. Two linguists who kindly read it for me wanted *more.* Jan Fornell, the top Swedish translator in Japan, thought my idea that certain linguistic differences were compensated for by other differences so that the same overall psychological effect could be achieved was better expressed by something called "the implicational universal" (I disagree, but should have mentioned the term and explained why my approach is different), while James Unger, head of the East Asian Language and Literature Department at Ohio State University, wondered if I had read this or that author (I *had,* of course, but the article was too long to begin with, so I minimized citations. Besides, I told myself, if Dale – one name mentioned – and others failed to mention *my* earlier work, why should I mention *theirs*? (As it turned out, Dale *did* – see appendix 3 "Picking on the Outsider.")

A piece of writing that reads well twice should not be messed with. Yet, I *do* want to please even the most critical scholar. And I also want to develop ideas found in this essay *here,* rather than leaving them to fester and spill-over into my other book on English and Japanese: EXOTIC TONGUES (2005?). *The solution?* Leave the original alone. It will please the poet in every reader. But add notes. *Lots of notes.* Some with citations to please the scholar, too.

foreword

Is Mistranslating Culture Inevitable?

Distant tongues, by definition, share little. Strictly speaking, they can not be *translated;* there is just too much that cannot be "carried across" the divide. All that the translator can do is *Mind the gap!* [1] as he or she strives to recreate a semblance of the original on the other side. It is impossible to do this without creating *some* misunderstanding. This essay describes how and why it occurs.

If the translator *insists* upon literal translation where no equivalent structure or term can be found, he or she risks creating not only awkward sentences but prejudice among his readership, for such language unintentionally feeds stereotypes about the "East" in the West and "West" in the East. In chapters **I** and **II**, these charges are substantiated with what I call *"the "honorable" problem"* (what happens to Japanese in English) and the *""I" of the monster"* (what happens to English in Japanese) respectively. Then, in chapter **III**, I try to put this *"prejudice in perspective,"* explaining why Occidentalism (mostly uncomplimentary stereotyping of the people and culture of the West),[2] symbolized by the pushy mechanical monster into which we are translated, is now a more serious problem than its far more studied twin, *Orientalism,* perhaps the third most infamous *ism,* (only trailing sexism and racism) in the business. [3]

If, on the other hand, the translator does *not* try to translate the untranslatable, but gives us language so natural that only someone who previously read the original might suppose the words were translated – Venuti's phrase, "the translator's invisibility" is apt – we and our language have no opportunity to recognize difference and grow from the experience. [4] Translation between exotic languages (no language is exotic but in relation to another) is, then, a damned-if-you-do-but-damned-if-you-don't effort. In chapter **IV**, *"The stuffed and the diced,"* I argue that most translators are better *not* trying, because leaving a reader ignorant is better than planting the seeds of prejudice, show why the different grammar of English and Japanese belies any claim to word-for-word translation even in the loosest sense of the term, and criticize the current trend toward an easily read but misleading "diced style" of English-to-Japanese translation. [5]

Anglo-American scholars who have read little of what is written about the West in Japan and less of English in Japanese translation have no idea of the seriousness of the *Occidentalism* problem. They do not understand how prejudice against the West is the reverse side of the Japanese identity – as much part of it as heads and tails of a coin – and ignorantly ask things like: "What is not clear is why the West should be fascinated with what the Japanese think of themselves." (Lynn Revell: *Nihonjinron: Made in the USA* in Phil Hammond ed. CULTURAL DIFFERENCE, MEDIA MEMORIES: Anglo-American Images of Japan: Cassell/ London: 1997) [6] I hope these scholars will seriously consider the implications of the charges made in chapter **V** *"a failure of the imagination;"* and I would suggest that while it is very gracious to hold the West (the scholars' own culture) ultimately responsible for all prejudice, this is itself a form of *Orientalism*, for it fails to acknowledge the contribution – good or bad – of the other.

Written Japanese may take a long time to master, but Chapter **VI**, *"a difficult language, English,"* explains why our native tongue is especially liable to be mistranslated. I go out a limb, perhaps a bit too far, arguing that while we can usually tell when we don't understand something in Japanese, Japanese usually don't know when they don't know English. Moreover, for a number of reasons, Japanese neglect to ask for the help of native speakers even where the need is clear, such as writing down the words to songs which a foreign ear could not possibly pick out. This is sad, but the results are very entertaining and help explain why the answer to Chapter **VII**'s leading question *"Do I complain too much?"* is "No!"

Unaware of the ubiquity of *Occidentalism* in Japanese discourse, Western critics commonly over-react when facing anti-Western or anti-American stereotypes mouthed by Japanese leaders or others whose banalities have the bad luck to come up against a sensitive interest group and receive international press. In chapter **VIII**, *"Occidentalism: the extent of it,"* I argue that censuring individuals for their utterly commonplace statements (Sony's Morita re. our (the Occident's) "never apologizing;" Novelist Kometani re. our (Judeo-Christian) religious intolerance) is not only unfair to them but unfair to us, for we fail to get at the heart of the matter, which is, in a word, a biased worldview that said individuals naively represent.

Orientalism and *Occidentalism* may be expressed in other, less obnoxious contexts. In the case of Japan, "*nihonjinron*," or, "theory/ies of Japaneseness," has long been *the* salient term.[7] Because everything said about Japan implies (and, often makes explicit) the opposite about the West, books about ostensibly Japanese traits are full of *Occidentalism* and, to the extent Japanese identify themselves with the East, self-professed (and proud) *Orientalism*. Moreover, since Japanese tend to identify the West with the rest of the world, and think the rest of the world (including China and Korea) is more Western in mentality than they are – not to mention the fact Japan *is* the first non-Western culture to industrialize and beat a Western power (Russia) in a modern war – the Japanese identify their side of the antithetical East-West stereotype with being "unique."

All cultures are unique. Of course. But my early experience in Japan (1972-3), broad reading, and experience with Japanese teachers in the USA told me Japanese were so hung up on their own uniqueness that it hurt their ability to cope with new developmental and ecological challenges and effectively participate in the international arena. [8] Moreover, I felt the incredible strength and number of Japanese preconceptions concerning "Westerners" or "Americans" stymied personal conversation, and this bothered me. [9] I thought a book deconstructing the *myth of uniqueness* was in order, and spent much of 1976 and 1977 doing research to that end.

Travel writers have long joked about a Japanese penchant for being different, [10] but, as far as I know, it was Edwin O. Reischauer who showed the first serious concern for what I later called "the *unikusa-shindoromu"* (uniqueness syndrome) – an excessive fixation on one's cultural uniqueness on the part of Japanese. He devoted a whole chapter of THE JAPANESE TODAY (1977, expanded in 1988) to the problem. I have yet to see his contribution recognized by a single critic of *nihonjinron*, perhaps because it would complicate their simplistic (=unfair) portrayal of Reischauer as the apologist for US Cold-War policy and, after Benedict, the leading maker or purveyor of stereotypes about Japaneseness. [11]

Most recently, the introspective, self-culpatory bias of our benighted scholars, who find it hard to allow others the right to do wrong, would have us believe that "not only did Western thinking create, mold and color Japanese perceptions of themselves, but the supposed Japanese obsession with their own uniqueness is but another facet of the Western imagination." (Lynn Revell again: *Nihonjinron: Made in the USA,* in CULTURAL DIFFERENCE, MEDIA MEMORIES: 1997) [12]

Anyone who has spent a long time in Japan (or reads a lot in Japanese) knows the problem is real. The only disagreement concerns the extent to which the West shares the perception, and the purpose, if any, served by the "myth of uniqueness." [13] Obviously, then, I would put myself on the same side as Reischauer, Miller, Sugimoto, Mouer, Taylor, Dale and others who have recognized and shown concern for the excessive fixation on uniqueness on the part of Japanese. But, at the same time, I think some of the analysis and criticism of the Japanese found in Miller, Dale and some others is unfair. In a world full of endangered cultures, I feel we need to show a bit more appreciation for difference.[14] Especially when it is so wonderful as the Japanese writing system. Chapter **IX** is written *"in defense of Japanese."*

We cannot help but appreciate our own humanity, the only reality we know from the inside out, more than that of others. [15] Translation, in the final event, requires an infusion of good faith to bridge the gap. Where may we find this? Chapter **X**, *"Songs from Xanadu,"* gives one possibility. It concludes on a poetic note I shall not risk ruining here.

notes

1. Mind the gap! This loud warning is heard at almost every "tube" station in London. Actually, there is little or no horizontal opening (what would be called a "gap" in the USA), but a large difference in height between the train and the platform. The warning is for those getting *off*, whereas, in Japan, the equally ubiquitous warning is, rather, not to take a flying leap (*tobikomi*) *into* the train!

2. Occidentalism. Most readers may be unfamiliar with my use of this term. It will be developed over the course of the essay, so I shall write no more here. A foreword must not spoil the fun.

3. The three ism's. The ranking of the ism's was not surveyed. It is only my impression. Judging from the hundreds if not thousands of boring books on sexism, racism and orientalism published by academic presses, submissions on these subjects are always considered worthy of publication, so long as they are written in proper and politically correct academese.

4. *The Translator's Invisibility* is the main title of "a history of translation" by Lawrence Venuti (Routledge: 95) to which we shall return later.

5. The stuffed and the diced. These are terms I use to describe the translation of English into Japanese. I will explain why "to cut or not to cut" is the dilemma for Japanese translators and the significance this has for Occidentalism.

6. Anglo-American scholars. According to the bio in CULTURAL DIFFERENCE, MEDIA MEMORIES, "Lynn Revell is a doctoral student at the University of Kent at Canterbury" and "has worked for the Commission of Racial Equality, and as a school teacher," and is a contributor to "Marxism, Mysticism and Modern Theory" (Macmillan, 1996). (I should add that Revell's chapter is a brilliant information-filled piece of scholarship based on material available in English. If only she had more experience in Japan and read more widely in Japanese her perspective might be different.) The introductions of most of the nine other contributors to this "unique media project undertaken by academics and working journalists to shed light on the West's long and uneasy relationship with Japan" likewise give little or no information concerning the nature of their expertise on Japan or their fluency in Japanese. For all their fussiness about qualifications and citations, English language academic presses rarely give enough relevant information about their authors. In fact, they usually give less than ordinary presses do in Japan!

7. Nihonjinron: how salient? Revell, correctly pointing out difficulties in defining the genre, debates claims that there was a *Nihonjinron* "boom" in the 1970's and 80's. I would suggest that the genre is hardly so "elusive," for one can ask the clerk in any bookstore in Japan where to find *nihonjinron*. In 1984, TBS Britannica insisted upon naming a book of mine "*Nihonjinron Tanken*," or "*Nihonjinron Exploration*," rather than "The Myth of Uniqueness" or "The Uniqueness Syndrome" as I had wanted. ***i*** They thought (wrongly) the word alone guaranteed sales. I think of *Nihonjinron* as roughly equivalent to our pop psychology (later developing a "new science" branch) and socio-biology, an equally amorphous yet nevertheless real phenomenon. But the ubiquity of *nihonjinron* in Japan must be experienced to be believed. I can remember watching chimpanzees playing in a Kanto (greater Tokyo) area zoo and overhearing one young woman tell another that compared to the very Japanese-like (*ikanimo nihonteki*) mannerisms of the tense hierarchy of the "vertical-society" (*tate-shakai* ***ii***) Japanese monkeys (*Nihon-zaru*: *Macaca sus-cata*), the chimpanzees were as might be expected (*sasuga-ni*) far more easy-going as might be expected from a Western (Africa, too, is West in the sense it is not East) animal. Japanese do not go out and seek *Nihonjinron* in bookstores; *Nihonjinron* is their worldview.

---

i. The myth of uniqueness. The editor felt that the figurative connotations of "myth" (falsehood believed by many people) were not well enough established in the equivalent Japanese word: *shinwa* literally, "god-talk." I disagreed. A uniqueness "complex" would also have been fine. The publishers used the lame subtitle "research on the uniqueness disease" (*unikusabyô no kenkyu*). The incompetent naming and marketing of the book that was supposed to be my best-seller taught me a lot about publishing the hard way.

ii. Tate-shakai (vertical society) is a term invented by Nakane Chie, perhaps the best known cultural anthropologist in Japan. Some scholars from the Kinki area (Osaka, Kobe, Kyoto, Nara) protest that she describes the more militaristic Kanto area (greater Tokyo), whereas the Japan they know and love is more like the Occidental *yoko-shakai* (horizontal society). A younger scholar, especially popular among avant-garde cultural elements, Professor Tanaka Yuko, goes even further than the Kinki-ites. She claims that even Edo (Tokyo's old name) was once full of horizontal ties and that country was so well networked that one might think of the Edo era (1603-1867) as the original Post-Modern society.

---

8. Preoccupation with uniqueness and international debate. "Writing in *The Financial Times* (12/13 August 1995), Betham Hutton argued:

> The Japanese have an entrenched belief in their own uniqueness. This has been used to justify barriers against imported skis (Japanese snow is different), imported beef (Japanese stomachs are different), and imported ideas (Japanese brains are different). (from Hammond and Stirner "Fear and Loathing in the British Press" in Hammond, ed. Ibid.)

What I find remarkable is not the perception of difference per se, (Japanese may well have comparatively smaller stomachs and longer intestines than Europeans and Africans – so what?) but the way it is indeed used to justify protection against foreign products. If, to give another example, foreign rice can not possibly make the proverbial Japanese taste-buds happy, why must its importation be fought tooth and nail? Logically speaking, the fact that foreign things do not meet the taste or needs of the consumer would seem to indicate rather that there would be absolutely no need for a formal import barrier. I ask those academics who would claim that Japanese uniqueness-mongering is a fiction, why, then, such an argument is commonly used as a rhetoric for exclusion by the Japanese even when it is a patently absurd?

9. Personal effect of Occidentalism. Preconceptions can ever so subtly poison the atmosphere. Say that something is broken or missing in your office. If Westerners do not admit wrong-doing (one stereotype) because they live in a dog-eat-dog world (another stereotype), you may find yourself under more than your fair share of suspicion. More generally, anything one says and does may be interpreted as the foreign opinion and not treated on its individual merits. I was called "strange" at my dormitory at Georgetown – not everyone skipped their senior year of high school in favor of Mexico, made etchings and used a switchblade to cut limes for tequila, etc. – but in Japan, anything I did was considered perfectly normal . . . . for a *gaijin.* (foreigner). Needless to say, that hurt my ego. I, who was used to being one-of-a-kind, found myself *a type*. On the other hand, my long years on the outside meant that I never tried to become just one of the crowd in Japan; and, never having tried, did not experience the pain of being rebuffed that makes some good ole boy types bitter.

10. A penchant for being different. See, for example, the page of the cosmopolitan journalist and critic George Mikes' THE LAND OF THE RISING YEN (1970) that follows these perceptive lines:

> I found the Japanese extremely scrutable. This seems to point to the fact that the Japanese are human beings like the rest of us, but they will strongly resent this insinuation. They want to be different."

11. For the record: E. O. Reischauer and uniqueness. Here are the first two lines of a page-long letter dated Jan. 8, 1980, which I received from the kind professor. He was responding to a messy ten-page outline of a partially finished manuscript by a total unknown, whom he had never met:

> I found the outline of your "anti-*Nihonjinron* book" fascinating and the whole concept an admirable one. There is so much nonsense being written on the subject of Japanese uniqueness that a book taking the problems head on would be most welcome.

He even wrote "You may send a copy of this letter to others if you wish to show my reaction to your proposals." Later, with his permission, I used a partial translation of the letter as a preface to one of the three books (*Han-nihonjinron*: Kousakusha) the manuscript branched into by the time three different publishers saw fit to publish me in early 1984. While Reischauer's work may pass along some stereotypes – mostly those, I would argue, with more than a modicum of truth – about the Japanese, it behooves his detractors to admit that he was among the first to see that excessive belief in uniqueness was a problem and elaborate what it means in terms of excessive self-consciousness and feelings of superiority and inferiority with respect to foreigners.

12. Japanese uniqueness – total fiction? In 1585, the Portuguese Jesuit Luis Frois wrote down 611 ways the people and customs of Europe and Japan were opposite. *[i] Japan is different from the West's point of view. It would be strange if this were not so, seeing that the cultures came from opposite sides of the world's largest continent.*[ii] Leaving aside religion-related matters, difference usually did not imply inferiority. Some clearly showed the Japanese in a better light than the Europeans. After all, most Westerners regarded the Japanese as uniquely – unlike other people met on their world voyages – equal or even superior to the West in respect to manners, literacy, goodness and courage. The Japanese agreed about the last trait. They took great pride in being braver than anyone else in the world and this "unconquerable self-respect," (to use Knapp's expression) helped keep them from being over-run by the belligerent West. Moreover, Japanese have long been exceptionally avid regionalists, harping upon and categorizing the unique cultural climate and customs (*fûdo* and *fûzoku*) not to mention dialect, personal character and products of their own countries (Japanese use *kuni* to mean both nation and one's home prefecture). And, finally, a broader cultural nationalism developed in the 1800's which attempted to set-off Japan, as a unique land of the Sun God and of Pure Language, from China, Russia and the Southern barbarians. *[iii] But pride/shame in being *uniquely unique* mostly awaited Japan's second meeting with the West, when the West had become almost synonymous with the world at large (rather than being another China) and identity no longer a matter for scholars but part of the process of modernization. Here is a line from a fine book published in 1896.

> In the case of this unique people, also, there is to be taken into account, not only the principle of inversion [what Chamberlain a few years earlier called "topsy-turvy"], but, likewise, the presence of extraordinary contradictions . . . (Arthur May Knapp: FEUDAL AND MODERN JAPAN)

Japanese had to find an identity in that. To explain how they did so is essentially to give the intellectual history of modern Japan. "Western thinking" *[iv] does indeed have an important role in this history, but that does not change the present situation. The Japanese I have known since my first visit to Japan in the early 1970's have clearly taken over the uniqueness game and made it their own. If it is a fiction, it is more their fiction now than ours.

---

i. Frois. The fact that two pocket book translations of the Frois contrasts sold for decades (and still sell) in Japan, while I am just now introducing it to the English language world may indicate the comparatively greater interest the Japanese have for black and white cultural difference. Paraverse Press will publish a translation with long annotations, ***Topsy-Turvy 1585***, on 21 June, 2004.

ii. Opposite sides of Eurasia. Opposite geography also implies a certain similarity, for both sides of a continent are equally distant from the center. See page 51.

iii. Edo Era nationalism. The movement was by no means limited to a few scholars. Even the rustic "every-man's poet" Issa was quite the nationalist and wrote hundreds of haiku touching upon his nation and the realm of the emperor. (If you read Japanese, see Aoki Michio: ISSA NO JIDAI [issa's time] 88, chapter 6 for the details). And, more surprisingly yet, haiku's bad twin, the vulgar senryu, despite its sacrilegious black humor that extended to the very gods, often boasted about Japan being a uniquely good place to live. Paradoxically, Japan was well primed for its eventual opening by jingoistic rhetoric developed in isolation.

iv. Western thinking: Japanese uniqueness. Media scholars and journalists miss the depth of *Nihonjinron* because they favor new sources in their research. Those who give all the credit (or blame) to Ruth Benedict and other Americans, would do well to read Dale on the Japanization of German nationalism – the "On Identity as Difference" chapter of THE MYTH OF UNIQUENESS. Dale provides ample examples of borrowing from Heidegger and ironically notes, "that

> under the incognito of a 'unique Japanese way of thinking' there often stirs the hidden form of an occidental ethnocentrism all but forgotten in the postwar West. . . . If the real problem posed to the world since the Meiji Restoration is that of 'how Western civilization will be Nipponicized', as Hasegawa thought, then we are tempted to remind him that his enthusiastic vision is second-hand, and all too familiar to those who have read Nietzsche's mockery of the German belief that their unique development would work 'to Germanize the whole of Europe." *[a] (Ibid)

All this is *true*, but it is not *all*. I think Dale is wrong to stigmatize all Japanese reflection on their culture that owes something to, or shows parallels to, ideas found in Germany; and, further, he is wrong to treat all ideas of philosophy other than our radical individualism as "fascist" simply because the fascists made good use of them and because many German intellectuals did indeed sell out. (What is so different with academics who follow the pc line? I think most men everywhere have always been either cowards who follow the latest trends in order to be successful, or naive believers in the latest truths).

---

a. Hasegawa Nyozekan. Perhaps I should add that twenty-odd years ago I read Hasegawa – the very book Dale quotes (THE JAPANESE CHARACTER, trans. John Bester)? – and found much of worth in him. For one, he did not fall for the standard line (already, at that time) about Japanese being especially appreciative of nature. He wrote that Japanese, as a farming people, feared woods as dark scary places and, as poets, failed to see the forest for the trees (or, even the individual falling leaf). He recommended they learn to love nature on a larger scale and introduce wooded parks into the city, as was done in parts of the West. Obviously, this sort of thing is not central to Dale's argument. My point is this: As good as Dale (and his predecessor, R.A. Miller) is, a reader who is not familiar with the work of the people he quotes would come away with a much worse impression of them than they deserve. Hasegawa and many others he summarily cuts are basically fine people, who honestly reflected – and are reflecting today – on their own culture. I wished we had more like them in Anglo-American culture. So, read Dale. But, for heaven's sake, don't *only* read Dale! (I hope Dale, too, agrees with this.)

---

13. Behind the myth of unique uniqueness. Reischauer saw it as an *obsession*; Miller as a *strategy* for regaining pride lost in losing World War II; Sugimoto & Mouer as a *tool* of political control; Taylor as a *burden* ("their profound and agonizing sense of just how different they are."); Dale as a mental *disorder*. I suppose I think of it as an *accident* of history, an ethnocentric defense against Westernization that has taken on a life of its own. Yet, even as I work to ameliorate the excessive uniqueness complex of the Japanese, I salute them for keeping different in a world where *our* way is wrongly considered *the* way. Take this misguided comment on the Japanese calendar system from the most recent Western book on Japan I've read:

> "The *gengo* system is not old. It was started in 1869 as part of the new imperial "tradition." Today it lingers uselessly on, too small a matter to be more than occasionally irksome,

> for one simple reason: Those who govern Japan prefer to keep it. It is one more reminder to Japanese that they must regard themselves as different from others, a nation apart and all the same under their shared timekeeper, the emperor." (Patrick Smith: JAPAN A REINTERPRETATION, Pantheon 1997)

The quote-marks on "tradition" implies the system was invented to back up the newly strengthened position of the emperor. That is right, but also wrong. The *gengo* system is not an artificial creation, but the modification, or rather combination of two traditional methods of dating. In the previous centuries, a *nengo* cycle extending from one major event to another, which might be anything from the completion of a temple to an earthquake and was decided upon by the Emperor coincided with another system more simply following the *dai*, or reign, of the Emperor. The former system using a formally selected two-character name, usually simple and reflecting what was supposed to be the keystone of the era and the latter were, essentially, combined in 1869 to create the *gengo* system (a concept that had been around for hundreds of years, but had not been applied) both because the resetting of the calendar for the *nengo* had become too frequent in the latter half of the Tokugawa period (1603-1867) and to shore up the native system in the face of the West's alternative calendar. By the old *nengo* system, the Showa era would surely have ended with the end of World War II, rather than waiting until the death of Hirohito (posthumously, the "Showa Emperor") in 1989. Perhaps, I should add that the Japanese also have a calendar dating back to some mytho-historical event, but they rarely see fit to use it. They passed their "Y2K " six-hundred and sixty years ago. The idea of the arrow of time is not as unique as we tend to think. The dating backwards, the BC part, is, as far as I know, the only unique part!

More important, it is wrong for Smith to attribute the survival of the old calendar to "those who govern Japan," as if the calendar is enforced from above so Japanese "must" feel different. Most Japanese, like me, may see no reason why a calendar based on the birth of the hero of the religious mythology of one civilization should be allowed to monopolize the time of the world. (Is this, or is it not, the Age of Reason?)

When the Japanese cracked down on the Dutch traders in the late 16th century, they said that they had thought their "Christ" was a different one from that of the Portuguese, whom they had already kicked out, but the "date of Christ's birth over all the doors . . . in the sight of everyone in our land" pretty much gave the jig away. The Dutch were ordered "to demolish forthwith all your dwellings which bear the above-mentioned date (without any exceptions), beginning with the latest built on the north side and so on to the end." (in C.H. Boxer: THE CHRISTIAN CENTURY) I, for one, do not think Japanese are under any obligation to accept Christian dating as a *fait accompli*. We need to find something more universal to date with, rather than forcing others to live in Christian time.

14. **Appreciation of difference.** The reverse side of "we are unique" is "you are different." If Japan were a tiny culture in danger of extinction, one could overlook the largely fictional difference maintained by the selective introduction of appropriate cultural elements (those not liable to create cognitive dissonance) and systematic mistranslation. Every culture has a right to its own delusions that help keep it from succumbing to the pabulum called "global culture." But Japan is a world power and no longer needs to alienate others in order to survive. Consider, if you will, Jared Taylor's children, back from years of being called "*gaijin*!" (a rude word for foreigner unless the foreigner uses it himself --- as a black might use "nigger") in Japan, running about the beach in Hawaii taking revenge, making little Japanese children cry by calling them "*gaijin*!" (SHADOWS OF THE RISING SUN: 1983)

15. **Appreciating our own humanity** (*but not that of others*) Jack Goody writes "they have customs ; we have sentiments" (quoted from memory, I may be a bit off) in THE EAST IN THE WEST. This is true for us, but the Japanese view of the Occidental *they* and Japanese *we* is not merely the reverse of this. The *we* side is the same, for only we, whoever we are, know how deep we are; but the other, the *they* is

different. Though Japanese tend to identify the Occidental with the childish revelation of emotion (a shallow behavior), they – or at least those who write Nihonjinron – do not grant(?) true human significance to it, for they explain us as hyper-rational, acting mechanically from calculations of self-interest, i.e., apparently emotional but *lacking* deep human feeling. In a word, the Japanese opposition, at least versus the Occident, is "they act, we feel." This dichotomy will be detailed later.

I

The Honorable Problem

(orientalism by default)

Compared to Oscar Wilde's obnoxious American child who "from its earliest years . . . spends most of its time in correcting the faults of its father and mother," the children of Japan, described by "Belle Brain!' in a 1905 issue of *Harper's,* behave like angels. [1] Two of the five stanzas in her rhyme include comically Englished samples of what is supposed to be Japanese.

> The little children in Japan
> Don't think of being rude.
> "Oh noble dear Mama" they say
> 'We trust we don't intrude,"
> Instead of rushing into where
> All day their mother combs her hair.
>
> The little children in Japan
> Are fearfully polite;
> They always thank their bread and milk
> Before they take a bite,
> And say, "You make us most content,
> Oh honorable nourishment!"

This is *Orientalism* in a nutshell. On the one hand, the children of Japan are idealized and – imagining the uses this rhyme was put to – dangled over the unruly heads of their American counterparts. As John Steadman shows in his well-balanced analysis of our often contradictory *Orientalisms*, THE MYTH OF ASIA (1969), the West has idealized the East – at least, certain aspects of the East, many of which are found in Japan – as often as it has denigrated it. [2] On the other hand, the words put into the mouths of the Japanese children psychologically belittle their entire culture. *Prejudice, like the proverbial pickaninny, can be very cute.*

Consider the "Japanese" in the verses. "Oh noble dear mama" is, denotatively speaking, not far off the mark. The imagined original may be *"haha-ue-sama,"* where *"haha"* is "mama,"*'ue"* "above", and "*sama*" a formal title (used equally for "sir" or "madam!' in Japanese), or *okachama.*, where the "*o*" is a prefix of respect and the "*cha* " a postfix of diminutive endearment, surrounding the significant "*ka*' of motherhood. [3] Either way, the connotation of the translation would be wrong for two reasons: first, because what, in Japanese, are unobtrusive prefixes and postfixes turn into separate words with a hopelessly strong presence in English; and second, because real Japanese children, like all of us when we speak our own language, use conventional expressions without giving much thought or significance to them. [4] Isn't a three-word transliteration ridiculous for what is, practically speaking, "mama!" (or, perhaps, "dear mama" in 1905?)

The absurd way the children address their food foreshadows the classic Orientalese of Hollywood fifty years later. Japanese do say something before they eat. While GIs memorized it as *eat-a-duck-if-you-must,* the address is but a single word: *itadakimasu*, or "I/we receive/accept!" There are many verbs for receiving in Japanese; this one says it in a humble and grateful manner. The gratefulness is, naturally, for partaking *of* the food and is not, heaven forbid, directed *to* it!

I find the Christian grace too specific, but feel perfectly comfortable with *itadakimasu*: a literal word of grace.[5] Unfortunately, grace, like poetry, is lost in translation, and we are given Orientals who "thank" their food.

"You make us most content/ Oh honorable nourishment." Again, Japanese *do* say something when they finish eating. And, again, the original is a single word (or two, depending on your definition): *Gochisosama-deshita*, where a kernel of meaning *chiso* – or "running-about," is sandwiched between a polite prefix and postfix, then turned past tense. Etymologically speaking, we appreciate the efforts made by the host to gather the food-stuff. "It was a treat" would be more than sufficient a translation. (In case "running about" still seems strange to any readers, let me point out that "treat" originally meant "to drag" and "scrumptious" stingy! To be literal about meanings is to be ridiculous.) [6] I say *more* than sufficient because what is said habitually has less meaning than the more seldom heard "it was a treat" or, for that matter, "thank you for a wonderful meal." Where English has no standard phrase to close a meal, *any* translation must be heavy-handed. *The translator is not a traitor; his language is.*

"Most content" was a standard phrase associated with the "the passive East." Coming from the spiritually inclined, it was meant to be a compliment, from the economically inclined, a criticism; and many, no doubt used it both ways as convenient. With the new "active East" of today, one might expect to find supporting evidence such as the fact that Japanese has a word for "more" but none for "less" bandied about more! [7] It wouldn't be hard to use comparative linguistics to reverse the traditional East-West stereotypes and balance the account (something the author has done in works published in Japanese). [8]

"Oh honorable nourishment!" As all readers know, the adjective "honorable" shares with "humble" the dubious honor of being the most commonly encountered Orientalese atrocity. In a book full of admiration for Japanese cleanliness, patriotism, bravery and intelligence (Japan has always been blessed with many admirers) published circa 1896, the utterly stock phrase *shibaraku o-me-ni kakari-mashita* is Englished: "It is a long time since I hung upon your *honorable* eyelids!" (my italics).[9] Considering the fact that many if not most Japanese eyelids lack a flute, or double edge, and their eyelashes do not curve up, I think this would be a difficult act for even an ant to follow; but sadly enough there are no eyelids in the original (only eyes) and no hanging going on (the verb in question is, like "do" or "get," of very broad usage – "to hang" is but one of *kakaru's* myriad meanings!

Excuse me for playing with a minor work. In defense, let me say that the outlandish character of the "translated" language, brings into relief (albeit comic) a major problem. *The honorable problem.* It is a sad commentary on our culture that this adjective could be appended to things it does not properly belong with, and that the ridiculous language resulting is believed to reflect foreign thinking. That this could pass without contest and be perpetrated by pulp novels and movies, entrenching itself as a stereotype, bespeaks of a warped frame of mind, one that permits us to speak of children thanking their food and men hanging from eyelids. [10]

The irony of it all is that there is no "honorable" as such found in Japanese. The "*o*" or "*go*" prefix is infinitely softer in impact and can, depending upon context, *simply indicate something pertains to the other party* (a directional prefix, perhaps?), or that something is considered precious. Green tea and money are often "*o*"ed, but cats and pencils are not. Some overly precious women affix it to almost everything in sight; many use it almost entirely for communicating what would best be translated simply "you" or "your." In cases where it is normally used, like our "you" or "your," no one gives it much thought; unless one were *not* to use it, in which case the absence would draw attention. The same thing can be said for terms of self-depreciation.

Perhaps we may conclude that the *Orientalization* of far Eastern languages was – and is (Hollywood still uses "honorables" now and then) – *an unconscious act of revenge by the English language* against forms of speech it was and is, unfortunately, incapable of matching.

ch.1 notes

1. Belle Brain's rhyme was found in a short book called THE TRUTH ABOUT JAPAN (Watt ed. 67). The rhyme bears the mark of that charmed window of good style open during the transition from fancy Victorian to plain Modern. The precise issue of Harper's in which it was printed is not given in the book. The "little children" in the poem need qualification. Today, at least, *older* Japanese children were and are on the whole more polite than their American peers; but *preschool children are a different story altogether.* Japanese mothers were the original "Never say "No!" Doctor Spock parents, and their young children have long reflected this total freedom. Many, especially the boys, tend to be rambunctious, if not spoiled, even by liberal American standards. Since the discipline in *buke* (samurai) families (between 5 and 10% of the population) began relatively early, we may assume the poem is really about "children of the samurai." (When BB wrote there were no samurai per se, but a hairdo, swords and title are more easily given up than a tradition of Spartan upbringing.)

Using the Japanese as paradigms of politeness was not Belle Brain's invention. Perhaps she was a student at Vassar in 1894 when the Japanophile Edward Morse (His JAPAN DAY BY DAY and JAPANESE HOMES are among the best books ever written on Japan) lectured "On The Importance of Good Manners." A few excerpts:

> The principal of a young ladies' school in Boston after hearing a lecture on the children of Japan confessed to the lecturer that one of her most difficult tasks was to induce her pupils to say "thank you" and "good morning." . . . [not so in Japan, where it came naturally].
>
> He said to me "do you realize that the behavior of these serving girls in their natural grace and gentle politeness equals, if it does not exceed, the manners of the most gentlewomen of our land?" One awakens to his own deficiencies in such matters by coming into contact with the refined ways of others.
>
> From this universal courtesy, I explained a problem which had long puzzled me. In Tokio and other cities I did not find regions where the more favored classes lived and other quarters inhabited only by the poorest . . . a gentleman could build his house in any part of that great city with absolute certainty that the manners of his children would not be corrupted by the wretchedly poor children of the neighborhood . . . (ibid)

Morse was the first Westerner to lecture on Darwin and Wallace's theory of evolution in Japan, where he had an easier time of it than in the United States with its fundamentalist blockheads. This, however, is tongue-in-cheek:

> . . . we find with the Japanese so many acts of the most unselfish nature blended with their good manners that one might be inclined to believe that the courtesy of the Japanese is a part of their nature . . . With the sharp definition of the classes in feudal times coupled with the dominance of the proud Samurai class over those below, it is possible that those who would not manifest good manners and a kindliness of demeanor have been exterminated and thus by a process of selection the well behaved have survived. Frankness compels me to confess that when confounded by the impertinence of public officials, the flippant serving girl and many other similar kinds of people . . . I have sometimes wished for the power of some selective action to weed out the rude and impertinent from our midst and to do it at once. (Unlike the poor Southern Universities who kindly lent me things for free or a cost-covering charge, rich Harvard made me pay $25. for the loan of this 35 page microfilm! A poor man like me could not research a book like this one if all universities were so heartless!)

2. John Steadman: THE MYTH OF ASIA. Asia, or "the Orient," does not exist. Not only is the reality diverse, but even the popular stereotypes reflect a plural Asia, or *Asias*. On the one hand, there is the gaudy and luxurious Byzantine East, on the other, the subtle Zen or Cha'an aesthetics that coincided with and encouraged modern minimalism. Steadman shows a far deeper understanding of the *natures* of Asian *civilizations* and the complex, even contradictory worldview of the West than Edward Said, whose influential ORIENTALISM reduces the East to the region we call the Near East (Japanese scholars **(i)** tend to consider this part and parcel of the *West* rather than the East) and the Western view of it to one of disrespect and denigration. Moreover, Steadman provides far more insight into the various ways in which cultural difference are exaggerated to generate and re-enforce stereotype than does Said (See "How to Make a Difference" (append.) for sixteen examples of Steadman's "ways" and mine. Yet, I have not found a single citation of Steadman, or even anyone who has read him to date! Can anyone tell me *why* he is ignored and everything is *Said this* and *Said that*? (Add. I am delighted to see he has a small but growing internet presence. I like to think my years of advertising him to people has something to do with this! But, still no citations in books.)

---

i. Near or Middle East as West. The Japanese are not the only ones to draw the line in different places. In a Time-Life book on *Historical India* (1968) published one year before Said and Steadman, Lucille Schulberg writes of the way "India has often puzzled or frustrated Western observers" who "have reported their sense of a vast cultural and psychological distance between India and the West," giving for her example the words of Alberuni, an 11th Century Muslim scholar. After quoting him to the effect that "they differ from us to such a degree as to frighten their children with us," she writes "Many *Westerners* tend to criticize India's differences as shortcomings." She examples the difference with "most *Westerners* adhere to a concept of absolute truth . . . Hindus believe that there are many kinds of truth . . . Indeed, one of Hinduism's objections to Judaism, Christianity and Islam is that they preach one truth for all men" (my italics). So she clearly considers the Near/Middle East part of the Occident. I would only add that some Japanese, go further and put India with its Indo-European languages and argumentative nature (not true for all Indians and the opposite not true for all in the Far East, i.e. Koreans) into the Western half of the world.

---

3. "Mama" in Japanese. While the principle is unaffected, I am not at all confident about my guesses concerning the Japanese term translated "noble dear mama." The reason is that the words used for "mama" in Japan were in the process of changing at the time of the poem and different regions and classes of people still used different terms. The samurai class in Tokyo may still have used "*okakasama*," and the townspeople "*okkasan*." "*Okaasama*" first appeared in primary school books made by the Ministry of Education in the 1890's, when the now conventional term was thoroughly disliked by the townspeople, who called the book introducing it, "the okaasan reader." (Kindaichi Haruhiko: KOTOBA NO SAIJIKI 1973)

4. Conventional Expressions. If conventional expressions are not accompanied by thought when voiced in their original tongue, neither are the overlapping category of conventional lines of rhetoric. This can cause confusion when one unconsciously uses such rhetoric in another language. The Mizutani's (a husband-wife writing team), in their excellent column for students of Japanese published in *"The Japan Times,"* once wrote of a Japanese woman in America who was surprised when her American girlfriends chided her husband and asked her if she was looking for an extramarital affair. The misunderstanding arose because she had been doing a lot of complaining about her husband as is customary when Japanese women get together. Where Americans tend to boast of their spouses, because they assume it will please others to know they are happy, **(i)** Japanese complain, presumably because they do not want to arouse jealousy or hurt the feelings of others in less fortunate circumstances. In Japan, the bitching was taken with a grain of salt, in America, however . . . I shall give no more examples of this type of misunderstanding, as there are many books available concerning the different communication strategies of Americans and Japanese – useful for business, etc. (One of the latest, and perhaps the best, Haru Yamada's DIFFERENT GAMES, DIFFERENT RULES lies on my desk) – I will try to stick with problems resulting from language *itself* rather than "communication strategies" from now on. My reason for introducing this is because the parallel with literal translation is very strong.

---

i. American boasting. The standard Japanese interpretation – what I have read many times, at any rate – of the different American rhetoric does not consider the possibility that boasting will please others. The interpretation is simply that "we Japanese" care about the feelings of others, so we downplay our happiness, while Americans, not thinking at all of the feelings of others, blithely boast about their spouses. That is to say, the difference is fit to the *Nihonjinron* stereotype of the social Japanese versus the individual Occidental.

---

5. Grace in a word. Let me be blunt. Unless you sincerely believe in the Christian (or Jewish, or Moslem) theology, a grace thanking a specific supernatural being or beings seems vulgarly concrete, juvenile and downright barbarian compared to the more subtle relationship with the Cosmos expressed by *"Itadakimasu!"* I simplified a little when I said the word was not directed *to* the food. The thankfulness expressed does *include* thankfulness for the food, in so far that it is life we kill – or have killed – in order for us to live. Feeling grateful for taking this life is, of course, in no way comical. "Thanking food" only sounds funny because we are used to thanking supernatural beings (think how funny *that* sounds to others!)," and because food is something already dead. Now, back in America, I regularly say *"Itadakimasu!"* at the beginning of my meals and *"Gochisosama-deshita!"* at the end. My friends think I am being Japanesey, but that is not true. *I just like the sense of closure.* If English could give me such grace in a word, I would gladly speak in English. But, the Japanese term is indeed a mouth/earful. Could we, perhaps, adopt more familiar sounding (less polysyllabic) terms with similar meaning from *another* language? **(i)** The French at least have *bon apetite* to begin a meal. And, a Croatian friend says they, like Japanese, have something to say at *both* ends of their meals that is not particularly Christian.

***i* Borrowing words from other tongues**. There is a book that attempts to help us do just that: THEY HAVE A WORD FOR IT. Howard Rheingold includes a large Japanese selection, but does *not* list *itadakimasu* or *gochisosama.* He also misses the most useful of all Japanese expressions: *yoroshiku onegai-shimasu,* which basically means, "Please see what you can do to help me on this matter, I'm counting on you!" and is perhaps *the* most common way to close a letter. He does, however, supply a simple adjective which might *sometimes* work as the Japanese participle "o-". He neglects, however, to tell us that this "Chinese honorific *lao* (rhymes with "cow")"**(a)** is written with one character meaning simply "old" (The founder of Taoism, Lao-tsu, for example, translates literally as "old-child," and that amber colored rice wine as "old-wine" and that *lao* is as much about *affection* as it is about respect.) In contemporary Japan, with its cult of the young rivaling that of America – although the emphasis is more on cuteness than on fitness – the same Chinese character is virtually taboo and anything pertaining to the elderly is given the foreign adjective *shiruba,* or "silver." But none of this matters for us. In English, *lao* would only be one more euphemism. We need to do to "old" what African-Americans did to the hitherto denigrated "black." If the former could reclaim its beauty, the latter can reclaim its respect. **(b)**

---

a. Speaking of rhyming cows, the *lao* may be pegged on them or crows for that matter, *anything.* You can find this usage in I.T. Headland's CHINESE MOTHER GOOSE (c.1900), which includes the original Chinese.

b. Rehabilitating words. Rheingold wrote "Perhaps the "gray rights" movement of the 1990's will be marked by your grandpa Tom's insistence upon being addressed as *Lao* Grandpa Tom." I'd say *keep* the "ole" of Ole Bre'er Rabbit and *make it* venerable.

---

6. To transliterate or not to transliterate. Who could disagree with Donald Keene when he writes the following:

> Any translator who attempts to "expand" English with the constructions or expressions of another language exposes himself and, more important, his text to ridicule. "Little grandfather," for example, surely does not seem as cute to a Russian as to ourselves, and "Where is the august umbrella of my honorable father?" is no closer to the Japanese original than Gilbert and Sullivan to the Mikado. The English language is not to be improved by these means: "grandpa" and "where is father's umbrella?" are close enough." ("On Translation" in APPRECIATIONS OF JAPANESE CULTURE.)

I might only add that Russian to Japanese or vice versa would work fine, for "little grandfather" can be handled the same way, with commonly used diminutives in both. In English, we have the diminutive suffix "y" (son/sonny, Jim/jimmy, dog/doggy, etc.) but it doesn't work with many words. "Grandpappy" would sound more like a dialect than a diminutive term of endearment.

7. A language without "less." You might wonder what Japanese translators do for "less" when Alice replies: "You mean I can't have any *less* tea" when she is asked to have *more* although she had not yet had *any*. The answer is she cannot have *"motto-sukunai,"* or "more little." While there is no single word for "less," there are still ways to express it. This is true for most missing words. And, speaking of "missing," Japanese has no such verb, either. You must say you "want" someone or are lonely without them. English, on the other hand, has no single word to express how you feel upon experiencing something that reminds you of a person or a place: *natsukashii!* We must make a sentence of it: "My, that sure brings back memories!" or "It makes me feel nostalgic!"

8. Comparative Linguistics as a Weapon Against Prejudice. I wonder if anyone else has done this or if my efforts in *Eigo wa Konna ni Nihongo* are one-of-a-kind. Glosses are welcome for a later edition.

9. Hung upon your honorable eyelids. In a book on PICTURESQUE EXPRESSIONS, I encountered Knapp's strange eyelids. There is an English idiom *"hang by the eyelids,"* – that, according to the lexicographer "requires no explanation – dating from the latter half of the 17th century. Its definition:

> To have a very slight hold on something, to be just barely attached, to be in a dangerous or precarious position.

While Knapp's 1896 book FEUDAL AND MODERN JAPAN gives a good deal of attention to the "principle of inversion", where the "far Oriental" is pictured as the psychological antipode to us (see his book, or my introductory essay to ***Topsy-Turvy 1585*** on the history of such inversion), this exotic treatment does *not* assume Western superiority, as Edward Said's ORIENTALISM might lead one to expect. Rather, Knapp takes care to explain how

> an analysis of any one of their [ostensibly backward and wrong] methods . . . will show that it possesses manifest advantage over ours.

The fact that "the Japanese saw" (pull-cut saws actually are found as far West as Turkey) which Knapp rightly found to have "superior merit" has only made real inroads into American workshops in the last decade of the twentieth century shows Said is not all wrong either!

10. Wanted: an *honorable* and *humble* history! When Europeans visited Japan in the sixteenth and seventeenth centuries, they were delighted to find that being polite was for all practical purposes part of the grammar of the language because the verbs and particles varied depending on the rank of the other party. "And so," writes Joao Rodrigues S.J.,

> it is impossible to learn the language without at the same time learning to speak with dignity and courtesy." (In Cooper: 65/81) **(i)**

The culture of our world has flipped over, and nowadays this *plus* is considered a *minus*, for Japanese makes it hard to be egalitarian. But, at the same time, we must realize that our ponderous "honorable" ("august/ly") and "humble" adjectives are a poor parody of the real thing. If anyone traces the appearance of these terms in English (and other Western languages) translation or representations of Japanese (and other Far Eastern people), I will be happy to append a summary of your findings to a later edition of this book.

---

i A Language of Courtesy. There are entire books about the honorific and polite usage of Japanese. I will not attempt to introduce it here other than to say that the use of different verbs for different levels of address bears a resemblance to Javanese (see the summation in Peter Farb's WORD PLAY), but is not quite so well developed; yet the system is more complex than that of syntactically related Korean and unrelated Chinese, because a Japanese speaker uses honorifics speaking to his boss but not when speaking about the boss with a third party, while the boss gets the honorifics no matter who is addressed in those tongues. The Japanese argue that one who belongs to a company would in effect be talking up his own side, rather than speaking with the proper modesty. **(a)** This subtlety is lost on many young Japanese. I have heard a young salesman fresh in from the farm use a very polite term to refer to his own boss on the phone and get a lecture for it. If "the American system of address is complicated by the fact that it attempts to do two things at the same time: indicate relative status and also the degree of intimacy felt for the person being addressed," (Farb: Ibid.**(b)** Japanese must also indicate the belongingness of the two parties.

(a.) Japanese *versus* Chinese and Korean. The difference is not so absolute as some Japanese linguists would have it, for Chinese and Koreans use denigrating terms for themselves and their spouses when talking with outsiders but not when talking within the family. In 1902, J.C. Calhoun Newton wrote of the foreigners having difficulty finding –

> a suitable word to apply to their wives so as not to offend the taste of the Japanese, nor violate their own sense of what is due to their wives. As to saying of my head that it simply aches, and of *your honorable* head that it aches or *augustly suffers*, we foreigners have no sort of objection, but when it comes to speaking of our wives as *stupid things*, we must draw the line." (Andrew Watt: 67)

Actually, Japanese uses less of these self-effacing expressions ("stupid-thing" for one's wife, "piglet" for one's child, etc.) than the Koreans and Chinese (at least, traditionally, I wonder about now!). I write "denigrating" and "self-effacing," but for those who use the terms they are not so. *They are simply the proper manner of speaking.* The Inuit have gone much farther than Chinese and Koreans, for they have developed it into a joking rhetoric, where husbands and wives heap whole sentences of what, to us, seem like horrid insults upon their spouse when discussing them before a third party. (See a wonderful article in *National Geographic*: November, 1978).

(b.) "The American system of address." Since we tend to be unconscious of the decorum required in our own tongue, and this makes reports on Asian languages (such as mine above) seem far more exotic than they really are, readers who are not linguists or philologists are advised to read the "Speech Situations" chapter of Peter Farb's WORDPLAY to put the seeming difference in proper perspective.

II

The "I" of the Monster

(Occidentalism by mistake)

Fifteen years ago, I took a course of comparative sociolinguistics from a Japanese visiting professor at the University of Hawaii. We were taught that Japanese use the first-person pronoun far less than English speakers do. This is true, and so obvious to anyone with even a smattering of Japanese that we hardly needed to be shown the evidence – comparative pronoun counts showing, say, 8.7 times more first-person pronouns in your average English language novel, or 10.2 times more in an American playwright's dialogue than that in a Japanese playwright's work.[1] We were also introduced to books and articles by leading linguists who seemed to take great pleasure in evaluating this undeniably enormous difference. To wit: Using the first-person pronoun is against Japanese good taste and moral sensibilities. It sounds pushy, egotistical and is hopelessly wearisome to boot. The more Japanese the Japanese, the more the offensive pronoun is omitted. *Unlike Western people, we prefer understated subtlety to overstated crudeness.* [2]

I was astounded; not so much at the readings but at the fact that our professor seemed to go along with them. How could someone so bright and well-schooled – including over a year of linguistic post-graduate work in the United States – be so naive? I would have expected any linguist worth her salt to look very long and carefully at the *syntax* (differences in overall sentence structure) involved, before making a blind leap from numbers to significance. She did not. [3]

Syntax matters. In Japanese the pronoun must be followed by a post-particle or, at the very least, a pause. It doesn't blend into other words like "I'll", "I'd" or "I'm." Whenever it is used, it stands out in the manner of something linguistics call "marked case" (eg. *I* did it (not him)). [4] That is, like a sore thumb. It, or its post-particle, may immediately be followed by a comma – imagine an "I" set off by a comma! – and is, practically speaking, a phrase or even a dependent clause of its own. *In Japanese, but not in English, "I" is indeed an island.*

What those gloating over Japanese subtlety fail to realize is that they are not really comparing Japanese and English. Their "English" is a monster born through mating the high frequency of pronoun use in English to the high impact of the Japanese pronoun. Had this monster been confined to the narrow reaches of the academic mind, it would probably have been put to sleep long ago; but such is not the case. The monster predates the professors, and is very much alive outside of academia, for it is, to be sure, the image of English held by most Japanese and confirmed by what is called *chokuyaku*, or direct translation. [5] This monster is the linguistic body of "proof" upon which Japanese *Occidentalism* (stereotypes about the West) naturally rides. Until it is slain, the Japanese can not help but be prejudiced with respect to the basic humanity of Western people. [6]

The first-person pronoun is not alone here. The same can be said for all of them. The incommensurability of the second-person pronoun in both languages is even more pronounced, for Japanese syntax dictates that the pronoun appears at the head of the sentence in cases where English allows it to be inconspicuously buried within. Compare the following sentence given in formal and informal style in direct translation into Japanese:

What are you doing?
Anata-wa nani-o yatte-imasuka?

Whachya doing?
Omae, nani yatteru-no?

The difference can be seen at a glance. "You" in Japanese, is the verbal equivalent of the German index finger. Indeed, it is often used to call people – as English speakers use the words "dear," "honey" or a person's name – and Japanese writers on comparative culture who are not aware of the difference in impact in the English and Japanese second-person pronoun occasionally describe an English language conversation as a duel or slugfest! [7] While "I" and "you" in English are much more interchangeable than in Japanese (for this reason few Japanese can master the unconscious art of switching back and forth between "I" and "you" in a purely first-person narrative), the monster says that these two pronouns stand in dualistic opposition, or antagonism, as do those frightfully aggressive creatures who use them. That is, dear reader, us.

If you like irony, there is something amusing in this sad situation. Take the case of Tanizaki Ichiro, my favorite modern Japanese author. [8] Like many other prewar intellectuals, he went through a period of infatuation for all things Western. His works of that time were so packed with pronouns, it's amazing the other words were not pushed off the page. The budding literary stylist creating monsters! Eventually, he came to his senses and to the exquisite mature style we find in his life-statement, INEI-RAISAN (in praise of the obscure).

What Tanizaki did, then, was to create a "Western" fiction, a monster, and then slay it. But nobody in Japan realizes this. They see it as he did, a rebellion against the West, or a return to purely Japanese aesthetic values. Neither he, nor anyone else that I know of, ever understood that his youthful style was not at all Western. This is shown by the way the Japanese judge styles of translation today. *The monster is called a direct translation* and thought to be close to the heart of the original, while good translation is accused of being doctored to suit "Japanese sensibilities." Considering the difference in impact of the words in languages of such different syntax, my point is that a pleasing Japanese style of translation, or "treacherous beauty' as some call it, is actually far closer to the spirit of the original English than the ugly but supposedly faithful monster. [9]

The irony deepens. Given the premise that the monster is a fair approximation of English style, any one with an iota of good sense could not help but look down upon that monstrous language and, by inference, those who use it. Many Japanese, however, are not burdened with good taste; they don't mind pronoun-heavy translation. Indeed, some may even *enjoy* the hard-boiled "foreign" style, deriving a vicarious pleasure in the rude assertiveness or feeling assured that they are reading something authentic. Moreover, monstrous translation has rubbed off on contemporary Japanese literature. There is nothing, mind you, as horrid as the prewar "foreign" style, but the influence shows. *Japanese is slowly monstering itself* and those who think they are on the side of "internationalization" and presume to share my foreign taste are usually tasteless fools, while the Tanizakis who oppose it and believe their tongue and heart to be at odds with mine are mates of my soul, if they but knew it.

ch.2 notes

1. Pronoun counts. I am not going to search for a proper citation. With an incontestably large difference, the details do not matter. The interpretation does.

2. "I" as bad taste. The Japanese playwright and novelist Inoue Hisashi was once invited to Australia. **(i)** In his book on the experience, THE REAL IDENTITY OF JACK (*Jyakku-no-shotai*), he comes up with a scheme for Japanese to make rapid progress in speaking English.

> First of all, we need to throw away our *bidoku* (good taste / etiquette / morality) that has us adjust to our surroundings and refrain from forcing ourselves on others by declaring "*Watashi-wa*" ('I') "*Watashi-wa*" ('I')". **(ii)**

What I translated as "declaring" here is the compound verb *ii-tateru*, or "say-standup." In Japanese, the "I" does not just *come* at the head of the sentence, it must *stand* there and blow its trumpet. Naturally, this makes native speakers of Japanese *"I" shy*, even when they use English, where "I" is not so problematic. It is not, then, their good taste, but their hyper-consciousness regarding pronouns that they must shed to speak English. (Some of this note repeats points made in the main body – but, what the hell, new metaphors are worth almost as much as new ideas. Wittgenstein, a good read for a philosopher, is at least 90% repetition!)

***i* Inoue Hisashi.** His short story collection BURIJITTO BORUDO (Brigitte Bordeaux), was the first entire book I read in Japanese. His "I" "I" quote was used to lead off a chapter on the first-person singular in one of my books. Talk about ingratitude: the book in which I found the quote was a present to me from the author! On top of that, a right-wing magazine (*Shokun!*) gleefully announced that I was making mincemeat of Inoue Hisashi *Dai Sensei* (Great-Teacher) – Inoue is liberal-to-left on all but the matter of rice production where he stands with the farmers against imports – and that reached the ear of his wife just before I called his house to request an *obi* (the belt on a kimono or a book sold in Japan) blurb for my next book. Boy did she give me an earful! How *dare* I sully the name of the Shakespeare of modern Japan, and they had been so kind to me . . . . Luckily, I already had in hand a postcard from the Great-Teacher saying he was delighted with the book!

***ii.* "I" as forcing ourselves upon others.** This concept is by no means Japanese alone. The big "I" is an inviting target for the speakers of other European tongues as well. So long as it was identified with the more reticent English, however, it was only regarded as a typographical oddity, but once Americans began to push their weight around, it became both mark and proof of the West's overbearing ego. Paradoxically, the "I" in English is absolutely necessary for modesty's sake. To start a sentence with "I think" or "As far as I know" rather than a straight declaration, or a statement ascribed to the impersonal "one," is to qualify it so as to allow for difference of opinion. (Japanese has a parallel problem: the sentence may be ended in the active form of "think" *omou* meaning "[I] think [that]," or in the passive form *omowareru,* meaning "is thought [that]. The latter is considered more proper, but I dislike it for the same reason I dislike the English "one.") It is people who pretend to speak for all of us that have an ego problem.

---

3. Our professor. After being so critical, I am not going to name her. She was an admirably enthusiastic teacher and later to co-edit an excellent comparative study on honorific and polite language that showed English had as many or more ways (meaning levels of speech) of asking for a pencil as Japanese.

4. Marked case AND absolute case, etc. My paragraph-long description of "I" as an island in Japanese is fine. But, my linguistic terminology is insufficient. Recently, reading a dictionary of linguist terms, I found this:

> **absolute case:** The case in which a noun is

said to be when it is the subject of a sentence but it is grammatically isolated from the other sentence-elements. (E.g., in Japanese, this case is usually formed by placing the particle *wa* after the noun.)

So, "absolute case" should be added to "marked case" – a word I first encountered in the above-mentioned professor's course. The *wa* is the reason why we see so many "As for~" beginning sentences translated from Japanese by Japanese, or poor translators. What interests me most is the fact – something I *know* by feel – that even without that *wa,* merely placing a subject at the beginning or end of a sentence in Japanese – and that is inevitably where it goes, even for a question – is enough to make it "absolute" in the above meaning of the word. "*Anta, dou omou?"* is every bit as *absolute* as *"Anata-wa, ikaga deshouka?"* (my comma). I suspect linguistics has more terms out there for what I want to say. (A gloss for the next edition, anyone?)

5. Direct translation. I have trouble discussing translation in English for lack of good terms to describe it. This term is my Englishing of *choku-yaku* (direct=straight=close-translation) and means a translation which preserves the words and the word-order of the original, sometimes at the expense of the style and even the meaning. It is more often than not used in a derogatory way and – as you will note from my argument – I think it *should* be. Its antonym, *iyaku* may be transliterated as "meaning-translation" and is supposed to give the intent of the original. This term tends to be viewed in a positive way than its nearest English equivalent, "loose translation." When languages are as different as English and Japanese, the "direct" translation will often throw you for a loop, whereas the "loose" one may be right on the ball. (I am Wittgensteining again.)

6. Cannot help but be prejudiced. As previously noted, most books critical of how Japanese view themselves and others find *motives* behind the prejudice, such as a self-serving national ideology (see Roy Andrew Miller: JAPAN'S MODERN MYTH) or psychological fixation (see Dale: THE MYTH OF JAPANESE UNIQUENESS). **(i)** There is an element of truth to this (and, much the same could be said about our world-view). But there are usually *bona fide* reasons for specific stereotypes; and people are not dogs. It does no good to rub their noses in their prejudice and call them "racist," "ethnocentric," or whatever. The reasons need to identified, taken seriously and proven invalid if we really hope to excise the prejudice. That is what all *my* anti-stereotype books have tried to do. **(ii)**

---

i Miller's book and Dale's. I learned of Professor Miller's book from a friend of a friend of the family, a CIA agent connected with the Embassy in Japan. Miller argues that the Japanese language, being the only thing that "survived intact" and the "only thing that the invading Americans did not have at their command and in abundant supply" came to assume an abnormal importance to the Japanese, some of whom worked and are still working to create – or, rather reinforce (for the roots are pre-War – the myth of the language's uniqueness. While Miller's polemic makes for thrilling reading, he is sometimes unfair with respect to Japanese scholars in his zeal to see a plot where none exists. (See my later comments on Tsunoda and Suzuki.) Dale's book relies heavily on Miller for the discussion of language, but is not confined to it. Still, if I were to recommend a single book written in English to convey the entire scope of Japanese uniqueness-mongering from primatology to psychiatry, it would have to be this one, which, unfortunately, shares Miller's penchant for rudeness.

ii My books. As noted already, I have tried as hard as anyone to help Japanese overcome their fixation on being uniquely unique – we are all, after all, unique. In 1984, I had three books published, each approaching the problem from a different field (language/nature/society). For more information on my books and the Japanese response, visit paraverse.org. But I do not think it helpful to write things like "the obsessive assertion of uniqueness reflects a desire to become father to oneself, and a narcissist complex" or speak of "the *nihonjinron*-inundated world of the Japanese media, which must be cleared and scoured in order to allow for an empirical science to grow upon the ruins of this totalitarian universe." (Dale: 86)

---

7. "I" and "you" as a duel. This perception of "I" and "you" as antagonistic does not come only from direct translation, but from the idea of the West as a dog-eat-dog hyper-individualistic world. "Thinking about Japanese from Japanese," (*Nihongo-kara Nihonjin-o Kangaeru:* Asahi Shinbun (the New York Times of Japan)), Araki Hiroyuki even claims what the West calls *love* is

> but a tenuous truce in the battle of life where existence itself includes the chance of killing the other, within a framework of absolutely uncompromisingly ferocious self-assertion. (Ibid.)

This type of rabid Occidentalism and the monster of direct translation grow big upon each other's feedback. There is, however, a kernel of truth in the Japanese perception of the first and second-person pronoun as antagonistic entities. Because pronouns stand out so strongly *in Japanese*, the first-person pronoun is intrinsically assertive (thumping the chest) and the second-person pronoun intrinsically denigrating (pointing). For proof, consider the fact that the terms – we might even call them euphemisms – used for the first-person in Japanese usually start in humility (*boku*=slave/servant), gradually taking on pushy connotations, while the terms used for the second person (*kisama*=noble-one) become terms of insult. (See the "Words for Self and Others" chapter in Suzuki Takao: WORDS IN CONTEXT (78/86 Kodansha) But, it would be wrong to say this "Japanese" consciousness of pronouns is completely absent in the West. Here is Percival Lowell in 1888:

> The Japanese language is pleasingly destitute of personal pronouns. Not only is the obnoxious "I" conspicuous only by its absence; the objectionable antagonistic "you" is also entirely suppressed, while the intrusive "he" is evidently too much of a third person to be wanted. Such invidious distinctions of identity apparently never thrust their presence upon the simple early Tarter minds. I, you, and he, not being differences due to nature, demanded, to their thinking, no recognition of man. (THE SOUL OF THE EAST: 1888)

Lowell, who – like a Bostonian acquaintance of mine at Georgetown – favored the presumptuous (for it presumes "we" are all with the speaker) "we," himself, was not interested in putting down the West by insulting its pronouns, but proving Japanese were, for better or worse, the world's most impersonal people. He found "this vagueness of expression a freedom not without its charm." The freedom "to speak of yourself as if you were somebody else, choosing mentally for the occasion anyone you may happen to fancy . . ." But, he also realized he was waxing overly poetic, for the next paragraph admits that "Japanese is as easy and as certain of comprehension as English. On ninety occasions out of a hundred, the context at once makes clear the person meant." (Ibid) Eager to find deeper significances, Lowell, like the *nihonjinron* writer failed to catch the relation of syntax to the ellipsis.

8. Not only Tanizaki. The other representative modern novelist in Japan is Natsume Sôseki, who may be found on the 1,000 yen note (much as Dickens is featured on the 10 pound note in England). I remember his famous BOTCHAN (which might be translated "little-master") was aggravatingly full of first-person pronouns. A sentence from his second best known work KOKORO (heart/mind) was quoted in English translation in Smith: 1997.

> It was as though his heart were encrusted with a layer of black lacquer, so thick no warm blood could ever penetrate it. (Seidensticker? (i) 1914/93 Tuttle)

What is remarkable here is that the original Japanese has far more pronouns than the translation! To be precise, in this sentence, *three times* more: "It was as though" is *<u>watashi</u>-ni iwaseru to,* or "If *I* am to say;" the "his" is there (*<u>kare</u>*=he+the possessive case *no*), and the "warm blood" is *<u>watashi</u>-no sosogi kakeyô to suru chinoshio* or "*my* injecting-try blood-tide." In Soseki's case, it is possible the strategy was deliberate; i.e., the more pronouns, the better to emphasize the painful self-consciousness of his young protégé. But I have my doubts.

---

i. Seidensticker? Patrick Smith's Japan: *A Reinterpretation*, published by Pantheon Books (1997), a fine publisher, and has not only proper notes (with page numbers cited) and a bibliography, but a useful chronology (!); yet, as far as I can see, a vital piece of information is missing: the name of the translator of the English translations of various Japanese books cited! If it is proper not to give the name of the translator in a bibliography in the USA, then our bibliographies are improper. The order of the date and the publishers name, etc. and the punctuation used is not important (unless a professor with nothing better to do threatens to fail you for improper style, as happened to me at Georgetown). But, it is harder to translate a book than to write one, so leaving off the translator's name is *wrong*.

---

9. The unfaithful beauty. A couple years after this essay was written, top Russian-Japanese interpreter-translator Yonehara Mari wrote a book titled: THE UNFAITHFUL BEAUTY OR THE CHASTE DOG? (*Fujitsuna Bijo ka Teishuku na Busu ka* Tokuma-shoten = 1994). **(i)** She holds the same opinion I do: the dilemma is a false one. The skill and care that goes into creating beautiful translations means they are usually accurate, while ugly "direct translations" tend to include many mistakes. They are far from chaste by any measure. This is because, first, it is the translator who cannot really comprehend the original who tries to stick close to it for fear of mistranslating (and the existence of idioms whose connotations are far from the denotation means this tactic often backfires); second, because the translator inclined to believe direct translation represents the intent of the author tends to be relatively insensitive; and, third, because of the nature of translation between Indo-European and Japanese, as I will argue at length in the main essay.

---

i. The chaste dog? English lacks a word for "an ugly" [woman]. Japanese has many, most of which are two character words. Yonehara's title uses one of these (*shujo*) and glosses the character with the pronunciation of the more colloquial word *busu.* (It is wonderful the way written Japanese is free to *choose* a word's pronunciation.)

III

Prejudice in Perspective

(a problem of identity)

There is a lesson in this tragicomedy of fawning Easterners and fearsome Westerners. You would expect it to have been learned long ago: superficial linguistic differences result from our shared human nature responding to deeper syntactical differences in order to establish a psychologically acceptable balance which varies far less across cultures than comparative word counts indicate. If the *frequency* of an honorific term or pronoun is 10 times more in culture A than in culture B, you can bet that the *impact* of the same will be 10 times less. Multiply the frequency by the impact and the total effect will be about the same. The very same parts of speech presumably showing how different we are, in broader perspective, may rather prove how very similar we are at heart. [1]

If linguists wanted to do so, this lesson could be empirically grounded easily enough, using a number of languages sharing Japanese and English syntax as closely as possible – at least with respect to its effect upon the pronoun – and the correlation of impact with frequency recorded. Korean is a perfect case in point.[2] While Korea neighbors Japan, you could not find a greater difference in speech styles. You may live in Japan for a year and hardly encounter a single raised voice. But cross that narrow strait and you will hear shouting matches around the clock (Korean gentlemen do not do this, but most of their countrymen and women do). The level of assertiveness is far above that of most white American speakers of English and, I would guess, in excess of the public-debate culture of urban black America. [3] And yet, this is important, these selfsame Korean speakers, just like the shy Japanese, rarely use the first-person pronoun. Why? You guessed it – Korean syntax is almost identical to Japanese. All of the gloating aesthetic and moralistic rhetoric of the Japanese professors of good taste crumble before this single fact.

Someone with knowledge of Japanese and linguistics might find my presentation too simplistic – as I write for the general reader this cannot be helped – and might want to bring in other factors. For example, *avoidance.* [4] Since Japanese has dozens of ways to say "I" (although only a handful in common use in any single dialect), and choosing one is to assert or admit a certain level of relationship with respect to the other party, there is a natural tendency to avoid saying it. [5] This may matter sometimes, but not usually. Japanese are less touchy (*more honest*) about accepting ranked relationships than we (American English speakers) are. My argument, however, is on a different level: what really matters is the unavoidable high impact caused by syntax. Since some degree of social inequality is common to most if not all cultures, high impact pronouns would always have to be avoided and expressed in other ways (indicative prefixes, directional verbs, and so forth), or multiplied into self-denying and self-asserting forms. That is to say "avoidance" is merely a byproduct, or symptom of the syntax.

Another factor, seldom mentioned in this respect, though far more important than avoidance, is the sheer length of modern Japanese. With all the fanfare about haiku and minimalism, you might think Japanese can say a lot in a little. As a rule, the opposite is true. Poems are written in a code of literary trope tied together with abbreviated or special grammar. Old poems rendered into understandable modern Japanese grow anywhere from 1.5 to 5 times longer than the original. Folk songs attempting to communicate a complex story or mixed feelings usually sound like *hayakuchi-kotoba* ("fast-mouth-words," Japanese for a tongue-twister). Translations from English grow from 20% to 40% in length. And all of this is even without a high frequency of pronoun use. Thus, high impact and sentence length both dictate that pronouns not be used. Not using a pronoun requires no explanation. No pronoun is natural. Using one is not. [6]

All of this should be old hat. But it isn't. Why? Three reasons come to mind.

First, there is an ideological obstacle to serious thought found on both sides of the Pacific: *cultural relativism.* It goes without saying that post-Boas relativism beats classic ethnocentrism; and I hold no truck for the late reactionary bloom of the Great Western Cultural Tradition. [7] But *"Thou shalt make no value judgments on cultural differences!"* is an unrealistic and dangerous creed. It is *unrealistic* because, disavowals not withstanding, we *will* form opinions, good and bad, about the object of our study. Denying or repressing such feelings can hardly lead to greater intercultural understanding. And it is *dangerous* because the premise that comparison can be harmless permits scholars to make irresponsible generalizations and publish (especially in Japan) mass-market books full of shallow comparisons that cannot help but increase prejudice. Unless handled with exceptional care, as the old English proverb says, all "comparison is odorous."

Second, the Western scholar is just too damn modest and self-denigrating. He or she is merciless with respect to his/her own culture's *Orientalist* and other racist sins, but tolerant of other cultures' *Occidentalist* drivel. (Note: I do not include here the patriotic ideologue and the Christian fundamentalist, for national conceit and blind faith are beyond the pale. I would only criticize those *worthy* of criticism.) True, there are those who boast the unmatchable greatness of the English language (usually citing the wrong things, like the large and multi-tiered vocabulary – where Japanese is probably superior in this respect) but they are usually restricted to the English department. The general trend is to contrast the hopelessly linear, dualistic or otherwise unattractive aspects of our mother tongue with some ideal language of inherently greater wisdom.[8] No one notes, for example, the fluid character of English where almost any noun can verb and verb can noun, or the relatively high content of what I call built-in onomatopoeia (such as the perfect word "stop").[9] Faced with *Occidentalist* stereotypes about English, most of our "intellectuals" would probably accept them at face value. They will graciously acknowledge the monster as their own.

Third, the Japanese scholar is faced with tremendous cognitive dissonance should he/she challenge the monster, for the Japanese cultural identity rides upon it. In PORTRAITS OF "THE WHITEMAN" (Cambridge, 79), Keith Basso writes: "in all Indian cultures 'The Whiteman' serves as a conspicuous vehicle for conceptions that define . . . what the 'Indian' is not . . . .[10] 'The Whiteman' comes in different versions because 'The Indian' does, and it is just for this reason – that conceptions of the former constitute negative expressions of conceptions of the latter (and vice versa) – that in rendering Whiteman meaningful, 'The Whiteman' renders Indians meaningful as well." The Japanese worldview, likewise, is predicated upon antithetical stereotypes of "the West." [11] Like the Angel-Devil print of Escher, the stereotypes define each other. Should, for example, a Japanese say that his language is ambiguous, he does not mean compared to the tongue of a cat or a Korean, but compared to Western languages. If he says French is clear and logically put together, it goes without saying his own language is *not.* [12]

Compared to the overwhelmingly important role played by *Occidentalism* in Japan (and increasingly in Korea, Singapore, Malaysia, and elsewhere), *Orientalism*, for all its hype, is no big problem for the West. Our identity is not for the most part based upon contrast with Asia, much less the Far East.

This is not to say *Orientalism* is dead. There may be few "honorable" and "humbles" in print today, but there are still too many "cunning" prostitutes and "slavish" wives. The image of the Asian woman, heightened by contrast to feminist ideals and change in the West – a century ago, "slavish" wives were more likely exalted as "faithful" or even "ideal" wives – has retained undesirable *Orientalist* attributes. Asian men, on the other hand, went from the kowtowing Chinaman to the blood-chilling slit-eyed Japanese and Korean soldiers of post-War comic books to the harmless eye-glassed nerd (who, however, might surprise you with his karate).

To the extent that the nerd is "goofy, asexual, effeminate" (Dr. Diane Fujino) [13] in character, he does seem a throwback to the kowtowing Chinaman, but, on the whole, his image lies within the range of ethnic stereotyping long considered essential for the creation of comedy, and is, thus, like himself: *harmless.* If there is any problem, it is with the ground upon which the stereotype is set, the puerile "less-wimpy-than-thou-ism" or "tough-is-cool" attitude of American popular culture, where a gentle superstar apes toughness and snarls *"Just beat it!"*, and even supposedly pacific New Age publications show a pathological attraction for the word "power." That we could be so nerdy as those we laugh at!

As a rule, cultural stereotyping in the United States is a vulgar activity. Pulp is full of it, decent publications have some of it, and academic ones have almost none. This is in marked difference to the case in Japan (and possibly most of the Far East) where *Occidentalist* stereotypes are found equally at all levels of discourse, with the only difference being in the sophistication of the wording. But please do not get me wrong. Though I credit our academics with being less prejudiced than their Japanese colleagues, we have not yet managed to break the back of something I'd call "deep-*Orientalism.*" Remember the "little Japanese children" in the rhyme *Thanking their Bread?* Most attempts to make sense of non-Western belief, even when written with the best of motives, fail to get far beyond this. A complex relationship with spirits of the natural world may still be called "animal worship" – words intended as ecological praise, perhaps, but condescending in their simplicity and misleading for they reduce the complex mind of the person who does not see the Universe in the black and white terms of religion with the big R, to the one-track worshipping mind of the true-believer. I have only read one book that I felt did full justice to the subtlety of the "savage mind" (though that, too, is a misnomer, for there is not *one*): THE APOTHEOSIS OF CAPTAIN COOK by Prof. Gananath Obeyesekere (Princeton Press, 1992).[14]

If we spend more time on *Occidentalism* than *Orientalism* in this essay, it is only because the latter is so well established in the academic world that you even find Japanese criticizing themselves for practicing *Orientalism* against other Asian countries, whereas the former has been ignored precisely because of its far greater importance.[15]

ch.3 notes

1. How very similar we are! The theoretical linguist says: "We already *have* proved just that. There is something called the 'implicational universal,' which says 'if this is true, that probably is, too.' In an SVO language, the subject (or pronoun) tends to be used; in a SOV language, it tends to be dropped. This *explains* your so-called psychological parity." I respond, "No, sir, *my* 'psychological impact' versus 'frequency,' or 'psychological parity' explains *your* correlations. Correlation by itself proves nothing. "Universal Grammar" is behind it? You might as well say God made it so! It is not surprising that such "explanations" do nothing to help correct the mistaken ideas concerning the first and second-person pronouns held by most Japanese, including linguists, while my writing – judging from the reviews, anyway – did. Linguists! Do not ignore the psychology behind the correlations, for it, not grammar *per se,* is the touch of nature that makes all tongues kin.

2. Korean first-person use. The first clear mention of Korean as proof that the subject-less sentence was born of syntax rather than cultural style that I have found is in a book called "Recommending Korean" (*Chosengo-no Susume*: 1983) by Korean-born Watanabe Kilyong and popular linguist Suzuki Takao, who deserves special commendation for confessing that he (and other Japanese linguists) had been remiss not to take Korean into account when writing about this and that feature supposedly unique to Japanese. Would more scholars be so honest! Professor Suzuki's name may already be familiar with readers of Miller and Dale, for he is one of their main bogeymen. Where Suzuki writes a clear essay on the problem of Japanese not accepting Japanese from the mouths of apparent foreigners – many Japanese simply cannot use the natural language when speaking with someone whose face is not similar to theirs – Miller makes it seem as if Suzuki is excusing or even condoning this! And the inflated *rhetoric* ("We must think of the Japanese language as the Nihongo Creed, and spread this new religion of Nihongo throughout the nations of earth." transl. Miller) of Suzuki's pep-talk to a convention of teachers of Japanese-as-a-foreign language is taken for gospel.

3. Assertiveness in perspective. In WORD PLAY, Peter Farb described the different way black and white Americans argue, and how this gives each a bad opinion about the other. In Japan, the tendency to keep quiet was found in *all* classes. The lack of arguments, shouting (and even punching and slapping by boys) even among the poor was observed by the Jesuits Valignano and Frois in the 16th century and again by many Europeans in the 19th century. It would seem that verbal violence was considered as dangerous as physical violence. One can, then, well understand the Japanese aversion to Koreans, and their confusion concerning playful argument, which continues today. To the Japanese, argument is unnatural, something that must be learned. Even Japanese intellectuals professing to like argument, claim that, in the West, children are taught the rules of debate and practice it at school, thus gaining this strange faculty Japanese lack. This, of course, is ridiculous, for the uneducated in the West are often as vocal as the educated. The problem is, rather, that Japanese children in primary school are taught *not* to argue. I find it most telling that even the great Japanophile Edward Morse, in the previously mentioned Vassar address of 1894, could not help but admit a few "absurdities" in the Japanese body politic:

> As an example, it is considered a rudeness, as it is with us to contradict another, but the Japanese consider it rude to have another opinion. The result is that if you express yourself ever so slightly, for instance, that a piece of pottery is old Satsuma, a submissive agreement with this view at once follows, and to the uninformed, endless confusion is the result. ("The Importance of Good Manners." 1895)

Rather than learn Western rules of debate from what some now put down as "an argument culture" (I'd call it litigation-crazy, selfish and dishonest, but not an "argument culture" because true argument is not bad), the Japanese might pay closer attention to the Korean way.

4. Avoidance. Below, an all too typical scholarly explanation of why words meaning "I" and "you" are few and far between in Japanese conversation. While, realizing that "the grammatical structure" enables a speaker to leave out the subject of a sentence because it "can be subsumed in the verb form," yet nevertheless "it is quite possible for someone to introduce a personal pronoun should s/he so desire" for the sake of emphasis" – so far so good – Brian Moeran cannot help going on to dish out (what I consider) the usual sociolinguistic malarkey:

> In general, personal referents are avoided wherever possible because, by so doing, a speaker takes the emphasis off certain individuals and their actions, and so breaks down the divisive opposition that tends to exist between 'self' and 'other.' . . . . . . By avoiding the use of personal referents, they are able to establish a 'selflessness' which contributes greatly to in-group solidarity. (LANGUAGE AND POPULAR CULTURE IN JAPAN: Manchester University Press, 1989)

5. Dozens of I's. Usually, we think of words multiplying because they concern a subject popular to the language-culture. Countless types of snow for Inuit, horses for Mongols, hawks for Arabians, cars for Usanians, etc.. In the case of the Japanese and Korean first-person pronoun, the subject is used much less, yet far more prolific. This anomaly calls for explanation. The prolific Korean essayist Lee O-Young (李御寧) provided a "post-modern" explanation in 1988. He cites a poll by a management expert showing the company was *far* less important in the private lives of American workers than in that of Far Eastern workers, and concludes:

> The level of privacy is different. In the folding-screen cultures [versus the walled-room culture of the West], the individual and the group, I and other, are not opposed and alternate [<u>*takuitsu-teki*</u>]. There is a permeability, circulation, where according to the situation, [the screen / psychological boundaries] it can be opened, closed and moved. The personal referent for the people of the East's three countries [China, Korea, Japan] is not like the absolutely unmoving one of the West, it changes: '*wata(ku)shi, ore, boku* . . .' This isn't saying there is no individual but that . . . (*Furoshiki no Posuto-modan*: Chuokoron 1988 [I have misplaced the date of the articles but Lee's book was published by Chuokoronsha that year, too.])

To Lee, the East is flexible poli-everything, while the West is frozen mono-this-and-that. What the West did to the gods, they did to the self. They impoverished and fixed it. The rich poliverse was cut down to a single "I." Maybe the question should not be why Japanese has so many "I's" but why *we* have only one self-referent. Moeran writes:

> The fact that Japanese children are taught to master about half a dozen terms of self-reference by the age of six, and that none of the options available is dominant, reveals how early the flexible nature of 'personhood' or 'self' is encouraged in Japanese society (*cf.* Smith 1983: 79). (Moeran:89)

I do not feel the use of different self-referents makes much difference to the development of the self, except in so far that ambivalence about using such terms – which make all too clear the nature of a relationship one might not be happy with – may make the speaker *more self-conscious* and increase, rather than decrease, the psychological distance between the parties involved. I believe that the abundant diary and first-person literature **(i)** not to mention the "nobody-could-possibly-understand-me" syndrome that runs riot in Japan – It seems every other drama on television concerns problems caused by the inability of people to open up to their friends and tell them what's the matter! – make nonsense of claims that the solitary individual is a Western thing. **(ii)** On this point, I am not alone. In his 197_ book NIHONJIN-NO-SHINJO, Sato Tadao argues that this "terrible solitude" (*hidoi kodokusa*) is at the very heart of the Japanese character. What is new in my argument is the hypothesis that the syntax found in Japanese and Korean, by making self-reference an all-or-nothing choice, may contribute to that hyperconsciousness.

(i) Diary literature in Japan. Donald Keene, who was later to write a book on the Japanese diary serialized in *Asahi Shinbun,* noted in his APPRECIATIONS OF JAPANESE CULTURE that the fondness for keeping diaries "dates back to the Heian period." That is to say, as soon as Japanese began to write, they wrote about themselves! He also notes that they did so and still do so despite the danger that is often involved in exposing one's thought. ""I shall have to be careful" wrote Takami Jun as he began what was to develop into a 3,000 page diary for 1945 alone!"

(ii) Dostoevsky's UNDERGROUND MAN, i.e., the hyper-sensitive paranoid type, with fear of eye-contact, body-smell, etc. is said to be far more common in Japan than America.

---

6. *Not* using a pronoun requires no explanation. The same thing can be said for the subject in general. The length of Japanese and the way the subject is emphasized merely by being stated makes it only natural to omit it. The *Nihonjinron* understanding has been closer to the following explanation by Japanese historian of philosophy Nakamura Hajime:

> "That the Japanese people can dispense with the subject in their linguistic expression is due to the fact that the intuitive understanding of the scene referred to in their discourse is usually attained beforehand by their close bonds and nexus with others."

To me, this is so much bullshit!

7. Great Western Tradition. I like the idea of having people learn their own roots. And that goes for white Indo-Europeans, too. The problem with Great Books courses is that they fail to take sufficient account of non-Western civilizations. so students end up with a warped world-view.

8. Self-denigrating Western scholars. I will give many examples (quotations) in a book EXOTIC TONGUES (2005?) Commonly, a writer reflecting on the separation of humans and the natural world, i.e., the fragmentation of Western identity contrasts one or two good aspects of an idealized Eastern or Native American language with the sorry reality of a Western language. Such contrasts tend to be naïve at best. Depending upon what aspects are chosen any language can be shown to be more or less close to nature or wholistic, etc. than another.

9. Built-in Onomatopoeia No dictionary would call the word "stop" a mimetic term, but the fact is that the "s" with its movement, followed by the friction/breaking "t" against the teeth followed by the powerful final "p" is about as onomatopoetic as a word can be. Compared to the Japanese "*tomare*" and the Japanese word seems as good as dead. I argue, as Australian (by now, possibly Japanese) Roger Pulvers (JAPANESE TURNED INSIDE OUT) once did, Frank Harris (1855-1931) in his MY LIVES AND LOVES, and Salvador de Madariaga ("And what could suggest a more peremptory obstacle than stop?") in ENGLISHMEN, FRENCHMEN AND SPANIARDS (1928) did long ago, that English is particularly full of such built-in mimesis. Japanese, on the other hand is blessed with a plethora of mimetic adverbs English lacks.

10. What the Indian is not. What is said about the Amerindian view*s* of the Whiteman not only applies to Asian views of the West, but how various countries see the Japanese. Harumi Befu neglects to mention Basso's book in his otherwise thorough introduction to Joseph Kreiner ed. OTHERNESS OF JAPAN: History and Cultural Influences on Japanese Studies in Ten Countries, where he writes:

> To individualistic Americans, Japanese seem group-oriented, and the group phenomenon defines the problematics for Americans. To Koreans, however, I wonder if Japanese groupiness is an issue.

Exactly. Unfortunately, the book's selections do not even *begin* to answer Befu's many fine questions.

11. Antithetical stereotypes. "Theoretically, any Japanese phenomenon is natural grist for the uniqueness mill, and is presumed not to exist elsewhere by virtue of the fact it exists in Japan." writes Dale (1986/8). *Absolutely.* I cannot remember how the discussion started, but I can remember an astounded Japanese man saying "You mean to say that you Americans have wet dreams too!" If Americans tend to assume universality, Japanese tend to assume peculiarity. Occidentalism works hand in hand with uniqueness-mongering because most of the world is not as far removed from Japan as the Far West in general, and America in particular. In other words, "elsewhere" means the West, and the part of the West most different from Japan at that. (I cannot imagine a Japanese being surprised to learn another Asian had a wet dream.) That is why I have written with only slight exaggeration that, for all the writing on the subject, there is no *comparative* (*hikaku*) culture in Japan. **(i)** There is only *contrastive* (*taishô*) culture, or contrastive anthropology. **(ii)** Let me hazard a list of stereotyped contrasts between "we Japanese" and "them Westerners." (Qualifications: the asterisk-marked items are sometimes reversed. For example, the Japanese may see Occidentals as generally more easy-going and less repressed than they themselves are, but if they were to think of fundamentalist Christians, the contrast might reverse.).

We Japanese	*Them* Westerners
emotion	reason
complex emotion	simple emotion
repressed emotion	violent emotion
alogical	logical
analogical	digital
software	hardware
fuzzy	exact
ambiguous	clear
human	machine-like
polyvalent	dualistic
polytheist	monotheist
animistic	Cartesian
nature-following	nature-fighting
vegetarians	carnivores
farmers	nomads
villagers	cosmopolitans
wet	dry
connected	separate
repressed	easy-going*
synergetic	antagonistic
dependent	independent
interdependent	independent
trusting	untrusting
humble	boastful
tolerant*	intolerant*
forgiving	vindictive
considerate	pushy
gentle	rough
pacific	aggressive
pulling	pushing/hitting
social harmony	social warfare
group-oriented	individualistic
feminine	masculine
responsible *	childish *
disciplined	wild
sensitive	crude
diligent	lazy
natural	artificial
soft	harsh
average	exceptional

Some of these pairs may not make much sense to the reader.

"Alogical and Logical" may require a bit of explanation. Shortly after World War II, when the Japanese had lost self-confidence, the contrast was "Illogical and Logical," but as Japanese came to feel that their culture was better in many, if not most ways than that of the West (this came to be true in the 1970's), "illogical" changed to "alogical," which is to say something beyond, and superior to mere logic rather than something inferior to it.

"Wet and Dry" means having soft-edged and ever-so-human sensitivity versus operating in a brusque matter-of-fact way letting nothing phase you deep-down. *Wet* at its worst can be melodramatic, while dry at its worst can be heartless.

"Average and Exceptional" refers to two things, the perceived lack of diversity in Japan versus the greater range in human types abroad=America(?) and the tendency of Japanese to identify with being average, supposedly with greater frequency than is the case in the USA. In journalistic terms, this

means America has many geniuses and people with extreme wealth but also many unintelligent and poor people, whereas the Japanese with few from either end of the spectrum, enjoy a peaceful, happy medium.

(i) Comparative culture in Japan. My books do include what little true comparison I can find. Umesao Tadao's Ecologicohistorical View of Civilization (*bunmei-no setaishi-kan:1974*) argues that Japan shares a common history with the Far West: at the fringe of the continent, both are able to escape much of the continual forced migrations and conflict, which periodically return all too many cultures to scratch, and build a thicker topsoil of culture. Secure, they are better able to actively seek out and copy other cultures – Japan was active on the high seas prior to the closing and was not really closed even when it was supposed to be – and incorporate this into their growth. (Not knowing of Umesao's work, I had independently come up with the same idea, although my main focus was on aesthetics. Luckily, I found Umesao's more thorough work and cite it in my ANTI-JAPANOLOGY (*han-nihonjinron*: 1984).) At the turn of the century, Nitobe Inazo pulled out no stops to find similarities in Japanese and Western tradition (Roman soldiers falling on their swords for *harakiri*, etc.). Today, scholars in Japan carp on the inaccuracies in BUSHIDO, forgetting the purpose of the book was to make friends for Japan in the West, which it certainly did (I credit Nitobe for TR's enthusiasm which helped in the settlement of the war Japan won with Russia and H.G. Wells's A MODERN UTOPIA, where samurai, as the modern embodiment of chivalry and service, administrate the world.). Nitobe was hardly as naive as they think. His essay "The East and the West" in THE JAPANESE NATION (1912) shows he *chose* to emphasize similarity:

> No small pains are taken to discover points of difference between East and West, and of these, there are many, especially of the superficial sort; but the very fact that attempts are made to discover differences, takes points of resemblance for granted. When I listen to the analysis of Japanese character and institutions by a hypercritical foreigner – and *vice versa* for that matter – I am reminded of an anatomist who dissects a woman's corpse and eruditely arrays all the points wherein she differs from man, and would lead us to the inevitable conclusion that man and woman are so irreconcilably opposed in every single aspect that the two could never be one.

I only went beyond BUSHIDO because of my interest in Carlyle's SARTOR RESARTUS, which Nitobe translated; but that is another story. In the fourth edition of my 1984 book (1991), I cited his fine challenge to the concept of island cultures as *insular*. He should be, but never is (as far as I know) cited by those who, since the late seventies, have been concerned with the bias for difference in Japanology (Befu Harumi, Ross Mouer, Sugimoto Yoshio, etc.). Lest anyone think that cultural reflection is a twentieth century discovery that came with hard-to-read deconstructionism, another quote from Nitobe:

> Every oddity in manners, every idiosyncrasy in thought is magnified into a distinguishing characteristic of the East or of the West, as the case may be; either way, most often for the Pharisaical [Said would not like this adjective!] purpose of self-exaltation. The very faults that are common to both, are deemed particularly blameworthy when committed by the other race. The atmosphere of the Pacific seems to possess the obnoxious power of throwing above the horizon on either side not only an inverted but a perverted image. (Ibid.)

ii Comparative and contrastive culture Not *hikaku-bunkaron*, but *taisho-bunkaron*. The point is made in all three Gill (84,85) books. I might have translated the *bunkaron* as "culturology" rather than simply "culture," but "cultural *anthropology*" is no option, because most of the writing my work deals with is pop-scholarship and has too little discipline to merit the academic term.

---

13. Image of Orientals in the US. Back in the States after 20 years in Japan, I find two points insufficiently developed in my brief overview. First, South-east and Far-east Asia now have a monopoly on the word "Oriental." (India is just India and the Middle or Near East is the Middle East.) But, at the same time, Cambodian, Chinese, Korean, Japanese, Thai, Vietnamese and other Far Eastern cuisine, clothing and such are all put into a single bogus "Oriental" category by our common culture. It is fine that small "Oriental food stores" can offer food from more than one culinary tradition, but Americans who would not call *pasta* "European" but Italian, should, by now, know better than to talk loosely of "Oriental" this and "Oriental" that (unless, like the pull-saw, the items are really is common to all of Asia (but, I find the saws are considered Japanese, rather than "Oriental."). Second, Japan's image changed. The *economic animal*, which bears some resemblance to the older view of oriental immigrants working too hard and taking-over California (even while the "passive East" stereotype remained in full force) mutated into something worse: *the un-ecological boogeyman eating up timber and whales.* Such criticism falls flat, coming from people who use twice the energy/resources per capita of the Japanese yet support big cars as national policy and think of "flyer miles" as something to be proud of and will not even pass a decent gas tax! At least, our national hypocrisy has little to do with Orientalism. (Two years later, I find we hear little about Japan, since the Japanese economy has weakened. No doubt China, with its growing surplus will be our next boogyman).

If I write little about the image of the Japanese in the West in this book, it is because there has been more written on it than of the vice-versa. Perhaps the best is Jean-Pierre Lehmann: THE IMAGE OF JAPAN (GA&U:1978) which treats "our" ambivalent feelings toward modernizing Japan (1850-1905). Ian Littlewood's more recent (S&W:1996) THE IDEA OF JAPAN fills in the twentieth century as well. Donald Richie's review (*Japan Times,* June 4, 1996) ends on just the right note:

> "Such a book on the Japanese idea of, say, the United States would be an interesting volume. But in the meantime everyone here (in Japan) ought to read this one."

14. Gananath Obeyesekere's Book An anthropologist friend told me that THE APOTHEOSIS OF CAPTAIN COOK was torn apart (for misreadings, false citations, unfair criticism, etc.) in reviews and advised me *to cut all mention of the book* from my essay lest scholars wonder about *my* judgment. Come on! Even if Prof O may have played hard and loose with some facts and created what amounts to a straw man, I think the straw man is not all straw and the book is worth a read. I think it more than enough to add this note as a *caveat lectore.* Checking on more recent developments, I notice Princeton did see fit to reissue the book with a lengthy *Afterword* addressing Marshall Sahlin's book-length response (HOW 'NATIVE'S' THINK) to it. I have not yet had the opportunity to read Sahlin's criticism or Obeyesekere's response.

15. Occidentalism: ignored for its greater importance. I fear I have been a bit too kind to Japanese academia. The difficulty of messing around with something so fundamental to their identity as Japanese partially explains their reticence, but scholarly sloth is just as important. Academics, like other mortals, jump on the bandwagon and ride what's hot. Orientalism has been a politically correct discipline for decades, while *Occidentalism* is only beginning to get recognition. In Japan, the concept is so new I failed to get the word into the title of a feature published in *Chuokoron* (my reply to Lee O-Young's *Furoshiki Post-modern* article: see pg 103-4) in 1988 (I did get it into the text toward the end of the article; and, in 1990, convinced *Asahi Shinbun* to use it in the title of my half-page essay: *Seiyô e no sennyûkan "okishisentarizumu"*(prejudice against the West: Occidentalism 1990/5/9 *bunka* page). There are, however, numerous newspaper articles warning of overdoing "West-bashing" on the part of Malaysians, Singaporeans and Chinese journalists.

The only sustained serious reflection upon Occidentalism to come from the East that I know of is the study by Xiaomei Chen, which shows that,

> In China – and perhaps elsewhere – Orientalism has been accompanied by instances of what might be termed

> *Occidentalism,* a discursive practice that, by constructing its Western Other, has allowed the Orient to participate actively and with indigenous creativity in the process of self-appropriation, even after being appropriated and constructed by Western Others. (OCCIDENTALISM: A Theory of Counter-Discourse in Post-Mao China; OUP 1995)

If "Orientalism, in Said's account, is a strategy for world domination," Chinese Occidentalism mostly serves competing domestic aims; i.e., the government uses it to oppress political opponents while critics evoke it in support of change. "As such, it is both a discourse of oppression and a discourse of liberation." She calls the latter "anti-official Occidentalism." Her basic tenant is that liberation, like the Establishment enemy, is ambidextrous:

> The leftist claims that are so frequently voiced in the West, no matter how positive a role they have or might play in the West in bringing about social changes, do not necessarily appeal to the contemporary Chinese generation oppressed by the leftist ideology. (Ibid.)

> . . . in many instances, being politically "correct" in the West might be at the same time politically "incorrect" in the East, where a totalitarian regime posits the West – or any form of "Other" – as antithetical to its dominant power. (Ibid.)

This is all too obvious. I only quote at length because it would seem this type of political validation is necessary to make academia look at Occidentalism, in the broad sense of the word used in this essay (as opposed to narrow meanings such as a style of art, or unneeded meanings such as Western ethnocentrism). Other than a categorical complaint that the "essentialist claim" that the "West is by nature or definition monolithically imperialistic" over all its history and the accompanying assumption that ""Oriental" cultures have never been imperialistic, or that they have only learned their "imperialism" from the West" is mistaken, Chen does not contest details of the content of Occidentalism.**(iii)** For this, in English, we mostly have the anti *Nihonjinron* literature I have already mentioned or will mention in this book, and some more general work of four basic types: 1) giving examples of views of the West and Westerners held by non-Western cultures, **(iv)** 2) challenging what might be called *myths of Western uniqueness,* **(v)** 3) showing the not inconsiderable influence of the East on the West, **(vi)** and 4) challenging stereotypes of the East or parts of it. **(vii)**

---

i The academic bandwagon. In OCCIDENTALISM, Chen writes:

> Western theoreticians – especially those 'Third-World-born' critics residing in the West – who speak of liberating the 'Third World' from the West's economic and political power – need to be more cautious in their claims, lest they unwittingly and unintentionally themselves become neocolonializers who exploit the cultural capital of the colonialized in a process in which those voices are appropriated for reinvestment in those 'banks' of the West that currently offer the highest rate of return to speculators in trendy academic markets. (Chen: Ibid.)

Chen's "bank" metaphor is well-taken. Too bad she had to write in the trendy French style of "discourse" that *diss*es our native tongue, and that the bulk of her book – all my quotes come from the best part, the Introduction – is (to my mind) the type of (boring) literary criticism loved by academic presses.

ii Chinese journalists. I have known only two people, one Swedish and one Chinese, who habitually responded to *anything* I said with a "No," to begin their sentence, even when they actually agreed with me! This is, of course, the opposite of the Japanese speech mannerism of saying "Yes, yes" (*hai, hai)* or "uh-huh, uh-huh" *(un, un)* regardless of the content of the other's statement! I wonder if there are many such contrary Chinese, and whether it would help explain their marvelous ability to criticize themselves. A few lines from a 1992 article by Tan Cheng Sun, "Cultural superiority goes before fall."

> Because of our frequent use of Western societies as negative examples, in addition to the fact we like to stress the merits of Oriental societies and Oriental thought, I notice that a 'superiority complex' and a 'great Chinese mentality' are beginning to manifest themselves in the Chinese community causing them to despise and reject all things Western. . . . //Their [the Chinese-dominated mass media of Singapore] reaction to reports of Greek seamen abandoning ship as the Royal Pacific began to sink was that it was the natural consequences of Western individualism and cultural tradition. Yet how do we account for the heroic acts of some Australian crew members who remained on board to help the passengers? . . . // We used to criticize Westerners for judging the Third World, particularly Asian societies, with a sense of superiority and in light of their own standards of morality and democracy. Now, are we not making the same mistake of treating others with a sense of superiority and prejudice? (*The Japan Times* Oct. 22, byline "*Strait Times*, Singapore" first published in "*Lianhe Zaobao*" Sept. 19)

iii. Content of Occidentalism in China. Chen does mention Mao's equation of the West with the City, and the East as Third World, with the Country. (In that case, *country and western* music might be the perfect way to break the ice.) But the broader popular images of East and West are not developed very far. Her notes, however, mention a collection of Chinese observations on America, and by extension the Occident: LAND WITHOUT GHOSTS – Chinese Impressions of America from the Mid-Nineteeenth Century to the Present. (U of California Press: 1989), edited by R. David Arkush and Leo O. Lee. I recommend it. Many of the selections are a fine read.

iv. The *first* way to approach Occidentalism is to note how others describe Occidentals. Examples I have read are Basso: IMAGES OF WHITEMAN and James Carrier ed. OCCIDENTALISM – Images of the West (Oxford U P: 1995 – same main title, same year, same publisher as Chen's book!). The former book works well, for one author concentrates on native Americans. The latter book reads like what it is, a disparate collection of talks and papers. Carrier's own chapter ("Maussian Occidentalism: Gift and Commodity Systems") has one fine line, I *must* quote:

> "what is critical sauce for the Muslim goose is likewise sauce for the capitalist Occidental gander."

And the chapter on "The Other in Japanese Advertising" by Millie R. Creighton is remarkably jargon free. Her fine presentation of the *gaijin,* a social construction" that "denies the individual uniqueness of Westerners, transforming all caucasians into an essentialized category that reduces the complex variations among them" is old hat to me, but will be new to Western readers who might not be aware that in Japan it has long been acceptable to use nude caucasians but not nude Japanese in advertisements. And she has something literary criticism neglects, good primary fieldwork:

> Commenting on the common usage of naked or near-naked *gaijin* women in advertisements, the librarian of Osaka Dentsu's advertising library says, "ads can't use Japanese women for such love scenes because it is too realistic, so *gaijin* are used." (Ibid.)

Carrier's book is a better introduction to Occidentalism than Chen's rather narrowly focused work, but it only hints of what we need: a carefully selected, more limited "Images of the West in Japan" or, at most, "in the Far East" (or, wherever) anthology. If the whole non-Western world is open for contributors, as with Carrier's book, the essays should attack a common theme – such as images of the West in advertising, newspaper editorials, best-selling non-fiction, as surveyed, etc. – in order for the whole to gain something not found in the parts: intercultural significance.

v. The *second* way to approach Occidentalism is to question myths of Western uniqueness – the West as home to a unique rationality and respect for the individual, etc.. Here, readers with a philosophical /sociological/ anthropological bent might best see Jack Goody: THE EAST IN THE WEST (Cambridge: 1996). He shows many of the "institutions" that were supposed to prevent modernization in the East were found in the West. "Our" family, labor, bookkeeping, not to mention rationality, were not so different from "theirs." I cannot think of another book like Goody's, perhaps because it is easier to lambaste prejudice, than challenge the suppositions.

A comment additional to my reading copy edition of January 2004: The myths Goody undermines belong to what might be called the "positive Occidentalism" (what supposedly made/makes West *superior*) that forms the reverse side, i.e. backing for "negative orientalism" (what supposedly makes East *inferior*). My work published in Japanese, generally uses the same approach (finding the East in the West and vice-versa, but with less primary research, I fear) to undermine the "negative Occidentalism" (what supposedly makes the West *inferior*) that provides the backing for "positive Orientalism" (what supposedly makes the East=Japan *superior*). That is to say, his work is largely a defense of the Orient (not so much for that purpose as to provide the perspective needed to truly understand development), while mine is largely a defense of the Occident (not so much for that purpose as to help Japanese overcome an unproductive worldview and, hopefully, create something new that was not based on reaction). I do not deal with the equation of the Occident with the (corrupt) City – as broached by Chen and further developed by Ian Buruma & Avishai Margalit in their recent *Occidentalism: The West in the Eyes of Its Enemies* (2004), for Japanese are as urban if not more urban than Occidentals and do not contrast the East-West in Country vs City terms. Buruma & Margalit's approach is closer to the first way, i.e. pointing out *how others describe the West*, but by stressing the fact that the West itself largely invented this Occidentalism themselves – as Miller and Dale have done attacking *Nihonjinron* – they indirectly cast doubt on the purity(?) of Islamic Occidentalism. I would not, however, have jumped from Babylon of the Bible and the Rome of Juvenal's satire to the romantic anti-urban romanticism and spiritualism of the Germans and the Russians quite so rapidly (Ah, but what a fine summary of Slavophilic Occidentalism! A book in a chapter!) Surely, the image of giant corrupt cities to the East (Constantinople = the Byzantine) – a factor behind "our" Crusades and the Conquest and destruction of Cities in the Americas in the Age of Exploration – long held by most of the West deserved a chapter. That is to say, our *Orientalism* also eventually bounced back as Occidentalism.

---

vi. The *third* way to approach Occidentalism is to show how much the East has influenced the West historically, thereby qualifying the occidentality of the Occident. While the idea of the West being the borrower is hardly new – McNeil's classic *Rise of the West* emphasizes the readiness of the West to take ideas from anywhere on the eve of its industrial development – the fact that Orientalism tends to make the East a victim, or a passive player even while it claims to support its cause – makes it all the more important to show that the West was not always the teacher. This has been done for science and technology by Needham and for fine art by a number of people (I have seen several good books but cannot recall their names.) A general reappraisal of the arts by John MacKenzie: ORIENTALISM – History, theory and the arts (1995), concluded that "the western approaches to the Orient have been much more ambiguous and genuinely interactive than Said allowed." (from publicity). He accuses critiques of Orientalism of "reading back . . contemporary attitudes and prejudices into historical periods" thereby "creating a monolithic and binary vision of the past" and shows that "in reality, Orientalism was endlessly protean, as often consumed by admiration and reverence as by denigration and depreciation." For religion, it has been done most successfully, I feel, by Joscelyn Godwin in THE THEOSOPHICAL ENLIGHTENMENT (1994) and by J..J. Clarke in his broader survey of the influence of the East on modern and post-modern spiritual culture: ORIENTAL ENLIGHTENMENT (Routledge: 1997). To look at the influence the East had and has on the West is to re-evaluate the meaning of Orientalism itself, and this Clarke does well in his short but sweet introduction, "Orientalism, some conjectures." While approving of the way Orientalism serves "as a corrective mirror" for the West, where "Eastern ideas have been used by the West as an agency for self-criticism and self-renewal," he does not forget to warn that explaining the rise of the West by our uniquely self-critical, indeed "somewhat patho-logical self-analysis" (Kraemer) cannot help but tie in with stereotypes of a dynamic West and a passive "endemically static and intensely conservative" East. He also points out the way Orientalism helped Eastern traditions rediscover their own worth and survive, where otherwise they might have been lost. That is to say, Oriental studies in the West can work against, rather than for cultural imperialism. Like all the books I have seen, even Clarke's fine study fails to cite Steadman's illusive THE MYTH OF ASIA.

I found an old book review titled "Rescuing Orientalism from the School of Said" by Donald Richie for what appears to be the best reappraisal of Orientalism since Steadman's *The Myth of Asia.* It is: *FIGURING THE EAST: Segalen, Malraux, Duras and Barthes*, by Marie-Paule Ha (Albany: State University of New York, 2000). Unfortunately, I have not yet read it.

Another IMPORTANT Additional Comment. Perhaps we should refrain from using the terms "Orientalism" and "Occidentalism" unless they are modified with the words, *positive* or *negative.* I do not feel we should let the word Occidentalism become synonymous with the most rabid varieties of anti-Western prejudice, as Buruma and Margalit would have it, for that is to repeat the mistake made by Said with respect to Orientalism.

---

vii The fourth way of approaching Occidentalism
This is to show things supposed to be *exclusively* Occidental in the Orient. Goody does this for Indian trade and commerce. The best-known work of this type is Needham's exhaustive research on science in China, which Goody often refers to in order to show that for most of history the difference simply wasn't there. As is the case for *Nihonjinron,* when the West is said to be this or that, the assumption is the East is not. Goody might have lengthened his title to read *" ~ and The West in the East."* In Japan, many scholars have pointed out modern characteristics of Edo culture which help explain Japan's rapid development. These include a higher literacy than in the West (and this, with a more difficult written language), fine logical argument (recorded by the Jesuits in the 16th century), original algebra (separate and in one case early discoveries in algebra), fine automata devices (mechanical toys and even clocks that could adjust their day and night hour length to fit the seasonal change), manu-facturing expertise (not only incredibly sharp swords but enormous quantities of guns produced and even improved: see Noel Perrine: GIVING UP THE GUN). More than anything else, however, individual Japanese combined a willingness to learn and the discipline necessary to achieve mastery of complex arts and sciences.

Yet Another! I think it would be good if someone could do for the Occidentalism of the Islamic world (in Arabic) what I and others have done for that of Japan (in Japanese), but I realize that the large number of Islamic fanatics preferring murder to argument make that an infinitely more dangerous exercise. Still, most Muslims do enjoy argument – though of strong faith, (unlike Slavophiles) they also take pride in their reason and would read if for nothing else to try to refute the book. Because of the danger involved, a governmental agency rather than a private press might need to publish such a book, or books, but any argument written by a non-Muslim that hopes to be read would have to start by admitting *there is more than a kernel of the truth in negative Occidentalism* – i.e., indulge in consider-able self-criticism – and find good in the other side to praise both for the sake of balance and to create good will (which we are *finally* discovering is as important as prestige, right?), and *that* is something beyond the mere toleration of bad news about our side to prove we do not spout propaganda. Or, if the writer were Muslim, he or she would have to be comfortable with his or her *own* culture. A book by someone who came to loath his own countrymen like Kawasaki's *Japan Unmasked* would be counterproductive. Like Orientalism, Occidentalism should be met head-on.

IV

The Stuffed and the Diced

(why precise translation is an oxymoron)

In a speech to UNESCO (1988), dialogue with Levi-Strauss (1989) and articles in the major media of Japan, the far-ranging literary critic Professor Eto Jun expressed his strong regret "that the Western reader can hardly confront Japanese literary works in the form and style in which they are actually written, but is obliged to be content with looking at his or her own shadow in the guise of Japanese protagonists," (UNESCO) unlike Japanese literature which "never tries to exclude different cultures with their own respective structures, but always tries to embrace them" (Ibid.). While he touches "upon the flexible structure of Japanese, which easily takes in heterogeneous structures" (dialogue) his major point would seem to be that the West has a mental hang-up: "Cartesian modern rationalism that requires the construction of a well-ordered and clear, i.e., mono-layer English text, even though the poly-layer Japanese original comprises in Bakhtin's terms, a heteroglossia, or diversity of languages, and a heterophony, or diversity of individual voices." (*Mainichi Shinbun?* 88-1-18?) [1]

Some of Eto's specific complaints hit the mark. Seidensticker *does* turn strongly distinctive dialects (not to mention individual mannerisms) of Tanizaki's SASAME-YUKI (literally, "light-snow" or, *snow flurries*, the English title is *The Makioka Sisters*) into uniform English. The sense of loss felt reading the original and the translation side-by-side is excruciating. A sentence translated "Excuse me, but I believe you are one of the

Makioka girls" could come from almost anyone's mouth. The original is spoken by an old geisha in dialect as thick as her make-up. (Other criticism of Seidensticker's turning *azaleas* into *lilies* [2] and such are misplaced – someone with a deeper feeling for language than Eto would realize that there are cases where one must be literally wrong to be right: when denotation and connotation are at odds, choose the latter). Seidensticker also *does* tend to journalistic medium-length sentences and unchanging tenses.

But to attribute this to the translator's need "to conform to the golden rule of modern Western narrative, at the expense of certain vital elements contained in the original" (UNESCO) is nonsense.

The sad truth is that few of us are fluent enough to translate, much less master dialect and the art of truly creative writing. Faulkner or Twain might have translated THE MAKIOKA SISTERS better than Seidensticker – but how many Faulkners and Twains read Japanese? My personal view is that publishers should employ the services of dialect writers to redo the dialogue of certain characters (forget the expense and difficulty of choosing your dialect), but no one does this, as far as I know, in the West or, for that matter, in Japan.[3] Moreover, Eto conveniently overlooks the fact that his criticism of Seidensticker holds true for most English-Japanese translation as well.

Not many Japanese translators even *try* to bring out the "heteroglossia" or "heterophony" of the original English. They make even less effort to keep the lively combination of past tense framing, the story-teller's present and subtle generalizations, more often than not forcing everything into uniform past tense – which, by the way, is far more monotonous in Japanese than English because it means almost every sentence will end with the same *"ta"* (end of the past tense conjugation of the Japanese verb which comes at the end of a sentence). They make far more real mistakes than Seidensticker and arrange minuscule vocabularies into sentences so boring that many Japanese, not unreasonably, avoid reading translations despite being interested in the contents. Eto *et al* have nothing to crow about!

My experience is mostly with fine non-fiction, but the little I've checked in fiction shows the same trend. The deliberately ungrammatical first line of THE ADVENTURES OF HUCKLEBERRY FINN was as proper as Seidensticker in every Japanese translation I found.[4] If Aunt Polly could only read Japanese she would hug Tom so tightly her pointy chin would skewer the poor boy! Or, even when they do try, with black English , for example, the result is almost always disappointing. The dirtiness of *the dozens* and bawdiness of urban black English in general is conveyed well enough by the abrasive vernacular of the *chinpira* (*yakuza* underling), but the art and the wit that make Black English the closest thing going to Shakespeare today are left behind, and the translator's effort only serves to reconfirm the stereotype of the black-as-body. Maybe Seidensticker knew what he was doing by *not* trying.

Professor Eto feels, and not unreasonably, considering our cultural exchange on the whole, that Japanese has bent over backwards to accommodate Western language, while the West has not repaid the compliment. There is truth in this observation. Not only countless words, but many forms of grammar (mostly new ways to control the flow of logic from clause to clause, or sentence to sentence), now considered as Japanese as Yoshino cherry blossoms, have enriched Japanese tremendously, thanks to the heroic efforts of past generations of translators. What Eto neglects to mention is that this difference was not a matter of philosophy but of necessity. Japan needed words for modern terms, not a few of which were neologisms almost as new to Occidentals as to the Japanese. The Western languages had, by and large, already done their borrowing and devising. Moreover – and this is crucial – Japanese happened to be weak in expressing relationships of degree, various types of comparisons and contrasts, and qualifying statements, without disturbing the train of thought. "Eventually, we see Japanese writing itself being changed to enable the original English or French text to be introduced just as it is" (dialogue), claims Eto. The truth of the matter is that, even with the innovations, Japanese is still a far cry from matching English.[5]

Why? Nakamura Hajime, the world-renowned philosopher and historian of Eastern thought, put it this way: "The language lacks the relative pronoun, 'which,' standing for the antecedent, that helps develop the process of thought. We find it inconvenient, therefore, to advance closely-knit thinking in a succinct form in Japanese." (THE JAPANESE MIND ed. Charles E. Moore, Hawaii, 1967) Were this all, the good translators of old would surely have supplied such a pronoun! Unfortunately, the relative pronoun is just the icing on the syntax, [a.] a syntax [b.] allowing dependent clauses to string out behind the statement [c.] they qualify, [d.] with or without specific words [e] "standing for the antecedent." (The a, b, c, d and e being five examples of modification without the relative pronoun).

Although some of the horrid translations I see sometimes make me wonder, I do not agree with Nakamura's strong Whorfian claim [6] that Japanese's "non-logical character naturally handicaps the development of ability in logical thinking among the Japanese has actually brought about grave inconveniences in their practical lives." (Ibid). I, also, do not think Japanese is "non-logical".[7] And, I would add, for those who don't know the language, that Japanese allows phrases and clauses, however humongous, to go *before* the word or phrase they modify, a trick English can not follow.[8] There is, however, a practical limit to the amount of qualifying that can be endured (even if understood) before the main point is made. *That* is why Japanese is indeed handicapped when it comes to the clear expression of long-winded, convoluted thought.[9]

Very, *very* few translators are capable of the complex bricole required to overcome this handicap. Most translations are simply *stuffed* or *diced*. By *stuffed*, I mean packed so tight with long prior-to-the-point clauses (imagine hyphenated modifiers running on dozens and dozens of words) that few readers can follow the argument. Until recently, most Japanese took the difficulty for granted – some even considering it proof of lack of logic and intelligence on their part – but today, in Japan, as in most of the world, complex, time-consuming sentences are out of favor.

So, what happens? They are *diced*. By *diced*, I mean that as soon as the independent clause ends, the translated sentence comes to a full stop, and the dependent clause turns into a separate sentence, as does *its* dependent clause, if it has one. What was a quickly flowing stream of logic graced with eddies of afterthought stretches into a plodding linear series of independent statements. The fragments are easy enough to read – if you don't think too much – but with every clause treated equally, given a full sentence of its own, the author's main point is weakened if not lost altogether.

The worst of it is that the subject (or other modified word) is usually repeated, all too often as the demonstratives *kore* (this) or *sore* (that) , which, like all pronouns in Japan dominate each newly sentenced clause – the feeling is "as for this" or "as for that" – and, with commas no longer sufficient, the translators artificially stay the shot-to-hell-and-gone train of logic with more conjunctive ties per paragraph than you'll find on an old railroad (I say *old* because the train no longer runs, and you have to walk those rails).

Hyperbole? *Perhaps*. But no exaggeration. Contemporary Japanese are addicted to conjunctions, even outside of translation. Syntax may play a role in it, but I feel the main reason is that most Japanese write poorly, having little chance to practice composition at their test-oriented schools. If you have not learned to dovetail, you will require nails and even big ugly bolts. A doctoral thesis by Kiyoko Mizuno Oi "Cross-cultural Differences in Rhetorical Patterning" (Ann Arbor, 1985) offers some telling statistics. Compositions by Japanese university students, whether in Japanese or in English, use approximately twice as many conjunctions as do American students. For some varieties the difference even exceeds 500 percent. Since *diced* translation involves at least two times the conjunctions (and near-conjunctions, such as "for example" and "of course") as found in original composition, this means an insufferably overbearing average of four times the number of conjunctions found in English!

Yet, what do you think Japanese think when they read a translation packed to the gills with their (statistically speaking) conjunctions? They think the style is very logical, the essence of the Occidental mind.[10]

Illogical as it may sound, both the hopelessly *stuffed* and the haplessly *diced* styles of translation justify their wretched existence on the basis of claims to be faithful *chokuyaku,* or direct translation, despite the fact they are as opposite as opposite can be to each other. The *stuffed* school claims (quite correctly) to have retained the logical relationship of the original whole. The *diced* school claims (again correctly) to retain the order of the original clauses. Personally, I prefer the older *stuffed* school to the *diced* one. If I *must* be misconstrued, I'd rather be thought too brilliant to follow, than a plodding bore.

ch.4 notes

1. *Mainichi Shinbun?* In my draft, the citation said *Asahi*. The style resembles that of articles found in the *Asahi Shinbun's Bunka-ran*. Rechecking for me, a librarian found an article on that date by Eto Jun in another top newspaper = *Mainichi Shinbun*. So *maybe* it is that. Or, maybe not. I vaguely recall receiving a packet of articles from Eto Jun, himself, when I lived in Japan. He died in 2003.

2. *Oops!* Azalea to Lily and Back Again. A respectable scholar would correct a mistake inside of his essay. Or, at the very least explain it first in the footnote, for not all potential critics are patient enough to read until the end. *But I will not*, for if I were the reader, I would prefer not to know yet. I would want to enjoy the suspense of not knowing.

It started with an E-mail from William J. Higginson, author of the international seasonal almanac, *Haiku World*. After reading my second mention of the *azalea* turned *lily* "as an [acceptable] editorial decision" (and not a mistranslation) in chapter 6, he took me to task:

> "I'm afraid I have to disagree with you. I seriously doubt it was an "editorial decision"! In the first place, it's certainly not uncommon to miss the right plant. I'm not sure on the Seidensticker example, but none other than Donald Keene misses one early on in his latest *Oku no Hosomichi* [Bashô's best known work] and by doing so puts the poem in the wrong season, screwing up the order of sections for the astute reader . . . . . Azaleas and lilies have almost NOTHING in common (different main color [lipstick red vs. white-to-orange], different type of plant altogether [woody vs. bulb], different shape and size of blossom-mass [bush of small flowers vs. large trumpets on clumped stalks], different season [spring vs. summer; azaleas bring us finally out of winter's last vestiges; lilies trumpet sweltering summer], different environment [dry woodlands vs. wet marshes]) and certainly no trans-cultural equivalence that I know of. How COULD *anyone* sensitive to the round of seasonal blossoms (a MAIN point of the culture of *aware* [Note: melancholic communion with nature] mistake one for the other? Impossible! This is a major flaw in your stream of examples (one you mention twice, for gawd's sake), and is a perfect (counter-) example of what you yourself are saying!"

Bill's spirited defense of natural rectitude told me I should have shared the Hirado lily passage from Makioka Sisters with my readers and that I had some explaining to do about why I excused Seidensticker for turning Tanizaki Junichiro's *azaleas* into *lilies*. Here is the passage cited by Eto Jun which I based my judgment upon:

> "Again the Hirado lilies were beginning to look dirty and ragged. . . . It came to Sachiko, looking out over the garden one afternoon, that exactly a year before, Teinosuke had noticed the tinge of yellow in her eyes. As he had done then, she went down into the garden and began picking off the faded blossoms." (*Makioka Sisters* from first paragraph of book 2)

Who could deny that discolored white lilies were a perfect complement for Sachiko's jaundice, whereas azaleas would do little for the Western reader? But, as Bill's e-mail notes "Just don't run that argument past a gardener or a woods-walker." My immediate reaction to that was *Seidensticker didn't plan to!* But, as I searched out all the "Hirado" in the book, I came to have second thoughts. I realized that while I had recognized the large amount of natural description in Japanese novels, I had not been aware enough of an element we might call seasonal registration that I had identified with haiku and classical Japanese poetry. As I quickly found Tanizaki's "hirado" in his huge novel by skimming from spring to spring, I marveled at how the seasonal phenomena subtly set many if not most scenes. To preserve that, I thought, were I the translator, I would have used *azaleas* and added a note about them. But Seidensticker's translation has no notes, and notes are so rare in fiction that I can understand why (though I do not agree) a publisher chose not to use them. Without notes, liberties must be taken with the translation if the novel is to read well for most readers. I considered writing Seidensticker to ask him whether the choice was deliberate or not . . .

Meanwhile, I conferred with a Japanese friend, a

translator. She agreed with Bill that it was wrong to change flowers, and felt his guess of mistranslation rather than editorial decision (as I imagined) was correct, because the original only speaks of a Hirato (or Hirado, for this geographical name has two possible pronunciations) and does not say what type of flower it is. Moreover, she had some of these large Hirato azalea in her garden by her country house and knew all about them (especially how dirty they could get). I had the first gloss draft finished when she wrote me again. Imagine my surprise to see the "subject" line of the letter:

"Seidensticker was correct."

When checking what the "Mosquiton" (in the first citation of the Hirado, which I skip here) was in the original, she noticed an indication of a note by the Hirado. Going to the back of the huge novel, she found the following note:

> "*Hirado*. The Hirado Lily. A perennial shrub of the lily family. The blossoms are orange. It resembles a sukashi-yuri (literally translucent lily), but has no speckles in the blossom."

The "orange" seems a bit odd when the passage that is noted mentions "a bed of red and white Hirado" (italics mine); but checking further I confirmed that cultivated Hirado lilies do indeed offer a large variety of colors. *So I had been defending Seidensticker from what turned out to be a false charge! It was the literary critic Eto Jun who was wrong.* This matters not a whit to the in/validity of my argument, but it is curious nonetheless.

Why, you might wonder, could a Japanese literary critic make such a mistake? First, *red* and *white* are, after all associated with the azalea rather than the lily and there is another passage where the red Hirado bloom blazes, something that will make most Japanese think azalea – I can attest to having looked twice at what I thought was a burning bush and turned out to be an azalea, but I have never been so fooled by a lily. Second, dictionaries are more likely to have the word "Hirado" by itself signify the *azalea* than lily for the *Hirado azalea* is better known than the Hirado lily (why Tanizaki must have added the note, which Eto, like my friend at first, must have missed). Third, the azalea bloom looks very dirty (lots of pollen) as it starts to wither away. Its little stamen hairs (called "whiskers" in one passage) resembling the filament of a broken burnt-out light bulb are uglier than the larger and fleshier ones of a lily, and the azalea, too, causes the gardener to wash his or her hands (mentioned in two passages). Fourth, the bloom was in Spring. The last mentioned Hirado in the book, a late bloom (*okurizaki*), was in late May or early June. As it turns out, the Hirado lily comes from a beach lily that shares the early blooming quality of the Easter lily, but most Japanese would not expect a lily at that time.

When all of these factors are combined, it is not surprising that Eto Jun made a mistake, but I am grateful he did, for it provided us with food for thought, which I hope I have not overcooked for you. (Because of the apparent mistake by Eto, I wish I had a copy of the Unesco Speech on hand to confirm, but I do not even have the exact date. My apologies.)

After reading this redone gloss, my Japanese translator friend added "For your reference, Sasame-yuki [fine snow = The Makioka Sisters] has nearly seventy notes . . . the great majority of which have to do with seasonal phenomena subtly included in many scenes."* While she added, "it is true that a novel rarely has such notes at the end of the book," the fact it has them, whereas the Englished novel does not, supports Eto's general misgivings over the standardization of literature in the West for, without explanation, there is a limit to the amount of difference that can be translated. With traditional publishers combining into a huge corporate institutions and few really novel books on the best-seller lists over the last decade, one might think the bland literary monoculture Eto criticized is here to stay, but I think the danger is past. With every writer capable of printing his or her book and selling it at prices competitive with the majors (not possible through a POD press, but easy if you are the publisher and use a POD printer/distributor) the current bookshelf is the last hurrah of the dictatorship of style. Let me make a prediction. By 2010, the self-publishing of books will be as common, and as acceptable, as self-production of music is today. And by 2020, not only will most books be self-published, but all major publishers will grant authors enormous stylistic freedom for it will be the only way they can keep them.

~~~~~~

i. The Makioka Sisters Edition. This is the
~~~~~~

Shinchôsha 1959 edition with the notes by Yoshida Seiichi, a prominent scholar (1904-84) of Japanese literature, edited (and originally published) with a postscript by Itou Sei (1905-69) , a famous novelist and literary critic also known as the translator of Lady Chatterley's Lover and Ulysses. Tanizaki Junichirô lived until 1965 and presumably cooperated on the notes.

---

3. Loss of dialect. The loss of dialect in translation is missed even more when you learn how much effort the writer went to in order to get it right. According to Donald Keene, "Tanizaki used assistants to render his own Tokyo speech into Osaka dialect." (APPRECIATIONS OF JAPANESE CULTURE)

4. The deliberately ungrammatical first line. Here it is:

> You don't know about me without you have read a book by the name of THE ADVENTURES OF TOM SAWYER, but that ain't no matter.

The matter of what's "ungrammatical" is now contested – but even if this might be correct for Black English, it would still be wrong for Aunt Polly and most of Twain's readers. The reason Japanese has trouble matching this in translation – or doesn't even try – is because there is no similar style in Japanese. There is avant-garde nonsense and there are many dialects. **(i)** The former only makes sense in its own world; the latter are sometimes so different Tokyoites can't understand them – and the television may supply captions – but *neither do anything considered ungrammatical.* (Unless you count the children who get into trouble at school because their dialects use personal referents Tokyoites – the national education is geared toward producing a style of Japanese similar to that of upper-class people in Tokyo – consider *rude.*) While there are a few mistakes in pronunciation made by foreigners **(ii)** that are picked up by novelists, there is almost no real *broken Japanese* in print. (I have never even heard the term "broken Japanese.") Is this because Japanese does not break? **(iii)** Or is it because of the greater rarity of something that might be called substandard Japanese? Is it too marginalized to make it into literature? This is a curious area that could be developed as a doctoral thesis – anyone?

---

i. Dialect. It is not only different in vocabulary, accent and conjugation style. Each has a different connotation. This gives the translator a lot to consider. When I introduced the FOXFIRE CHRISTMAS BOOK to a Japanese translator, I wondered if she might put the old folk into Tohoku dialect, which she knew. An isolated farm-region famous for heavy snow, Tohoku, is the country bumpkin capitol of Japan. The *dambei* for *da* (an *is* and *do* in one, this helper verb with numerous levels of formality puts the tail on a large percentage (10% 20%?) of Japanese sentences) has a country feeling even to the ear of an English native speaker. But the *hillbilly* connotation – a similar prejudice to that in the USA – made the translator chicken-out. But, that was only part of the story. She was hesitant to use it anyway, for there is always something artificial about foreigners speaking in dialect. If I directed a movie with characters from Kyoto, they would speak in a soft Southern drawl. *Would you like it?* Any dialect is too multi-faceted to perfectly match any other. The high-faluhtin archaisms in Hillbilly is not found in Tohoku dialect. And Kyoto's culture is a hell of a lot thicker – in the historical sense of having depth – than that of our South!

ii Foreigner's Japanese. Koreans [and Chinese?] do not differentiate between some voiced and unvoiced consonants and this is sometimes picked up by novelists. The Japanese make little effort to go much further at transcribing the accent. Part of this may be the limited number of phonemes they have at their disposal. But, even the American tendency to harden the "a" sound – which could easily be captured with Japanese vowels – escapes print. Instead, Japanese often put the "Japanese" of the foreigner (especially if he is white or black) into their stiff-looking syllabary, *katakana,* and leave it to the reader to imagine the pronunciation. Once a foreigner speaks with fair fluency, this *katakana-izing* stops. I still made grammatical mistakes – wrong postpositions, wrong pronunciations, wrong level of conjugation – but they were always, thank goodness, smoothed out when the interview was published. Unfortunately, the editors often added plentiful first-person pronouns to Westernize me. Their favorite choice was *"boku,"* a self-referent suitable for a young male – this, one of the "I's" taboo to women – that I never use, because it sounds too explosive for my taste. **(a)** Japanese think it especially appropriate for Americans who are stereotyped as cocky types – you know, someone who chews gum with his mouth open – and childish because, on the whole, they lack the self-control expected of a real adult. Since I happen to be American . . . . **(b)**

---

a. Self-referents and taste. I am not the only one who dislikes *boku* – except coming from a tiny child, from whom it sounds cute, especially when they stick on the diminutive *"-chan,"* (which they pick up from being addressed with it) to refer to themselves (English has nothing half so precious). Yanagita Kunio, "the all-but-sainted founder of folklore studies in Japan" who "is revered as the champion and discoverer, if not actually the inventor, of almost everything that is held to be truly and essentially Japanese over an enormous range of fields" (for the rest of this splendid quote see Miller: 82) detested *boku.* He found it harsh to the ear, like most of the "b + vowel" *syllabets* (short syllables used in a syllabary – a transparent coinage I hope will replace the opaque *mora,* a term linguists lifted from Latin), which come from Chinese. Japanese call syllabets beginning with a voiced consonant "muddy," a term with bad connotations. *Boku* began as a term meaning "slave" or "servant" and was picked up by literatae as a modest way to refer to themselves when writing patrons. But others began to copy it and carry it into the spoken vocabulary, where its naturally explosive sound made it a male, good-ole boys thing. More on Yanagita's *boku* thoughts in my book-to-be EXOTIC TONGUES (2006?).

b. The childish American. How ironic to find the American so viewed by the Japanese whom MacArthur called 14 year-old children. On the whole, I'd have to agree with the Japanese evaluation of us. We are less disciplined and more spoiled and, like children, don't even know it. But, our image is worse than reality because it tends to be based on our military personnel, many of whom *are,* for better or worse, exceptionally childish. (Playing war is, after all, a child's game.)

---

iii Japanese doesn't break? Some say Japanese is the earliest pidgin language. Can a pidgin, then, not be pidgined? I find that, in Japanese, the grammar *is* the language, in a way it is not in English. I hear Japanese children speaking so as to strongly accent the articles and post-positions, the "*te, ni, o, ha*" which are themselves the informal term for "grammar." (formally written *bunpo* or "writing-law." Imagine, if you will, strongly accenting "the" and "in" and "for" and "by"! In English, these minor parts of speech – what is left out of a telegraph – are not stressed by anyone in his right mind. In Japan, even young adults put a strong stress on the "*te, ni, o, ha*" when they wish to sound formal, although when they overdo it – as they did toward the end of the twentieth century – they sound so juvenile that some adults take umbrage (as they damn well should!). Yet, there is at least one place where Japanese is clearly breaking. The conjugation meaning "can" – Japanese have a separate verb for "can" (*dekiru)* but the verbs can do it by themselves – is being simplified, i.e., *shortened* by the young. Some adults are resisting, but they are bound to lose, because the conjugation *-rareru* is too long for people familiar with a faster language, English!

---

5. Japanese: still a far cry from matching English. In response to Prof. Eto's claim that the original can be introduced "just as it is," I can only reply that neither language will ever come close to matching one another. *Thank goodness!* On a less happy note, *both languages can not match their own past either.* I discovered a completely mistranslated "modern" version of Milton in a book that had undergone 17 printings (Rudolf Fleisch: HOW TO SPEAK AND WRITE EFFECTIVELY cited in my EXOTIC TONGUES (2006?)! Milton's train of thought is just too much for modern readers. The same is true for Japanese; and it is why Tanizaki was wrong to use the modern English translation of THE TALE OF GENJI, where "the meaning becomes clear, but at the same time becomes limited and shallow," for proof that:

> We do not make such useless effort, but use those words which allow sufficient leeway to suggest various things . . . [whereas] the sentence of the Westerner tries to restrict the meaning as narrowly and detailed as possible and does not allow the smallest shadow, so that there is no room at all for the imagination of the reader. (Kawashima Takeyoshi: "The

> Status of the Individual in the Notion of Law, Right, and Social order in Japan" **(i)** in Moore: The Japanese Mind: 1967)

Comparing ancient Japanese to a modern translation is ridiculous. Ancient Japanese literature may have enjoyed a somewhat higher level of ambiguity than English at a similar stage, but this does not justify Tanizaki's generalization. And fifty years later, at the start of the twenty first century, whatever may have been true in Tanizaki's contrast is, I fear, true no longer. Most Japanese *gendaiyaku*, or modern translations, of Japanese classics are *more* wordy and supply *more* information than the English translations. Some are – I kid you not – three or four times as long as the original. **(ii)** If that is because the Japanese have been Westernized, than they have already out-Westernized us and had better copy our translations to regain their more subtle past!

(i) Tanizaki on translation and "The Status of the Individual." Professor Kawashima prefaces the Tanizaki quotation with things like "The language habit of the Japanese people is not suitable for detailed and determinate expression or communication" and follows it with the type of tongue-in-cheek boasting that would soon – as Japan's economy waxed – be typical of *nihonjinron* cultural comparison = contrast:

> Viewed from this [the Japanese vantage point of Tanizaki and the style of the original *Tale of Genji*] cognitive and evaluative perspective of naive realism, men and society appear with immense variety in their subtle nuances and do not fit the abstractions with concepts by postulation. Each individual appears as a discrete entity with its own status and value. There is in this viewpoint no room for the existence of the image of an individual who is 'equal' to every other on the ground that he is 'independent' of each other. In a society with such assumptions, law and ethics aim at maintaining the social order consisting of the statuses of men with immense variety as they actually exist and not imposing a social order which is postulated by ideal or intellect.

Professor Eto and Professor Lee's later claims are foreshadowed in this description of a pluralistic postmodern Japan *versus* a monotonous West. Considering the amount of nonsense that has been written about the "individual" in the West – both untenable claims of total autonomy and patronizing ignorance concerning non-Western people, I am half-happy to see this type of scholarly doggerel from Japan give the West its come-uppance. But I can't help wondering if Kawashima knew that Burke wrote something similar reacting to the allegedly French concept of "the rights of man."

> I never govern myself, no rational man ever did govern himself, by abstractions and universals . . . Circumstances are infinite, are infinitely combined, are variable and transient: he who does not take them into consideration is not erroneous, but stark mad; *dat operam. ut cum ratione insaniat* (He labors to make his mind unsound by means of his reason); he is metaphysically mad.
>
> Nothing universal can be rationally affirmed on any moral or any political subject. Pure metaphysical abstraction does not belong to these matters. The lines of morality are not like the ideal lines of mathematics. They are broad and deep as well as long. They admit of exceptions; they demand modifications. These exceptions and modifications are not made by the process of logic, but by the rules of prudence.

ii *Gendaiyaku*, or modern translation. The term is more ambiguous in English; I feel like saying "modern *version*," instead. The fact that the Japanese translator of ancient texts of his own language expects the reader to try the original as well *partially* excuses the poor translation. To be fair, there are some excellent modern translations of ancient prose, but the translations of ancient poetry are almost always plodding glosses twice as long and half as witty as the original. (No hyperbole: not a few are four times as long and have zero wit!) I believe modern translations – in English or Japanese – should not explain too much. Rather, they should combine ample notes with a translation lively enough to be called poetry. If the poetry is used to explain, it should do so in multiple translation – I call this *paraverse/paraversing* – each version developing different facets of the original yet retaining the brevity (and *snap*) of wit. (Easier said than done? See the examples in RISE, YE SEA SLUGS! The thousand, mostly old, haiku have an average of two translations each, and some boast half a dozen or more.)

---

6. Whorfian claims. Not being able to write a complex – make that convoluted – thought succinctly does not rule out having that thought. Style does not make the man *that* much. A writer knows this from sad experience. Part of me wants to play up Whorfian claims, for nothing is more romantic and wonderful than increasing the types of intellect on the planet; but the other part of me says that the ability of mind to go beyond language is more fantastic!

7. Japanese as non-logical. R. A. Miller also catches this Nakamura quotation and pans, "If we are to believe Nakamura, to live in Japanese is to live in a labyrinth of illogic and inconvenience." I am certain Nakamura would disagree with the "illogic." Japanese writers – even ones who are not philosophers – take great care to differentiate between "illogic" and "alogic." The "non-logical" would have to be the latter. Unlike the illogical, the alogical as previously mentioned, may be interpreted favorably, for it can always be touted as logic beyond logic. This was to be the case in THE JAPANESE AND THE JEWS, a best-seller in the 1970's, which contrasted the black and white logic of the Jews to the more subtle logic beyond logic of the Japanese. Everything Ben Dasan (Yamamoto Shichihei) wrote about the Japanese style of thought can be found written fifty years earlier about the English by Salvador de Madariaga (1886-1978). I know the quotation is long, but his work has been overlooked too long by Japanology and I wish to show the entire parallel for the sake of the minority of readers who have read a lot of *nihonjinron.*

> The Englishman evinces a strong tendency to what we might term allogicalism. The word is necessary. Too often, particularly recently since they have begun to be better known, the English have been reproached for their *illogicalism,* and, with their usual awkwardness in these matters, they have themselves accepted and commended this view. It seems a little exaggerated to lend them a tendency contrary to logic. If now and then they have manifested such a tendency, it must have been when they found the machine-guns of unreasonable logic aimed at them. But to attribute illogicalism as a normal feature to the English would be tantamount to granting them a preoccupation with the world of thought, which is far from being a part of their constitution. The Englishman is not illogical, but allogical, for logic is a thing which he does not trouble about.
>
> Which, by the way, allows him an attitude towards logic far more complex than mere illogicalism, for, after all, if he were merely illogical, there would be a certain method in his madness. But the Englishman is more complicated than that. He is both logical and illogical. . . . We have seen that English allogicalism is due to the fact that, faced with the dilemma life-thought, the Englishman stands by life." (ENGLISHMEN, FRENCHMEN AND SPANIARDS: 1928)

Note the double "ll" spelling. It pairs better with "illogical" but "allo" seems to suggest "other" rather than "outside-of/beyond" as "a" by itself would, so I think we would do better to use just one "l" though O.E.D. wrongly defines "alogical" as "illogical." Perhaps, I should also add that Nakamura Hajime wrote things about Chinese thought that are remarkably similar to what he wrote about Japanese thought, considering how different the languages are.

> The non-logical character of the verbal expression of Chinese thought is, of course, intimately connected with the characteristics of the Chinese language. Words corresponding to the prepositions, conjunctions, and relative pronouns of Western languages are rare. There is no distinction between singular and plural. A single character can denote "*un homme, quelques hommes,* or *humanite* . . . . (in Hansen: LANGUAGE AND LOGIC IN ANCIENT CHINA, U. Michigan 1983)

Bare bones Chinese. Chad Hansen writes "there is no reason to suppose any of these facts render verbal expression illogical." True, but like Dale and others he is wrong to jump from "*il*" to "*non*" – the implication, as we have seen in the quote about the Englishman, above, is a bit different.

8. A trick English cannot follow. Arthur Knapp, who was good at seeing the advantages of the *inverse* way of doing things puts it like this:

> Relative pronouns are equally unnecessary. All you have to do is to transform your entire sentence beginning with "who" or "which" into an attributive and you will never miss your relatives. "A man who comes" is "a comes man," "a man who has come" is "a went man," and "the carpenter who fell off the roof and broke his leg" is "the fell off the roof and broke leg carpenter." It is all admirably simple, and the acquisition of the Japanese language with naught but the noun and verb to vex us is, from one point of view, as easy as Japanese housekeeping with nothing but floor and walls to keep free from dust. (FEUDAL AND MODERN JAPAN vol.2:1896)

[He is right except that long qualification/ modification is difficult to understand because it all must come before one knows what it is about.] Knapp continues, "but to think in Japanese. *Hic labor, hoc opus est.* For this requires an absolute inversion of every habit of thought to which we have been accustomed. [I would say that though the sentences are inverted, what is required is not an inversion, but a suspension of judgment until the subject is reached.] A sentence in English translated into the corresponding Japanese words would make absolute nonsense." [True, and equally true, of course, for the vice versa.]

9. Japanese is handicapped A handicap is not necessarily a disability. I find I write *better* for having my wings clipped. If Japanese cannot qualify itself as much as English can, it cannot become convoluted so easily. It is safe from people like me. To some process philosophers, this may be a problem but, to most of the world, it is not. A Yiddishism comes to mind: *that English should be so handicapped!* (This sentence, an example of rhetoric English could import, but Japanese could not.) Yet even as I joke, I know I do miss my freedom. Lest the reader wonder if the fact Japanese is not my native tongue has any bearing on this, I give you a top Japanese humor writer, Maruya Saichi, who put it far better than the philosopher/historian Nakamura, or, for that matter, any linguist when he wrote that, in English,

> the logic clings together in many directions, and has the power to rise like a spiral staircase; [on the other hand] in Japanese, it just spreads out and makes a flat floor. – WORDS, OR JAPANESE (*kotoba aruiwa nihongo:* Lost Date/publisher)

French, with its more restricted vectors of modification, might then make a straight staircase?

10. Logical style. I limited my discussion on logic to sentence style rather than argument style because the former has more to do with translation problems. Differences in essay organization are fun to Whorf. E.g. American students are far more likely to state their main ideas in the first paragraph. ← *English is far more likely to begin a sentence with a subject.* E.g. Japanese students are more likely to introduce associative material – beat around the bush, if you prefer – before coming to focus on the main point. ←*Japanese syntax allows looser, rambling sentences.* But, before getting too enthusiastic with our *Whorfing,* we must remember that such parallels can contradict, too. The English sentence saves its object for last – many have said Japanese is ambiguous for having its verb last, but one could say the same for having the object last, no? Yet, how many essayists (especially students) writing in English can refrain from broaching their agenda earlier?

Be that as it may, *good writing in any language is more similar to good writing than bad writing is to bad.* It gives enough information up front to grab the reader's attention, yet holds back to work slowly toward a conclusion by way of deductive logic (For a more finely nuanced – and more responsible – discussion see Kubota Ryuko: "An Investigation of Japanese and English Essay Organization: Difference and Similarities": *Canadian Modern Language Review* v54 1998)

11. On lazy readers: a note for the whole chapter. On second thought, perhaps I have been a little too harsh on Professor Eto. Most writing today (in English and Japanese **(i)** is seamless, stripped of all complicating items, such as parenthesis, brackets, footnotes and, when translation is involved, the original text. Our publishers and their lazy readers apparently want writers to lie by omission. They are like the good-natured spouse who says "just don't let me know." Something needs to be said for honesty. Lawrence Venuti writes:

> Anglo-American culture . . . has long been plagued by domesticating theories that recommend fluent translating. By producing the illusion of transparency, a fluent translation masquerades as true semantic equivalence when it in fact inscribes the foreign text with a partial interpretation, partial to English language values, reducing if not simply excluding the very difference that translation is called on to convey.
>
> . . . insofar as foreignizing translation seeks to restrain the ethnocentric violence of translation, it is highly desirable today, a strategic cultural intervention in the current state of world affairs, pitched against the hegemonic English language nations and the unequal cultural exchanges in which they engage their global others. Foreignizing translation in English can be a form of resistance against ethnocentrism and racism, cultural narcissism and imperialism, in the interests of democratic geopolitical relations."

Venuti qualifies this over the course of his entertaining book (He provides good examples which more than make up for the overblown ideology). For all his gung-ho espousal of foreignizing, he knows it is no easy business:

> Pound shows that in translation, the foreignness of the foreign text is available only in cultural forms that already circulate in the target language, some with more cultural capital than others. In translation, the foreignness of the foreign text can only be what currently appears 'foreign' in the target-language culture...

I find myself in the strange position of being both more *and* less optimistic than Venuti about the possibilities of foreignizing translation. I am *less* optimistic for the reasons given throughout the main body of this essay. My experience with foreignized English-to-Japanese translation says that "the very difference" conveyed is most likely to reflect and re-enforce prejudices held by members of the target language. Yet, I am *more* optimistic because I do not believe that what holds true for Pound – whose splendid control of archaic native forms allowed him to use what others would need to invent – holds true for any translator. **(ii)** But, even assuming a genius translator manages to really foreignize, we run into a genuine paradox: Will not our reading of the literally exotic text be far from the way the original was read? Using period instruments to hear Bach as he would have been heard is fine, but the people of his time would have been so familiar with the squeaky frets and whatnot that they would not hear the noise, while we do. In that case, would the genuine experience require cleaning up the noise? **(iii)** Or, should the good listener – reader – keep listening (maybe years) until the noise disappears on its own? And would that be any different than listening to it cleaned up?

---

i. **Foreignizing translations in other languages.** I can only speak for English and Japanese. I note that Italians sometimes put all quoted foreign text at the bottom of the page – I have seen this on a mass market paperback! So not all people are as frightened of anything difficult looking as we are. But I don't know *how* Italian's translate, or anything, for that matter, about the current situation for European languages other than Eto's claim. Venuti does supply some good historical background for English, French and German. He sees foreignizing translation as a forte of the Germans and introduces its main proponent Schleiermacher, who puts the dilemma of translation as follows:

> Either the translator leaves the author in peace, as much as possible, and moves the reader towards him; or he leaves the reader in peace, as much as possible, and moves the author towards him.

"Schleiermacher" writes Venuti, "privileges the first method, making the target-language reader travel abroad . . ." He also boasts about it being a particularly German strategy because of Germany's "respect for what is foreign" and because of the flexibility of its language, not yet "bonded" to the classical (like French). To me, this attitude sounds very Japanese, it could be a *Nihonjinron*. As does this:

> Our language, because we exercise it less owing to our Nordic sluggishness, can thrive in all its freshness and completely develop its own power only through the most many-sided contacts with what is foreign.

The French, on the other hand, according to a satiric dialogue by A.W. Schlegel (1798),

> look on a foreign author as a stranger in our company, who has to dress and behave according to out customs, if he desires to please.

That is similar to Eto's description of the Western approach. Yet, the French are not always so staid. Venuti mentions a "modern French Cultural practice" of homophonic translation. He gives no examples of this *traduscon,* but introduces rarer English ones by Zukofsky, where Catulus' *"Nulli se dicit mulier mea . . ."* becomes "Newly say dickered my love air . . ." (Zukofsky is in some book by Guy Davenport (the only critic I know who is readable) too.) I see this as another dimension of direct translation. It is diverting, useful to rub in the ear of a tone-deaf translator, and more honest than a effort to directly translate meaning (at least between languages as different as Japanese and English), for the sound experience does, however imperfectly, reproduce the original.

ii. Pound's translation. Venuti did not pay any attention to what I regard as Pound's finest work – the only thing I *really like* of Pound's – his SHI-CHING. But he did give us this punning tidbit from a letter Pound wrote to Mary Barnard (famous for her Sappho translations):

> "utility of syntax? waaal the chink does without a damLot"

To my lowbrow taste, Pound's SHI-CHING stands with Fitzgerald's RUBAIYAT as a uniquely readable translation of foreign poetry. And, unlike the RUBAIYAT, the SHI-CHING has something of the original style in it. True, Pound goes to anything from old English ballades to modern American blues for his styles but, even so, the translation is close to the Chinese in its remarkable terseness. Pound, too, does without a damn lot. If some of his translations were any tighter, the English would be telegraphic, and that is what ancient Chinese poetry is all about (although the extent to which the poem might have been fleshed out by the reader is currently under debate). This is completely different from bogus *foreignizing,* which follows the latest conventions of exotic style or otherwise works to create "just the right outlandish flavour." (G.A. Simcox's favorable review of Morris' translation of *THE STORY OF THE VOLSUNGS AND NIBLUNGS* (1870) found in Susan Bassnett-McGuire's pithy TRANSLATION STUDIES, the finest outline of what translation is about that I know of.) Unfortunately, most translations retaining something of the original language's syntax seem outlandish whether they are intended to or not. I wonder if any Germans who were in favor of capturing the original style in translation reneged upon reading Carlyle, "who used elaborate Germanic structures in his translation from the German" (Bassnett-McGuire: Ibid.)! If it is anything like the words of Herr Teufelsdrockh in SARTOR RESARTUS (the effect is comical, a parody of the German philosophical style – but it apparently fooled some readers, who believed the quotations were those of a real German!) I don't think they will buy it.

iii. **Music reproduction and authenticity.** I read a fine book about it once and lost its name. *Sorry!*

V

Failure of the Imagination

(how prejudice translates)

A Japanese magazine requested an article. Assuming that a native speaker could write in a better style than he could, translator John Bester wrote in English and "got a Japanese friend to translate it." This person, "was a good, careful English speaker. He'd lived abroad and seemed thoroughly conversant with the ways of thinking and expression of English-speaking people. So I hardly thought it necessary to check his translation . . . .".

Luckily, he did: "My first impression on reading the Japanese through was of unfamiliarity, both with the content of the piece and with the personality of the author." The flow of thought no longer did. And, ". . . worse,

> where its general tone was concerned, the article had become a caricature of the one I felt I'd written. What I'd intended as persuasive had become pushy; the conciliatory had become patronizing, and the logically reasoning downright overbearing. I sweated at the thought of all those Japanese readers out there, and how neatly the picture they'd get of Bester would fit in with the caricature-image of the full-of-self, contentious, implacable foreigner." (*Mainichi Daily News,* 1984/7/9)

With the assistance of a sympathetic editor the monster

was excised. Bester then asked himself, "Why should my friend, whose person seemed such a pillar of international understanding, have unintentionally ratted on me like that?" One reason, he surmised, might be that his friend, knowing he too was a translator, took special pains to be "faithful" to the original he believed best conveyed through "direct translation." A modest American turned into the Monster just like that!

> In short, although he and I were more or less at home with each other, he was still capable of compartmentalizing his mind so that he felt no contradiction between the human being he knew and the "foreigner" ostensibly responsible for this rather unpleasant piece of prose he'd just turned out. (Ibid.)

Bester concluded with an understatement.

> There's an important failure of the imagination lurking somewhere here. (Ibid.).

As Bester writes, "to varying degrees, the same thing happens all the time" in Japan. The only difference, of course, is that 99.9% of the time the author of the original has no way of knowing he has been *monstered.* Luckily or unluckily, he can not read Japanese.

Bad as it is, direct translation is not all of it. The *monster* is also fed with mistranslation, much of which is biased in a predictable direction: translators rarely make mistakes that soften the tone of the original, but often manage to harden it.

Take the adverb "apparently." The nuance intended is usually not "apparent" but "tentative," i.e., something *seems* to be the case.[1] Yet, about half of the translators whose work I've checked routinely turn it into *akiraka-ni,* or "clearly"; and this even when the slightest consideration of the context would indicate that things are not so cut and dry! Some translators manage to do this for decades without catching on. How can they do this? *Because that is how they think we think.* Sure, it may seem a bit strange to be so certain about something that any fool knows is not [2] – but that is the way Westerners are. *Vive le difference!* It is our identity.

In my opinion, this identity-constituting difference rests less upon "a *failure* of the imagination" than upon its collective *triumph,* whereby the ambiguous gray gestalt of reality has been replaced by antithetical black and white images, which are constantly reinforced by translators and, as we shall now see, others." [3]

A music critic comments about a popular song, "*Kôshuûdenwa*" (The Public Telephone), in which the singer gives up her man for his sake despite her never-ending love:

> An Occidental wouldn't understand this at all; they either love and stay together or hate each other and part. [4]

Too bad he never heard one of the biggest hit songs in country music history, Dolly Parton's *"I will Always Love You,"* (later, popped by Whitney Houston), which expresses an absolutely identical situation!

The psychiatrist Doi Takeo made the following equally outlandish claim in his best-selling book ANATOMY OF DEPENDENCE (orig. 1971):

> When a Westerner says "thank you" that's the end of it; not like the Japanese where the feeling lingers on and on. (trans. John Bester 1973) [5]

Doi is discussing a Japanese expression for "thank you", *sumanu* (literally "end-not," or *never ending.*) He doesn't seem to know the casual English expression often used by my grandfather: "much obliged."

Unawareness of the existence of certain songs or words in a foreign language can hardly be held against some one. What astounds is that these people seem to believe that we Occidentals have "On-Off" switches embedded in our hearts. Now this would be a very convenient thing to be sure, and Japanese occasionally express jealousy for our alleged *dryness.* But, I, at least, feel insulted. They complain about being called "economic animals?" We should complain about being depicted as monstrous machines! [6]

"It is often said" writes the president of a major Japanese engineering research corporation, that

> Europeans are analytical, logical, digital and hardware-like in thinking while the national character of Japanese is feeling-like [sic], analogical and soft-ware-like. (Shirozaka Toshikichi [?]: *Nihonjin no Sôzôsei Kaihatsu*, 1980, cited in Robin Gill: *Eigo wa Konna ni Nippongo: 1984/9*)

Were he writing today [1995], his countrymen would have surely have been granted another adjective, "fuzzy." The man's language shows he is no egghead – but he has done a fine job of reducing the *Occidentalism* of the intellectual establishment to its bones. The work of the Ruth Benedict of Japan, anthropologist Nakane Chie, contrasts our "culture of confrontation" to her "culture of continuity;" the highly respected linguist Toyama Shigehiko's work compares our "clarity-oriented" linguistic style to his language's "obscurity-oriented" one, and philosophic sociologist, Aida Yuji equates our "rationalism" to Japanese "intuition."

All say the same thing – you Occidentals are cold bricks; we Japanese are warm clay – and the conclusion being known from the outset (kind of like a John Dee murder mystery), the fun is figuring out new ways to get there.

One of the more creative efforts was made by the highly-awarded geologist, Suzuki Hideo in his best seller SHINRIN-NO SHIKO, SABAKU-NO SHIKO (Jungle Thinking, Desert Thinking, NHK Books, 1978).[7] He says that in a desert everything is clear and choices are strictly alternative, i.e., this way leads to water, that does not. Thus, the desert-born Judeo-Christian West is dualistic by nature; as opposed to the wishy-washy East, born of a jungle culture where abundance and easy living did not require decisiveness. This is confirmed, he contends, by the fact that Germans will say they know something even when they don't, whereas Japanese feel most relieved when they say they don't know (For evidence he mentions being badly misled on numerous occasions when asking directions in German. I hate to have to tell him but I've had the same experience in Japan and now often ask more than one person to be safe!)

Suzuki indulges in some philology – *de rigor* for this type of book – contrasting the Japanese way to say "[I] don't know," that is, *wakaranai* to Western equivalents, pointing out that the former is related to the "jungle religion!" Buddhism's central tenet: All things are indivisible, or, *wakerarenai.*

True. The significant part of *wakaranai, "wa"* is usually written with a Chinese character meaning "divide/part" (分). What intrigues us, however, is what the professor overlooks. By the same token, Japanese must literally *divide things to know!* "[I] know" is *wakaru* (*wakatte-iru /wakatta/etc.*), or "I divide." And, we could add the fact that the word most commonly used for what we most modestly call "*under*standing" is *rikai,* where *ri* is "reason" or "principle" and *kai* means, basically, "take to pieces." What could be more fragmenting than that? Further, I would argue that Japanese actually show a strong penchant for dividing and categorizing things, so much so that you tend to get thought that is far more discriminating (in both the good and bad senses of the word) than understanding.[8]

Maybe my rhetoric got the better of me, but what can you say when the very people who claim they don't divide things divide the world in two with a vengeance?

And, if a brilliant scholar like Suzuki Hideo can completely overlook the reverse side to his logic, how can an ordinary translator ever figure out that "apparently' may not be synonymous with "clearly" (Dictionaries don't help much because they give almost all of their space to the adjective form, which usually *does* mean "clear.")? Or, for that matter, how can they cope with any number of subtle problems that inevitably arise when transforming a sentence from English to a language as different as Japanese?

"My question again is a rather simple one," writes Professor Eto: "Why do translators of Japanese literature not translate Japanese texts in the same way as we have translated Western texts? *Are we wrong, or are they?* (JCLA speech, italics mine.)

Were Japanese translations half as close to the originals as Eto believes them to be, I would say "they!," meaning us. Unfortunately, they are not. Most Japanese-English translations may be far from ideal, but at least they do not make the Japanese authors look inconsiderate, or, for that matter, falsely humble. There is little *Orientalism* in them. On the other hand, if I am not mistaken, much if not most English-Japanese translation follows and reinforces the Occidentalist prejudice held by Japanese. A more realistic question for Japanese and English-speakers alike might be:

Would you prefer to be Seidenstickered or Monstered?

ch.5 notes

1. How apparent "apparently?" English and English-Japanese dictionaries should share blame for the mistranslation. Most of them fail to give a separate definition for the *-ly* form. But I was surprised to find a well-known pundit of the English language (to whom I wrote) did not feel that the first meaning of "apparently" differed from the first meaning of "apparent." All I can say is that when you *judge* instance after instance of "apparently" for correctness *in translation*, you will find the word is used most often to *soften* the statement rather than to *strengthen* it, like "clearly" would. It usually means that something *seems to be so, but is not necessarily so.* As rhetoric, its vector is opposite from "apparent," as it serves the interest of modesty. Possibly, my writing (1989) or that of Bekku Sadanori, **(i)** who has published similar thoughts, influenced English-Japanese dictionary makers: I was delighted to find separate listings for "apparently" in a number of new dictionaries I checked in a bookstore in Spring of 1998.

---

i. Bekku Sadanori. While I may be the first person to tie in Japanese mistranslation to Occidentalism, in year-after-year of columns and books Bekku has done more than anyone to call the public's attention to the large amount of ridiculously bad translation in Japan. He brings to bear not only good English comprehension but the broad intellectual interests and judgment which allow a translator to go beyond language to the thought that makes it intelligible. I think he did not read all of my books (I don't read all of his either – *Why?* I know I'll agree with all he says!) or he would have cited me when he wrote on "apparently."

---

2. "Certain about something that is not" as a translation strategy. After reading the following words on translation by Donald Keene, it occurred to me that I have failed to comment upon the relationship of translation style to the *reader's* expectations:

> . . . readers are far less tolerant of translated work than of those in English. Any obscurity in a work translated from, say Chinese, is laid to he workings of the mind of the inscrutable Oriental or to the failings of the more scrutable translator; obscurities in English works are quickly leapt over and taken for granted. If the translator has to deal with a work which is ambiguous in the original and susceptible to varying interpretations, it is probably best, except in the rare instances when the original ambiguity is easily transferred into English, to choose one of the possible meanings and state it plainly. ("The Translation of Japanese Culture" in APPRECIATIONS OF JAPANESE CULTURE)

Keene's observations are, sadly, true. Only someone who does or checks translations made *from* one's native tongue discovers its obscurity, how much the language or the author fails to make clear. Unfortunately, the ambiguity of the original is often behind its wit and tied to the author's discrimination, or *taste*. I hate to sacrifice *that* because the reader may well use it to re-enforce his idea of inscrutable Orientals. The Japanese translator and reader, however, are in the opposite situation, because not only scrutable, but clunky black and white language is *expected* from the Westerner. So, if the idea is to buck the stereotype, the Japanese translator should perhaps do the reverse of what Keene suggests! The only problem is that the Japanese reader might not believe the ambiguity, or subtlety, to be genuine. He might assume the translator *created* it to Japan the work. In order to avoid having to defend himself, the translator might adopt the Occidentalist style of translation. Personally, I favor translating as much ambiguity as possible (I assume, here, that the translator really understands the original text, for much ambiguity is only so to the poor reader) even when it is not easy and requires more brackets and footnotes (chapter notes alone won't do) than most publishers will permit. A Translator's Foreword could warn readers about making Orientalist/ Occidentalist assumptions. Where a quick-paced work of fiction won't permit this luxury, perhaps the translator can make up for the loss of ambiguity in translation by creating it in places where English/Japanese can do so without being obvious.

3. Black and white images. "Apparently" is easy to correct because Japanese has many ways to express things that *seem to be*. Indeed, they can do it better than English can because they can conjugate it in at the end of the sentence. But that is not true for many problematic words and syntax. "Many" – which is to *quantity* what "often" is to *frequency* – is a perpetual pain in the neck. We use it frequently and it usually doesn't mean a hell of a lot. Sometimes, the Japanese expression *takusan* works, but it is clumsy as an adjective and must be used sparingly. As a result, it tends to turn into *"ôku-no,"* or *"~no ôku"* meaning "most." In other words, what was meant in the original to mean "not a few" turns into what amounts to *a vast majority!* I teach Japanese translators to use "not a few" *(-sukunaku-wa-nai)* as a translation for "many," rather than "most" (*oku*) *when possible*. But it rarely *is* possible because it is long and grammatically limited – it must usually close the sentence. Regardless, it doesn't bother many translators, for *mosting* "many" fits the image of the Westerner overstating things in black and white terms. The diced style of most post-War translations contributes more to the problem then the vocabulary, but this can only be discussed *through example in a bilingual format*. (See my GOYAKU-TENGOKU and EIGO-WA KONNA NI NIPPONGO if you read Japanese.) Suffice it to say that, in Japanese, complex degrees of comparison, the qualifying-as-we-go (that only relative clauses make possible) often fragment into simple serial statements, each of equal (rather than dependent) weight, that lose the narrative of the original English.

4. They either love or hate. This is a common Japanese Occidentalism. It makes us (Occidentals) all emotional lightweights, fairies. Although Tinkerbelle was no light-weight for a fairy – Barrie describes her as *embonpoint*, or pleasantly plump (To think that many English and Americans conflate her body with that of Peter Pan so she is occasionally charged with promoting anorexia!) – she was still deemed too small to hold more than one feeling at a time. It also makes us like the dog as described by Freud:

> Dogs love their friends and bite their enemies, quite unlike people, who are incapable of pure love and always mix love and hate in their object relations. (found in Jeffrey Moussaieff Masson: DOGS NEVER LIE ABOUT LOVE. He adds "In other words, dogs are without the ambivalence with which humans seem cursed.")

While Barrie is neutral and Freud is favorable with respect to pure emotion, Seneca, who, as far as I know, originated the idea, probably meant it as criticism ("A woman either loves, or hates, there is no third thing" – translated by Nash in THE ANATOMY OF ABSURDITIES). I once defended our ability to hold mixed emotions on Japanese radio and had them play the teary recitation part of "I Will Always Love You" for the proof. Even if they had to depend on me for the explanation, the grain of Dolly's voice said it all.

5. THE ANATOMY OF DEPENDENCE. For an academic tome, this one sold more and sold longer – you'll still find stacks of it in all the campus bookstores – than any other book I know of. "Dependence" is a make-do translation of *amae*, a word for which there is no close English translation, the fact of which gave occasion for Doi, a psychiatrist, to write his *nihonjinron* **(i)**. Bester's translation made the concept well-known in the English-speaking world and Howard Rheingold includes the verb *amaeru* in THEY HAVE A WORD FOR IT: "To presume upon another's love, to act like a baby in order to be treated like a dependent." He is wrong with his pronunciations *AH-may-roo* and *AH-may*. Using his weird, but unfortunately necessary American style of phonetics, it should be *"ah-mah-eigh-roo."* But his half-page introduction is fine, except that in stressing the relationship of the word to the "meek dependent role of women or a child "ingratiating himself to his father," he fails to develop the general idea sufficiently to make the lack of a verb in English seem a problem. Think of a step-child or a new dog, adopted from the pound. Suppose they distrust you, or simply won't fully relax and let you love them. In Japanese, this situation can be expressed easily: they don't or can't *amaeru*. We do not have a transitive verb for being *open to care* or *accepting love*. The closest verb, *depend* usually works for adults, but won't for, say, a puppy. **(ii)** Where (I think) Doi goes wrong is in using this gap in English vocabulary to indulge in cultural contrasts galore, rather than treating it as a linguistic quirk.

---

i Cultures that *amaeru* and cultures that don't? Doi's *nihonjinron* contrasts a Japan where people *amaeru* too much and a Protestant Western culture – he allows for a touch of *amae* in the Catholic concept of *agape* – where individualism does not allow any *amae*. He sees the greater *amae* in Japanese parent-child (especially mother-boy) relations and in the company-worker relation, but he fails to see that there are parts of Western culture where, word or not, people indulge in more *amae* than Japanese: namely, couple relations, neighbor relations, and trusting in God. I hypothesize that the total amount of *amaeruing* enjoys a cultural parity. (Read Doi. See my *Nihonjinron Tanken* if you read Japanese, and the "*Omnia Vincit Amae*" chapter of Dale: 86, for more biting criticism. Dale claims Doi merely dresses up old theory in exotic Japanese words.) This is also discussed in the body of the book. I repeat for I think it important.

ii Dependence in the USA. The title of John Bester's translation, THE ANATOMY OF DEPENDENCE was well chosen, for even as Doi made the insulting Occidentalist generalizations I mention in the text, he criticized the lack of independence of modern Japanese, where the differences between male and female, child and adult, truth and falsehood, melt together into mush, for the urge to *amaeru* is one to be incorporated in something else. "Dependence" is also perfect because in the years following publication of the translation in 1973, *dependence* has become a catchword for addiction in the USA, where one is not supposed to be dependent upon anything or anyone, even a lover! The equation of dependence with psychological pathology in America also shows that exaggerated or not, Doi's contrast contains no little truth. The contrast was made earliest by someone he does not mention, Alice Mabel Bacon:

> A [Japanese] man . . . rarely makes provision for the future, and looks with scorn on foreign customs which seem to betoken a fear lest, in old age, ungrateful children may neglect their parents and cast them aside. *The feeling so strong in America, that dependence is of itself irksome and a thing to be dreaded, is altogether strange to the Japanese mind.* The married son does not think to take his wife to a new and independent home of his own . . . but takes her to his father's house, and thinks it no shame to live upon his parents. But, in return, when the parents wish to retire . . . (*my italics*. JAPANESE GIRLS AND WOMEN: 1890)

6. Westerners as machines. There is some poetic justice in this, coming in an era when "economic animal" was the common description of the Japanese. There is also not a little humor in it. In a book published in 1983 (*Nihonjin to Obeijin:* PHP) to help Japanese "become better cosmopolitans by pointing out the differences between the culture of Japan and that of the West" (from jacket), we find a cartoon of a Japanese man furiously kicking a vending machine while a Westerner "rationally" calls for help. Allegedly, this is because the Christian Occidentals maintain a strict difference between humans, with their souls, and mindless things, while Japanese, being animists can't help treating the machine as if it is alive! With Westerners usually depicted as lacking self-control, this opposite image is welcome. But, still, if we read between the lines, it is one more case of Japanese as all too human and Westerners as something else again.

7. A brilliant scholar like Suzuki Hideo. I discovered his work because the chief editor at the publisher where I worked kept telling me that the *nihonjinron* I challenged were worthless to begin with. "Well, then," I asked, "tell me of a good one!"

8. A Japanese penchant for categorizing. This is seen in their rectangular "50-sound" syllabary with its neat rows of syllabets: *ka, ki, ku, ke, ko; sa, shi, su, se, so* and in their enormous and diverse dictionaries. In the Edo era, one finds everything from *monowa-tsukushi* "listing" (see pg. 143) collections, tourist spots – places to see the Fall moon, places to see the geese splash down, etc. – to types of male and female private parts, categorized and listed according to their desirability. The large *saijiki,* sometimes Englished as a haiku almanacs, are now four times as large as Webster's and chop up the whole damn year into a fine chain of seasonal events, natural and cultural. The West only does better with quotation collections. Borges's weird list of Chinese things is amusing, but the perfectly scrutable categorizing mania of Sino-Japanese civilization deserves serious attention. "Japanese categories" – the last example of which could be the line-up of *pokemon* creatures – would make a fine doctoral thesis would it not? (Jacqueline Pigeot's book on *Monowatsukushi* as a Japanese rhetoric comes close to dealing with this, but this *listing* is but part of categorizing.)

VI

A Difficult Language, English

(just plain mistranslation)

All intercultural exchange is a form of translation. It, too, does not "carry over" as directly as one might assume.

Take *country music*. To me, country is a cross between metaphysical poetry and homeopathic medicine.[1] A more typical view would be that expressed by George F. Will a decade or so ago. He had doubts about the authenticity of the "miserable slice of life" depicted, but generously conceded that the music was defending an endangered constitutional right, *the Right to be Unhappy!* Japanese are surprised to hear that country in the US is ridiculed for its high number of *hurtin' songs* and *weepers.* To them, country music is as happy and "dry" as "Home on the Range" and "Oklahoma." This, of course, is just the opposite of *their* country equivalent *enka*, which is "sad and wet". [2]

True to form, Japanese go for *happy* country. (John Denver? *"Yes!"* George Jones. *"Who?"*) If the selection of songs ("Jambalaya" remains in *karaoke*, "Your Cold, Cold Heart" is long gone) doesn't do the trick, some editing will: In the translated versions of "The Tennessee Waltz" and "The Green, Green Grass of Home" there is nothing about a lover being stolen by a friend or the singer's ending up *under* that green grass. The part that sends the shivers running up and down your spine is gone, and all you get are stale memories and nostalgia. If mindless violence is "A" side, prime-time America, this is the musical version of the sweet inanity that defines its stereotypical "B" side.

Many Japanese do not like sad and wet *enka*. They say the same uncomplimentary things about it that certain Americans have long said about country. But fan or not, they all agree that *enka* is very Japanese – the tear-stained crystallization of the long-suffering Japanese heart. And country, therefore, being quintessentially American, is *by definition* the exact opposite. Then, this imagined "country" is dismissed as a mindlessly happy music by those who might appreciate it best in Japan, and lauded by those who might hate it if they but understood the words. We are back to Tanizaki.

I repeat: *All intercultural exchange is a form of translation.* Then, how do we decide what gets *translated?* In his classic book on the influence of natural environment on culture FUDORON (1935), Watsuji Tetsuro hypothesized that Christianity succeeded in northwest Europe because the people living in its cold, wet and dark forests welcomed the dry desert light reflected in the pages of the Bible. [3] On the other hand, most Japanese scholars in the post-war period have explained the lack of Christian success in Japan by the fact that their "wet forest country" or "monsoon culture" is temperamentally at odds with "desert thought" (None of these authors mention Islam's success in Indonesia!). As the proverb says, *Opposites attract / Like attracts like.*[4]

Since cultural compatibility can, thus, explain *everything* that does or does not happen, logic tells us it explains *nothing.* Besides, as we have just seen with respect to country music, the foreign element to be (or not be) adopted may itself be a figment of one's own culture's collective imagination. I would argue that the translation of culture has little to do with compatibility, and everything to do with prejudice. Like love, it is a historical accident and often involves self-delusion.

Take literature, for example. Most Japanese probably believe that America's best work is translated. As a matter of fact, this is not true – and probably never has been for *any* country.

Around 1990, the Japanese press was raving American (mostly New York?) "New Generation!" novelists. My personal opinion of their work accords with that of the '*L.A. Times*' critic who wrote that a glass of cold water in the face would do more for them than a review. Each to his taste. Japan has a similar school – I almost wrote *shoal* – of young writers, and *they* have readers. What stung me is that these twerps were getting written up and translated while writers far more worthy of the honor were still unknown here [I wrote this while living in Japan]. I am referring to two traditions of writing which make me proud of – or, at least diminish the embarrassment of – being an American.

One is *the nature essay*. Despite the fact that nature essays became a major literature in the 1980s, with bookstore shelves and a half dozen major anthologies to prove it, there were very few translations of Abbey, Dillard, Ehrlich, Eiseley, Lopez, etc., and no attention given to the genre. A new translation of WALDEN comes out every few years; but the first fall translation of CAPE COD (I corrected the translation after it was done at my instigation) didn't appear until 1993, at which time – i.e., after the "New Generation Writers" – nature essays *finally* began to be noticed here in articles that invariably began with the mandatory lie of the news world: "Most recently, in America . . . The latest fad in American literature . . . " – when it is the critic and his paper that was late!

The other is *Black American literature*. Langston Hughes and Alice Walker have followings. But they are exceptions. Hughes is "avant-garde" and Walker "feminist." The greatness of black English writing *per se* is not acknowledged. Only part of one book by Zora Neale Hurston and one book by Toni Morrison have been translated to date [i.e. 1994: no doubt, the Nobel

Prize has changed things for the latter's work].

We have already touched upon the difficulty of expressing black wit in Japanese (despite Mr. Eto, a rather uptight language). But it must be said, the Japanese don't make much of an effort, either. They don't, I believe, because even those translators who love black culture – for its warmth, attunement to what's important in life, etc. – simply can not accept the fact of black intellect. The sophistication of the language goes right by them. Blacks in Japan are synonymous with the physical. A common Japanese proverb says "Heaven gives us but one blessing." If blacks have good bodies, how can they have good minds? If black literature is given the attention it deserves, the Japanese are in for a surprise.

What, then, has held back nature essay translation? If intellectual wit is not expected of black Americans, intellectual maturity and grace is not expected of *all* Americans. We are supposed to be writing hard-boiled novels, acerbic columns, science journalism, shallow polemic . . . .

The Japanese are not alone in this respect. A few years ago, I visited London and was surprised to find almost no American nature essays, not even a selection from Mr. Hoagland's Penguin Nature Library – Penguin a British company at that! If the English had good nature essayists to boast of, I'd have shrugged it off as an understandable case of competitive exclusion. But *no*. They only had local detail. Political ecology. Animal stories (Mr. G. Durrell, very cute!). The only decent nature essays I could find were from the olden days. W.H. Hudson. Jefferies. I don't know. Maybe the English do not want nature as literature any more. But I expect the reason is simply prejudice, "for English people are far more interested in American barbarism than they are in American civilization," as Wilde once remarked.

But in the Japanese case, there is another big obstacle.

Translation. There just aren't enough translators capable of *literary* non-fiction. Most of the translators capable of writing with a modicum of style are not able to comprehend difficult English, much less the ideas it may subtly express. And even those who are capable (judging from their own writing) and seemingly comprehending, may well pander to the juvenile easy-to-understand style publishers have been demanding over the past twenty-five years or so, that has given birth to increasingly boring versions of Shakespeare (or, for that matter, ancient Japanese literature) that explain his wit so thoroughly it vanishes to all but the dullest reader. [5] We'll just have to see how much of the better nature writing gets the translation it deserves.

This problem of comprehension leads to another, less interesting but perhaps more important problem. While my main interest is the big picture – mistranslating culture – plain old mistranslation also calls for our attention, for the incredible amount of it found in Japanese-English translation speaks in itself of *something.*

Let me define *mistranslation.* Turning an "azalea" into a "lily," though you knew it was an azalea, is *not* a mistranslation. It is *an editorial decision.* Shaving off adjectives to help the train of thought through a narrow pass may be necessary to keep it from being derailed. No mistranslation there, either. Mistranslation is not mere misjudgment or stylistic sins. It is what happens when the translator does not understand the original.

No one is perfect. Some mistranslation, like occasional weevils in a bag of rice or grain, is expected. In any finished book, I would say a handful of first-degree mistranslations (author's intent completely reversed, or turned into something comically or tragically removed from the original) and a few dozen second-degree mistranslations (a word mistaken, sentence's intent lost) would be acceptable. The problem is that the majority of English-Japanese translations have a first-degree mistranslation every few pages and a handful of second-degree mistranslations on every page.[6]

Why? English is difficult. Japanese is difficult for people outside of the Sino-sphere because of the time needed to master thousands of *kanji*. But once we can read with out trainer-wheels (dictionaries), it is fairly easy. At least in this sense: *you generally know when you don't know*, and can ask a Japanese friend for help.[7] English, unfortunately, is far more devious. Most Japanese – even with years of study abroad – *don't know when they don't know*. Though the translator marks all of the places he is uncertain about to review with an English checker, he will be lucky to catch ten percent of the "ambushes".

Rhetoric is one reason for this. President Clinton, happy to get a question he'd been waiting for, tells a reporter, "I thought you'd *never* ask!" – and the superimposition tells millions of Japanese television viewers "What a shock! I never thought you'd ask me something like that." Japanese are supposed to be intuitive when it comes to reading *silence,* but let me tell you when it comes to reading *words* they definitely are *not*. Rather, they are almost entirely rhetoric-deaf. Any sentence with the least tad of english on it is liable to be misunderstood and, oftener than not, turned on its head.

Part of the problem comes from the enormous syntactical distance between the languages. Japanese put their feelings on the tail of the verb at the butt of the sentence. It may take a while to get there, but if you are patient you can hardly miss it. (When further emphasized by certain foreshadowing adverbs or particles earlier in the sentence, it is just *too easy* to catch). The subtlety of rhetorical English, where meaning can completely reverse by the use or non-use of italics, goes right by the Japanese. Indeed, if it's italicized, chances are it will be mistranslated!

The other part of the problem is not so much inherent to the language itself as the nature of modern Japanese speakers. Ancient Japanese were much more versatile linguists. They would have had much less trouble with English. They could write things like "When heaven and earth are no longer, than we will stop meeting" or "I'll stop loving you when the moon disappears from the sky" (MANYOSHU poems #2419 and 3004, respectively) and understand the meaning – as any English (or Chinese) speaker still can! – without having a scholar explain, "This is reverse rhetoric. Since that won't happen; love won't stop." They would have been astounded to even imagine people so dull as to require an explanation for something so simple.[8]

Most ambushes involve idiom. Knowing that English is full of idioms helps. But not much. Idioms do not come with labels dangling from their necks [smart tags, if I may add a new metaphor]. The translator will never know the words he faithfully translated had a completely different figurative meaning. Japanese is less idiomatic than English (or, English is exceptionally idiomatic) so Japanese speakers may have less experience with recognizing which words to take at face value and which not to. Still, if translators were more concerned with understanding and communicating rather than translating for the sake of translating, they might catch more rhetoric and idiom from the context. As it is, the tendency is to shrug ones shoulders (*who knows what the foreigner is driving at?*) and go on. For too many translators, translation is a mere business – who has time to think?[9]

The tragedy is not that mistranslation is rife, but that so little is being done to reduce it. Nothing will be done until the publishing industry realizes that mistranslation is not the exception but the rule, and hire native speakers of English with good command of written Japanese to check translations. Considering the relatively small size of the market and poor publishing conditions, this will not be financially possible unless the original publishers and authors care enough to contribute, or translators marry native speakers to obtain "free" assistance. I am not optimistic.

There are a number of books arraigning particularly poor translations, but the overall situation has been studiously ignored. I believe the *Occidentalist* view of Western language as clear-cut may be the main reason things are as bad as they are.

ch.6 notes

1. My country. Black blues lyrics are frequently included in anthologies of poetry while country is not. This bespeaks of bias against non-urban white culture on the part of the establishment intelligentsia. Country has more good lyrics than the blues because more people are writing it and words are relatively more important in country music. Take one favorite theme, cheating, and you will find hundreds if not thousands of clever plots that put opera to shame. **(i)** I get sick and tired of seeing books full of really lame pop lyrics by New Yorkers and Hollywoodites when country has the real thing! Look, have Gershwin and what's-his-name ever closed a song with a couplet as good as this one by Tom T.?

> "I'm glad I met you Mr. Hall.
> But I guess there ain't no song here, after all."

Or, how about the e.e. cummings-eat-your-heart-out lines of a 1980's Johny Rodriguez hit?

> But if he makes her happy,
> I guess I should be glad;
> Cause I didn't every chance I had.

Establishment columnists love to spout off about "Stand by Your Man" – one even compared Hillary=Tammy to a door-mat(!) **(ii)** – but I've yet to see the most touching line of the song mentioned: "he's only a man." **(iii)** Here is a song that off-handedly patronizes men and the educated idiots can't get beyond the title! You don't have to go to Japan to find cultural misunderstanding!

---

i. Country versus opera. I have read a number of books on the content of opera in English --- since I cannot read Italian very well – including Paul Robinson: OPERA AND IDEAS – From Mozart to Strauss (Cornell UP). Believe me, country is the more highly developed art-form. Opera is lucky not to be sung in English!

ii. "He's only a man." The fact that country can draw shivers or tears in less than three minutes says everything about how finely crafted some of the stories are. But the little lines are also impressive. If the following titles of "uplifting ballads" found in a Kevin Cowherd column (the title, "I was drunk the day my Mom got out of prison," a line from a David Allen Coe song) Baltimore Evening News found in the Yomiuri Daily News 89/1/23) belonged to the blues rather than country, the *New Yorker* (etc) would love them:

> "From the Gutter to You (Ain't Up)"
> "All My Ex's Live in Texas (That's Why I Live in Tennessee)"
> "She Took My Last Dime (And Called My Wife)"
> "I'd rather have a bottle in Front of Me (Than a Frontal Lobotomy)"

iii. "So why is Hillary Clinton smiling?" "Feminists will long ponder how it was that the first lady became wildly popular only when she played the doormat. (Excuse me, I mean played Tammy Wynette.)" – Maureen Dowd wrote this for the *New York Times.* She also calls Mrs. Clinton "the single most degraded wife in the history of the world." What nonsense! Why should Mr. Clinton's being a billy goat degrade *her?* Has Mr. Clinton said a single thing bad about her? Does Dowd want Mrs. Clinton to run after Mr. Clinton with a carving knife? For all we know, Mrs. Clinton said "Bill, you know I hate to go down, if you want head you better get it somewhere else!" What do *we* know about their private life! And, what a cruel way to use recently deceased Tammy Wynette! Does Dowd have any idea how insulting she is to all of Tammy's fans? No wonder country folk love to hate New York!

---

2. And *theirs* (*enka*)! While some Japanese will say "*enka* is our country," the image remains opposite if not antipathetic to C&W. When a comparison to a *similar* Western form is intended the chanson usually receives the honor, partly because the French woman who *is* chanson has the *tortured voice* Japanese find the *sine qua non* for "wet" singing – and they don't listen to George Jones – partly because the instrumentals are closer to *enka* (indeed *enka* melodies seem like chanson with a touch of Japanese traditional folk-song in the form of two regularly missing notes), and partly because *enka* is mostly written and produced by city-slickers who graduate from top Universities. **(i)** There is one difference between country and *enka* that fits my *cultural-parity hypothesis* very well.

Where a country song may become a man's or a woman's song depending upon who happens to make it a hit, *enka* are almost always gendered from the start. "Male tears" (*otoko-namida*) are allowed, but a man could not sing:

> Now I don't mind this waiting,
> don't mind this running round;
> But if you're going to cheat on me,
> don't cheat in our hometown.

like Ricky Skaggs, or

> Hurt me as much as you want to,
> If tears make you happy then I'll cry.
> Do anything that you want to.
> But don't ever tell me "goodbye."

like (sorry, lost your name). They could not sing the songs as *male songs*, that is. "We Japanese men aren't so degraded," as one man put it to me. But they, nevertheless, often *do* sing even more pitiful tear-jerkers, the *enka* equivalents of "I Will Always Love You" and D.I.V.O.R.C.E.. How? Why? As *female songs*. They sing in their own voice. We are not talking about imitation. But the understanding is that they are singing from the perspective of a woman. In other words, Japanese men must be more manly with male songs but may sing from the female point of view where American men are allowed male songs with more "female" feelings but are not allowed to sing as women. This is another example of my theory of cultural balance, where different choices result in overall equality.

---

i City-slicker music The sad sight of a man's suited back is common to both *enka* and chanson. And, it is a sad fact that a handful of male intellectuals, called – you guessed it – *Sensei*, produce almost all *enka.* The stars, typically come from the country and put up with years of making Sensei's dinner (in Nashville we find occasional star-to-be chauffeurs) until they are *given* a good song that makes them a star. Very few of the singers write any songs. Of course, there is the occasional *novelty* number – in this, *enka* is like country – that speaks for the boondocks. A favorite of mine had lines going something like this *"In my hometown, there is no video, no walkmans, no . . . .. no nothing!"* And, *enka* introduces more maritime songs every year – the sea is rightly seen as a lonely and "wet" place to work (male teardrops soaking through a thick seaman's raincoat) – than modern country has in its half-century history. And the country-bred singers do these songs in country accents, so *enka* is strongly supported in the country even if it does have men wearing suits. And, I almost forgot to say, there is a touch of nationalism in *enka* that reminds me of country. From a book about Kitajima Saburo (a top *enka* singer) this crap:

> In America, there's jazz.
> In France, there's chanson.
> In Japan there's enka.
> I am Japanese.
> I love Japan's music, enka;
> And will keep singing it forever.

Merle Haggard's concern lest we ever see "spuds stamped "Made in Japan"" (see his best album: "Amber Waves of Grain") is far better done.

---

3. Climate on Culture. *Fudoron* is literally "Wind-land-argument." The "wind-land" part means "natural features." Add "water" and you've got the name of the classic by Hippocrates. Until the mid-part of this century, many Europeans and Americans took it for granted that civilization thrives in the temperate zone because heat addles the brain and the cold causes stupor, and so forth. And, some supplied much more detail. If Alexander Humbolt, after contrasting the forests in the temperate zones and those of the equator, could *ask:* "How does this **. . .** appearance of nature, rich and pleasant to a greater or lesser degree, affect the customs and above all the sensibility of people?" Then, others less cautious would *answer*. W.J. Cash took it to the limit in THE MIND OF THE SOUTH:

> **. . .** there was the influence of the Southern physical world – itself a sort of cosmic conspiracy against reality in favor of romance. The country is one of extravagant colors, of proliferating foliage and bloom, of flooding yellow sunlight, and, above all perhaps, of haze. Pale blue fogs hang over the valleys in the morning **. . .** the dominant mood **. . .** is one of well-nigh drunken reverie – of a hush that seems all the deeper for the far away mourning of the hounds and the far-away crying of the doves – of such

> sweet opiates as the rich odors of hot earth and pinewood and the perfume of the magnolia in bloom – of soft languor creeping through the blood and mounting surely to the brain . . . It is a mood, in sum, in which directed thinking is all but impossible . . . . But I must tell you also that the sequel to this mood is invariably a thunderstorm. . . . The pattern . . . was to enter deeply into the blood and bone of the South . . ." (1941) **(i)**

While we still talk about the influence of spaces and frontier on our culture as the twentieth century ends, we do not tie geography and climate into our mentality in quite the same way Cash did and the Japanese still do. When Shintaro Ishihara (the politician who co-authored A JAPAN THAT CAN SAY *NO*) writes "Given our millennial cultural heritage and even *a common worldview developed out of environmental conditions such as the monsoons,* the present deepening of economic ties create very advantageous historical conditions for a new feeling of unity throughout Asia" (*Daily Yomiuri* 1995/1/26: italics mine) – one can't help wondering what *Los Angeles Times* Syndicate readers got out of it. *Monsoons?*

---

i Poor drunken South and white culture. Anyone fixing to study Orientalism might first look closer at how the poor white culture is treated here. Like Asia, it is plural. The gothic deep South, the redneck crackers, and the hillbillies. Here is Toynbee on the latter:

> They are the American counterparts of the latter-day white barbarians of the Old World, – Rifis, Albanians, Kurds, Pathans and Hairy Ainus; whereas these latter are belated survivals of an ancient barbarism, the Appalachians present the melancholy spectacle of a people who have acquired civilization and then lost it.

And, this is *polite* stuff. In moving from Japan, I misplaced files with horrendous quotations from Mencken and others which describe them as less-than-human degenerates! If you see a movie called "Tobacco Road", which is supposed to be by a director of progressive sensibilities, you can see something every bit as bad as the worse *Orientalism*. Moreover, the Appalachians were colonialized by outside interests. They experienced cultural imperialism in the USA in the twentieth century. But rather than giving a poor outline, I recommend a fine analysis: David E. Whisnant: ALL THAT IS NATIVE AND FINE (Univ. of N.C. 1983).

4. Cultural compatibility of two types. Watsuji did not actually divide cultural compatibility into two types. That, as far as I know, is my invention. I found myself more satisfied with his FUDORON than with recent *fudo*-related claims; and, searching for the reason why, came to the conclusion that Watsuji argued both ways and saw no contradiction worth mentioning in doing so, while people today simply ask whether or not something "fits the Japanese taste" (*kuchi-ni au / hada-ni au*) – i.e. is *familiar* to them or not. To follow a strictly homo-compatible approach is to shut out all fresh ideas from a culture. In HAN-NIHONJINRON (anti-japanology), I chided contemporary thinkers for having a more narrow concept of cultural compatibility than that of Pre-World War II thinkers and suggested that hetero-compatibility (opposites attract) deserves a new hearing.

5. Increasingly boring. Having the benefit of previous translations, today's translators of Shakespeare make less mistranslation than ever. The problem is that none have even a tenth of the wit of Tsubouchi's (1859-1935) translations. **(i)** Mistranslation and all, it is still head and shoulders above the rest. Why should this be true? Partly, it might be because Tsubouchi Shôyô was a genius and the world does not have many such. But I fear that decades of translation from English has made Japanese drop their standards of wit. The different syntax means that all too often the punch-line (usually a punch-phrase or punch-word) is no longer at the end of the sentence. I show this with examples in ENGLISH IS *THIS* JAPANESE! (*eigo wa konna ni …*) **(ii)** If you can learn to think something with the punch in mid-sentence is funny, you can accept anything! And worse than that, even humor that is *unnecessarily* lost – that is to say, it depends on neither syntax nor word-play – in translation simply because the translator doesn't get it) is often explained away as the result of a different sense of humor held by Japanese and foreigners. Take the *Playboy Japan* article (July, 1977) on jokes Saturday Night Live could not use, where a renowned critic translated:

"If Helen Keller were alone in the forest and fell down, would she call out?" (my back-translation from his Japanese); and, then, pontificated: "Japanese wouldn't find this very funny, but foreigners have a different sense of humor . . ." The professor, whose specialty was French literature, must not have been familiar with the English philosophical tradition involving Berkeley and stone-kicking, limericks about a tree in the quad and so forth, for he mistranslated the original "make a sound" as *koe-o dasun ja nai-ka* or "call out!" I say *humor is humor*. If you don't get it, either it is not really humorous, or you are missing something.

---

i Shakespeare in Japanese. The modern translators do *try* to recreate Shakespeare's puns, but they are so intent upon making sure *every* reader – even a child – can get it, that the joy of wit (when you figure out you've been had a bit too late) is lost for all. I give examples in MISTRANSLATION PARADISE (*goyakyu tengoku*).

ii Examples. When I write for intelligent Japanese, I have the luxury of including examples in English because most readers know enough to follow. Writing in English, I fear the number of readers capable of reading Japanese does not warrant such treatment. So I can only suggest readers see chapter 9 of EIGO-WA KONNA-NI NIPPONGO, scattered examples in GOYAKU TENGOKU and pages 215-17 of NIHONJINRON TANKEN.

---

6. Problems with most English-Japanese translations. I realize that is a serious charge. Here is how I came to know it true. First, the seven books I wrote in Japanese include scores of quotations from English-language sources. I preferred to use extant translations both because it is the proper procedure, because translating into a foreign tongue is harder than writing in it and because different styles of writing spice up a text. But, I found that about half of the quotations – although they were usually only a paragraph or two long – had serious problems. (That is how I discovered the way Peter Farb's WORD PLAY was butchered and came to write *Goyaku Tengoku* (MISTRANSLATION PARADISE) which is subtitled "word play and mis-play.") Then, as an acquisitions editor for a small but very good publisher for twenty years, I took it upon myself to check translations to over a hundred entire books. Since most of the translators were experienced, I knew that most of the mistakes (some would be found by the Japanese editors) that I discovered would have been published as is at any other publisher. By nature, I am an *im*perfectionist. I don't give a hoot about slight discrepancies and small mistakes, and love very loose translation. Japanese sometimes write ridiculous things about me like, "he is also feared as an utterly merciless mistranslation hunter." (Yonehara Mari: *Fujitsuna Bijo* . . . 1997) But, believe me, I have *never* gone out hunting. The mistranslations always came to me!

Addition for second printing: I was asked to elaborate on the *mistranslation* in Japan. It depends on the difficulty of the original, but a translation by an experienced translator (with, say 10 books-worth of experience) will usually have a major mistranslation once every 10 or 20 pages, whereas a poor translator will have one or two on every page and the worst ones in almost every paragraph! Minor mistranslations occur on every page of most translations. I find, however, that the destruction of the flow of the argument *despite not a single word being mistranslated* can be far worse than any minor mistranslation. I am afraid that concrete examples can only be grasped by people who read Japanese and English, my audience for 誤訳天国. Suffice it to say that translation is like making music, to do a good job, it is not enough to hit the notes. You must master the melody (W.H., sorry, I could not locate my writing on *first, second and third degree mistranslations* I promised to add here!)

---

7. Known ambiguity in Japanese. *Kanji* is hardly all of it. I simplified for brevity's sake. But my assertion that English is *more* obscure stands. Japanese does use more aposiopesis – where a sentence stops midway through and allows the listener/reader to figure out the rest. To the novice in Japanese, this often seem unclear. As Knapp put over a century ago:

> The first word of a sentence which has been employed from time immemorial to express a certain idea is amply sufficient in itself. The rest has become superfluous and has been dropped. And so it is that the stranger in that land, more than in

> any other, is left to find out for himself the meaning of a language of which little is left of all the commonplaces of conversation, save a list of extraordinary and seemingly irrelevant ejaculations. (FEUDAL AND MODERN JAPAN)

But, this is only unclear to the outsider, to the person who should not be translating, anyway. When I hear *"shitsurei-desuga"* (excuse me) from someone who answers the phone I *know* it means ". . . could you tell me your name and, if necessary, who the heck you are!" As for the lack of singular and plural – it usually does not matter. Consider "you." Does its lack of singular and plural bother anyone? Ambiguity only arises when the need to know (for translation) makes it so.

8. Rhetoric-deaf Japanese. One does not have to go back to ancient poetry to find Japanese who knew simple rhetoric. In Shogakukan's encyclopedia of quotations *NIHON MEIGEN MEIKU NO JITEN* (1988) we find under "Japan" the following line by a Meiji era writer upset at the rampant Westernization of clothing and architecture:

> Where is our pride as a nation? Where our dignity as a race? And where our honor as folk [a culture]? (*kuni to shite-no puraido, izuku-ni-ka aru. Jinshu to shite-no sondai, izuku-ni-ka aru. Tami to shite-no eiyo, izuku-ni-ka aru*) (Kitamura Hideya: MANBA[?])

The editors feel the need to explain to the modern-day reader that "*izuku-ni-ka aru* (where is?) is a rhetorical question (*hango-teki hyôgen*) and means 'is no where.'(!)

9. Translation as business. The fact there is a lot of English-Japanese translation means there is more training, more dictionaries and, now, Internet reference resources available; but, at the same time, it means a lot of publishers and translators are in it to make money, and that, as I have explained, means the help of native speakers like myself is out of the question. (*Fluency in exotic tongues cannot be bought except at a price no one will pay.*) Minority languages, where people translate for the love of it, probably fare better despite the considerable handicap of lacking good dictionaries. I think these observations on Japan may help explain the sorry state of French-English translation deplored by Oscar Wilde (See the fine OSCAR WILDE AS CRITIC anthology) over a century ago.

VII

Or Maybe I Complain Too Much?

(*the joy of mistranscription*)

Here are some of the words to a couple songs printed on a Lightning Hopkins album jacket released in Japan

Now you know I been wanna see one
For night and done goanna fell in. . . .

Darlin' you love me
I need, yes I love you, Sam
. . . she kissed me and say I love you
Oh lord till can't no come.

The album was graced with exceptionally good liner-notes by Japan's top popular music critic and music publisher.[1] It was called a "masterpiece of masterpieces" and "the acme of dirty aesthetics." Yet had the record company asked a native speaker of English to transcribe the songs, the words would go like this:

You know I been overseas once
And, whoa, Lightnin' don't wanna go there again!

"Darlin', do you love me?"
I said 'yes, I love you some'
. . . she kissed me and say "I love you
Oh Lord, till Kingdom come."

That makes a bit more sense now, does it not? Likewise

for another record company's luxurious three-record set, *"Mercury Country."* Presumably, because it is White English, the grammar is clean as can be. But that wouldn't help the Japanese listener figure out that the words supplied on the liner:

> *Jesus brought me a blue owl in my caboose.*

were actually,

> *Jesus brought me through all my troubles.*

Then, again, one must admit the misheard Japanese version is infinitely more interesting than the original!

If there is anything for which native speakers are absolutely irreplaceable, it is for transcribing songs.[2] But even when you are talking about a top blues record or a luxurious set, record companies are not bright enough to do this. Neither are movie importers. For all the money involved, native speakers are seldom if ever asked to help. The translator may ask a foreigner – even the director or producer – about a point of difficulty he or she is conscious of, but 90% of the errors slip by unnoticed.[3] Television is even worse. I am constantly finding mistakes, even on politically sensitive interview programs that surely should be checked and double-checked.[4] Some producers, like publishers, may not be able to afford a check by a native speaker fluent in Japanese. But my impression is that even those who can afford it usually do not bother. They must think it unnecessary.[5]

ch.7 notes

1. Japanese Popular Music Critic and Publisher. Nakamura Tôyô and his *Music Magazine* played a large role in making popular music – especially various ethnic musics (and not just the going rage in world music) *cool* in urban Japan.

2. Who needs native speakers? For years, well-meaning family back in the USA showed me this or that piece of comically wrong English and told me to write the company and maybe make some money correcting it. The last time, if I recall right, it was something made by Matsushita, one of the largest electric appliance makers in the world. I would rather write books and starve than do that type of work. But even if I were to write said company, chances are I would not get paid enough to make my corrections worthwhile. If they had wanted to pay for decent English, they could have asked one of their foreign employees for help. They did not. Besides, the meaning of the instructions was clear enough. We should think of the funny English as a *bonus*. It is quite all right to laugh. **(i)** After all, Japanese treat English as a *linguistic free-zone*, a mental space where they can do whatever they please, write inane things they would blush to write in their own tongue and use it for pr, or just to decorate notebooks and bags and T-shirts. **(ii)** A native speaker would only ruin the fun!

---

i Delightful Japanglish. Miranda Kendrick has compiled a book of GEMS OF JAPANIZED ENGLISH. It includes dry humor, such as this warning sign:

> CARS WILL NOT HAVE INTERCOURSE
> ON THIS BRIDGE.

And wet humor, such as this explanation found in a brochure coming with Shichimi togarashi (seven-spice chili pepper):

> It is the origin of this [Shichi-mi] house that the red pepper was given persons to encourage who meditated under the fall named Otowa of Kiyomizu Temple by being struck themselves by the water fall at that time . . .

Then, there is outrageous humor, as this ero-gastronomic statement from a steak house in Tokyo that "fosters authentic beef with deep affection."

> Beef has characteristics and physical property and mind as human fair sex has them. You will never eat the beef with the same taste as you are now eating for ever!

The back-cover of the book tells us "If you've ever had the uneasy feeling that Japanese do things better, this book may be the ideal antidote." The supposition (*Occidentals feeling inferior*) is not unique to the book-cover and explains why Said's ORIENTALISM makes some people roll their eyes in the Far East. But, considering how little Japanese most of Kendrick's readers know, Japanglish should not make us smug! (The point to remember is this: Since Japanese and English are far removed, bilingualism is very, very rare. So, if we are in close contact, there is bound to be a lot of funny language. We might as well enjoy it.)

ii English, a linguistic free-zone. The last example given by Kendrick may well have been written only in English. The store owner might have felt it all right to compare beef to women in a foreign tongue but not in his own. Some Japanese, mostly older men, feel that the overuse of English in Japan is a sign of a slavish attitude toward foreign things on the part of the young. I feel it is rather that English allows Japanese to be outrageous – every man a Humpty Dumpty, deciding for themselves what their English means – the old men should be happy that English takes the brunt of the idiotic and the trendy! (See my EXOTIC TONGUES, someday) Would they rather inanities like "Produced by Hello Juicy" or "Itsy Bitsy Buddies. It's so nice to chum up."? (both egs. from Kendrick: Ibid.) appeared in *their* sacrosanct language?

---

3. Movies and translation. Because the dialog is not always available, difficulty with hearing or transcription may be behind many of the glaring errors in translation. Whatever, the cause, a bilingual, or a native speaker of English with near-fluency in Japanese should be hired to review the entire movie. Witty lines are far more common on the screen than in most novels. The short space available *should* help to stimulate the translator's creativity but, in most cases, it only gives them an excuse to give up trying. (That means the services of a pundit are also called for. If a producer pays me enough *and* the movie is good, I will be happy to try to help: translating wit is my *forte*.)

4. Politically sensitive programs. I write these notes *years* after writing the essay and no longer have my library/examples at hand. Suffice it to say, I have even seen the slow talking Henry Kissinger misconstrued on several occasions on Japanese television shows that were far from live (No excuse, for there was time to check and correct). Even more surprising, I have seen full page anti-whaling advertisements in top Japanese magazines – can you imagine how much that costs?! – with the expression *shuwan,* meaning political "ability," "skills" or even "clout" used where it was obvious to me as a native speaker of English that the word "statesman" or "statesmanship" (as opposed to "politician," which is to say, *rising above mere politics*) was intended by the USA-based environmental organization. Since Japanese has no equivalent term, or rather antithetical terms, a creative copy-writer would change to "long-term" versus "short-term" interest, or being a "leader" versus "follower" – but, then again, the American environmental organization used a picture of a whale (either sperm or blue, I can't recall) that had *nothing to do* with the mink whales the Japanese caught! I can imagine one of the NGO's smug young lawyers impatiently telling a Japanese pr firm to "Just translate it *as it is!"*

Mistranslation can even happen in the ridiculously over-credentialed world of American academia. I have documented a horribly mistranslated survey, where the author, a Dr. K, responded to my inquiry, claiming "professional bilingual social scientists" had translated the survey and that it was retranslated into English again for a "translation compatibility test." (If you read Japanese, see my KORA!MU pgs 112-3) Obviously, translation checking is a difficult art or skill that has little to do with professional degrees (gaining doctorates leaves one little time for learning an exotic tongue.) Even when one pays, one doesn't necessarily get what one pays for.

5. Translation check unnecessary? Theoretically speaking, translation checks *are* unnecessary for novels and movies. If the aim is entertainment, accuracy is not important so long as the translation works. In fact, any one not publishing for a scientific journal should *prefer* a fine mistranslation to a lousy but correct translation. The problem is that most mistranslation is, in reality, uninteresting. The translator, having missed something that is usually interesting – good lines tend to be difficult/subtle – simply does his or her best to tie the dialogue together. Producers should (but do not) know that a translation check of *the entire dialogue* is vital if they wish to present a truly entertaining movie.

VIII

Occidentalism, the Extent of It

(when Koreans unite with Japanese)

A weird thing happened about five [now, ten] years ago. A novel written by a Japanese woman living in America (California) and the Japanese committee that gave it a prize were strongly criticized for discrimination by social critic David Goodman, and made the subject of an article given prominent space in the *Asahi Shinbun* (The *New York Times* of Japan). I say 'weird' because she was only using a worn *Occidentalist* saw – the one that hacks on the belligerent, unforgiving patriarchal Judeo-Christian West with far less of the humor that redeems Mark Twain's *Letters From the Earth* – that has long been acceptable in Japan.[1]

The newspaper was, no doubt, happy to cooperate since it prides itself on being progressive. But, it was dishonest not to confess that its best-known reporter, Honda Katsuichi had already written a book (*arabia yûbokumin* = Arabian nomads c. 1970) which included the same argument with an afterword by another well known intellectual (Ishida Eiichiro) putting it in terms that couldn't be more discriminatory if you tried. [2]

A splendid chance to debate the widely held tenets of *Occidentalism* had been offered to us by the novelist, yet the social critic and the oh-so-correct newspaper reduced it to the prejudice of one woman and indiscretion of a prize committee!

Then there was the case of the Japanese CEO who excited some American tempers by saying "Americans wouldn't apologize even when they are wrong." [3] This, too, was an excellent chance to have chased *Occidentalism* out into the open – but, no, the man was chastised by our leading media for his prejudicial views, as if he was merely voicing a personal opinion. Maybe he did *say* it was just a personal opinion. That doesn't make it one, any more than a Christian's belief that Christ rose from the dead and to sit on the right hand of God makes *that* a personal opinion. Catechism is catechism. The idea that Western people never apologize (except for minor things like burping) is an *Occidentalist* tenet of long-standing.

Let me tell you, there is a lot of uncomplimentary stuff in *Occidentalism*. If there were not, you wouldn't see schools in Japan treating "returnees" (*kikoku-shijo* or Japanese returned from long stays abroad) as they do. [4] Americans don't believe children returning *from Japan* need to be mentally decontaminated. But Japanese believe returnees have been spoiled, turned into egotists, who must be retrained to be sensitive good Japanese. Most Japanese *claim* to look up to the West and that they suffer from an inferiority complex. Survey statistics and the attitude toward returnees – which has, however improved some in recent years – show the opposite. As early as the 1960's, more Japanese felt "superior" than "inferior." [5]

From the mid 1980's, the Japanese mass media reported an allegedly new phenomenon: Japanese "arrogance" vis-à-vis the West. The self-criticism went like this: We have always had a problem with arrogance vis-à-vis other Asians, but economic success has gone to our head and now we are beginning to look down on the West, too. We had better be careful or we are going to get ourselves in trouble. Remember what happened the last time we under-estimated the West. Besides, we really should be more humble and respect other cultures.

Just like the American concern for the behavior of the

"ugly American" a quarter of a century earlier failed to reach the *Orientalist* roots of the problem, the "arrogant Japanese" editorials failed to recognize the *Occidentalist* world view that provided the grounds for the prejudice. In other words, the editorials say "Oh, we really shouldn't feel this way!" and everyone feels ashamed for themselves, but *deep inside they do not feel they have done anything wrong* – for, if their antithetical worldview is correct, the West *is* a pretty base thing.

Does this "arrogance" matter? Most scholars on both sides of the Pacific evidently think it does *not.* The Japanese believe their strong inferiority complex nullifies the significance of anything that might appear to be the opposite, while Americans are downright condescending in their tolerance for "reverse discrimination." Indeed, the very term "reverse-discrimination" implies that discrimination is necessarily something done by the West, or by whites at others, whereas, as we shall soon learn, discrimination has no inherent vector.

Consider. There are already far more Americans working for Japanese than vice versa. [I am not sure this is true, now][6] If one's worldview, i.e., opinion about one's own culture and that of others, makes a difference in how they are treated, we should be *very* concerned about what Japanese think about us.

Moreover, it is not just the Japanese. Occidentalism is widespread in Asia and growing. In an article of mine published in the leading political monthly *Chuo-Koron* in May 1990, entitled *"Professor Lee, Knock-off the Cultural Imperialism If You Please!"*, I recorded how the cross-cultural comparisons written by the brilliant essayist Lee O-Young began by placing Korea, Japan and the West (see his poetic early work IN THIS EARTH AND IN THAT WIND, in excellent English translation by David I. Steinberg) in triangular contrast (or separate comparisons) and, decades later, arrived at a dualistic worldview, with Korea, Japan, and to a lesser extent, China, on one side contrasted against the West in his

1990 book FUROSHIKI CULTURE'S POST-MODERN. The *furoshiki* is a square piece of cloth traditionally used to carry things in Japan and Korea. It fits itself to the proportions of whatever it carries and can be folded up when not used, whereas the Western suitcase or trunk is hard and, accordingly, not adjustable. The author contrasts the post-modern poly-use flexibility of "our" fuzzy thinking "*furoshiki*-culture" to "their" old-fashioned single-use and single-minded "trunk-culture." That is to say, he finds the Far East inherently more suited to the software age than the stiff out-dated West.

Attempts to justify success can be every bit as amusing and strained as attempts to rationalize failure.

In America's heyday as an economic superpower, we find John A. Krownhauser (THE BEER CAN BY THE HIGHWAY, 1961) explaining that Americans are less concerned with the old fashioned question "How does it come out?" than with process:

> "How are things *going*?"

Yes, indeed. The sentences in our comics often end *in progress*, with an open *"and . . . ."* Our great blue-collar workers perform feats of industry unequaled throughout the world by getting into the *process* of manufacture, operating with jazz-like "swing rhythm."(Ibid.) Look at chewing gum, Krownhauser says. It is inedible and its only appeal is in the *process* of chewing. The fact that Americans invented it and spread it throughout the world is enough to prove they are a uniquely *process-oriented* people.[7]

This is *just* the type of thing Japanese would soon begin to write with a vengeance, followed in turn by other Asians as their nations' economies took off. Perhaps it can't be helped. Justifying one's success would seem to be a basic human need.

Unfortunately, however, the Japanese and the Koreans

tend to be a little too eager to put down the other, i.e., the West, in order to raise themselves. Krownhauser praises American grace in the factory; he doesn't go out of the way to put down foreign clods. The typical Japanese book *does*. So does Professor Lee. Let us look at three points of linguistic comparison:

> . . . the thing we call simply a *de-iri-guchi* (lit. leave-enter-mouth or *exentrance*?) Westerners must divide in two and call either an "exit" or an "entrance". Western people call this 'the law of the excluded middle' and think it very logical; but from the eyes of an Oriental it can't help but seem a block-headed way of doing things.

Were Western scholars writing *Orientalist* polemic in the style of the Eastern *Occidentalist*, they might counter Lee as follows:

> "Easterners tend to apply singular appellations to singular objects. *A* is always *A*. An *exentrance* is always an *exentrance.* Nothing changes in their static world. We *Occidentals*, on the other hand, are capable of viewing objects differently in light of our relationship with them, so that the very same door or gate may become an "entrance" or an "exit" according to whether we are going *in* or *out.*

But, no one writes such things in the West; not even those who boast of the "Great Western Tradition" could do that type of thing and keep a straight face.

An even dumber, but more typical example. The professor claims that, contrary to Western languages (represented by one well-known pronouncement of what French is *supposed to be like* accepted as a fact and true for all the West), overly clear language is not Korean." [8] The East values moderation. Koreans and Japanese may go to the barber and ask to have their "head cropped." If an *Occidental* heard this, he might even mistake it for a case of suicide or head-hunting. This vagueness (not specifying that *hair* is what is to be cropped) is characteristic of Eastern communication. If speech is too clear, the listener must "play a passive role" and "the communicative function cannot help but become machine-like," so "we *Orientals* leave a blank, a vague space in our words" and this "is not merely communication, but human communication that reads a person's heart and the air." (Ibid.)

The professor does not come right out and say Westerners practice an inhuman machinelike form of communication, but the all-too-clear space between *his* lines does. I do not know how idiomatic Korean is on the whole, but I do know that Japanese is far *less* idiomatic than American English. So if *un*literal expressions are Eastern, English is more Oriental than anything Lee describes. The ability of English to turn a word as strong as "fucking" into a virtually meaningless adjective or adverb is nowhere matched by the more literally minded Japanese (and, I would guess, Korean).

Now, let's see our last example.

> "It is said that English didn't have words for spring or fall until the Middle Ages ended; certainly the culture of the West is weak when it comes to things between hot and cold."(Ibid.)

Yes, it *has* been said. Many, many times by Japanese Occidentalists over the decades. And Koreans jumped on the band-wagon. In a book on "THE AESTHETICS OF KOREANS"(*Kankoku-no Bi-ishiki*) published in 1984, Hon Sajun tells us that

> "Korean seasons change subtly in a hard to notice way . . . this is not so in the West . . . indeed, "spring" only entered English in the 16th century and autumn had to await the Age of Chaucer. So it is hardly surprising that, compared to Westerners, Koreans are steeped in especially delicate and warm emotions."

Hardly so sophisticated as the post-Modern theorizing of Lee, but basically the same recycled Occidentalist stuff.

Reader. Do not be too quick to think this is absurd. After all, Western intellectuals *do* continually accuse their own civilization of being "dualistic", do they not? If you could not easily rebut the above, you surely can not expect Japanese and Koreans to do so. Or, could you, perhaps, respond as I did, pointing out that *four* seasons tend to become a fixed grid dividing and holding down the year, whereas *two* seasons dynamically interact – that is to say, winter and summer battle (or play tug-o'-war, if you prefer) and the missing spring and fall are essentially *processes* rather than *states*? This idea of a pair of seasons is very Yin-Yang. The ancient West was East as East can be! [9]

Sometimes I wonder, *Does it matter what these people think about us?* If the antithetical *Occident* serves *Oriental* purposes, fine. Let it be. Why should I stick up for the West? The *Orient* so self-defined is such a fine place you hate to bother it. Then, there *is,* of course, a bit of that Monster in all of us. [10]

ch.8 notes

1. Antisemitism and Antisemitism! David Goodman wrote a book JEWS IN THE JAPANESE MIND (1995). On the whole, it is a fine piece of research. He details the contradictory image of the Jew as beloved: Anne Frank being so popular in Japan that menstruation came to be called "Anne's Day" (Anne-no-hi), leading businessmen and scholars call themselves "Japanese Jews," **(i)** and "theories that identify the Japanese and Jewish peoples" abound – yet the Jew is so distrusted that theories of Jewish conspiracies to manipulate the global economy and destroy Japan sell millions of books. But when it came to Kometani's novel PASSOVER – or at least the passage cited – I feel his criticism lacks balance. Goodman cites this passage:

> The people sitting here [around the seder table] are wondering why I don't convert to Judaism like Marilyn Monroe or Elizabeth Taylor. Other religions don't exist for them. Christianity and Islam inherited this intolerance from Judaism, and they ended up killing each other. That's the meddling West that won't leave people and their beliefs alone! That's colonialism, missionizing, and Nazism.

Goodman claims "the clear implication is that Judaism is a particularly intolerant religion and the source of all intolerance in the West, including Nazism." After being criticized for anti-Semitism, Kometani "sanitized her translation."

> ". . . For them, no other religion could have any possible validity. *This exclusively, this clannish conviction that they alone were the sole repositories of ultimate truth, is something found not only in Judaism but also in Christianity and Islam, and in the end they often killed each other because of it.* In the West, ideologies and theologies traditionally proselytized, unable to leave foreign cultures alone; resulting in imperialism, evangelism, and even in Nazism." (italics = Goodman)

Then Goodman writes that "where in the Japanese original, Kometani clearly implies that Judaism is the source of the West's "unique" intolerance, **(ii)** she has altered the passage for English readers, denying the special responsibility of Judaism and blaming all the monotheistic religions instead."

Stylistically speaking, the first translation is fine, while the second looks like one made under duress! Everyone knows that Judaism is older than Christianity and Islam. It is a fact that they inherited their monotheism and Old Testament ferociousness (righteous massacres and eye-for-eye-ism) from it. So, the difference is cosmetic, anyway. I should add that the Japanese word *haitashûgi* loosely translated "intolerance" in the first translation, is literally "exclude-other-ism." So, the switch to "exclusively" and "clannish" in the second translation is actually closer to the original. *But all this is not important.* If Goodman read more *nihonjinron,* and had a better feel for the broader canvas of Occidentalism, he could not possibly have jumped all over one poor woman for putting in her novel *utterly common ideas* mouthed and written thousands of times over by Japanese intellectuals (I dare say it is the standard line of the aggressively animistic Kyoto school), and not a few of ours. Charges of "anti-Semitism" should be saved for the dastardly conspiracy books. Kometani, in her naïve way tossed up ideas that should be a matter for philosophy, for debate rather than attack. **(iii)**

---

i Japanese Jews. Goodman didn't explain *why* "well-known anthropologist Yamaguchi Masao fancies himself "the Jew among the Japanese" or "Fujita Den, a highly successful businessman who owns a 50 percent share in the Japanese McDonald's franchise and 20 percent of the Japanese Toys "R" Us chain" [no, the dinosaur pun did *not* make it into Japanese.]. I assume it means they think of themselves as a successful minority. There is a way in which Japanese and Jews are similar which has nothing to do with legends or subjective identification by individuals like Yamaguchi and Fujita. In *NIHONJINRON-TANKEN,* I explain that Jewish American mothers are like Japanese "education-mothers" (*kyoiku haha)* in that they, too, rely on creating strong empathy with the child which they use to push the child to study. The Japanese is also a life-long "mother's boy" by WASP standards, and the family relationship. Jewish women are also satirized on WASP TV (and the Jewish writers willingly go along and even write the scripts) for kindly *pushing things on* guests rather than *making them choose.* **(a)** And, finally, Jews do not train their children to be independent, but give them the psychological and financial support needed to do grow and work as a professional. **(b)**

---

a. Serving guests: two perspectives. Doi wrote that being *forced* to make up his mind what to drink, rather than having coffee, tea or whatever supplied by his host at an American house is what set him off his studies of *amae!* (dependence) If he had gone to the house of a typical Jewish American, he would never have written that book! Of course, I wrote "making them choose" to show you the Japanese perspective. On the other hand, pushing things on guests (including relatives) is the standard Jewish-American sitcom perspective. The Japanese would not see it as pushy, but natural, and simply avail themselves (*amaeru*) of the offer. (Doi wrote in the sixties, before our fixation with allergy and individual diets; I suspect that today even Jewish grandmothers ask about their guest's preference!)

b. Independence: two perspectives. In "DIFFERENT GAMES DIFFERENT RULES – Why Americans and Japanese Misunderstand Each Other," Haru Yamada contrasts the "empathy-training" Japanese mothers provide their young children and the "Individual Action Talk" fostered by American mothers, who insist on making the child make choices. She also mentions American students paying their own way through college "demonstrate financially how Americans celebrate independence." All of this is backed with episodes. *It is true.* It is also, like Doi's *amae*, dependent on purely WASP contrasts. Jewish Americans who count themselves among the Dr. Spock mothers have never pushed children out into the cold, cold world. They strengthen them so that they can go farther into that world, accomplish great things out of the confidence that they are loved and have a family to fall back to. They gladly pay their tuition as their children in time will gladly pay their children's tuition.

---

ii "Unique" intolerance of the West. Goodman is right to challenge this claim, as I have many times, by citing examples of persecution in Japan and the "particularly egregious example" of "colonialist policy in Korea during the period from 1936 to 1945, when Koreans in their own country were not only forced to speak Japanese and take Japanese names but were also required to worship Japanese gods." (Ibid.) Nevertheless, this had more to do with the Japanese political insistence upon *total* control, than religion per se. And, I dare say our vaunted present day tolerance may well be ascribed to a reaction to the intolerance engendered by our monotheism.

iii A matter for debate. While I am neither Jewish nor Christian, I dislike facile *Occidentalism* and cannot help but react against charges made by Buddhists with respect to the Judeo-Christian tradition. See my article published in the Japan Times called *"Christianity, Buddhism and Ecology"* at the end of this book.

2. Honda's Books Honda Katsuichi is truly a remarkable reporter, for he went around the world living with people in various extreme environments and turned that into newspaper articles (and, later, books) for Japan's top newspaper. He found the ex-cannibals in the New Guinea Highlands compatible with Japanese sensibilities and world peace but, despite an initial kind welcome, found the Nomads just the opposite and either he or Ishida (or both, I can't recall) extrapolated that into a condemnation of the Judeo-Christian-Islamic civilization and its harsh attitude toward life that led to the atomic bomb. There may be some validity in such a conclusion, but I found it remarkable that it created no controversy whatsoever in Japan. In the early 1970's, the Occident was not very popular in Japan. I think this is important today, for those in the West who would split the world into Christian *vs* Muslim are forgetting something.

3. Americans never apologize. If I remember right, it was Sony's Morita who said that. Someone in my family sent me a slap-on-the-hands editorial from the *Wall Street Journal.* Details don't matter, for we are only talking commonplace. Japanese think grownups should willingly apologize, *even when it is not at all certain they are in the wrong*; and find rationalizing or otherwise defending one's wrongs a mark of immaturity or insolence. One is far more likely to see parents teaching a child to apologize than teaching one to "stick up for himself," whether or not he is in the right. Not surprisingly, travel guides must teach Japanese *not* to be quick to say "I'm sorry!" if they are in a traffic accident in the West – especially litigatious America – for this expression of sympathy (and, perhaps partial blame for being in the wrong place when the other party went through the light) would be taken as proof of liability in a country where people only apologize (occasionally) when they are dead wrong.

Ironically, this stereotype (which like many stereotypes is not entirely wrong) was to reverse itself the year after I wrote this essay. Here is England's *Daily Mirror* on the reason for Japan's failure to apologize properly for their War-time cruelty:

> . . . much of the Japanese culture is derived from the Busheido [*bushido*] Code drawn up during the time of the Samurai warriors. For them to admit a mistake and say sorry was unthinkable. (14 August 1995)

Unlike the Japanese prejudice, which has both some *theoretical* validity ("an eye for an eye and a tooth for a tooth") and some *practical* validity (saying one is sorry can be easily conflated with guilt, so it is discouraged in situations where Japanese might encourage and admire some voluntary sharing of responsibility), the *Daily Mirror* spouts *utter nonsense*, cultural libel, for the proverbial *bushi* not only *could* admit he was wrong, but willingly kill himself to atone for his own wrong-doings, or even to cover the wrongs of his superior. The *Daily Telegraph's* Defense Editor made it out to be a tribal fault:

> . . . It is one of their tribal customs not to admit that the tribe itself has done wrong, either in the present or the past. It would indeed be wrong to make such an admission: wrong for the tribe, wrong for the individual member. (15 June 1995)

There is *some* truth to this. Japanese in this century (but *not* 500 years ago, when the "tribe" was chronologically speaking more primitive) *do* tend to be loyal to their country and their company. The idea of the Japanese as the surviving tribe has been well developed in a complimentary direction by the Australian Gregory Clark, whose books sold millions in Japan; I cannot remember if he mentioned the inability to admit that one's country has done wrong.

Judging from the tenor of the English editorials and articles cited in Phil Hammond and Paul Stirner's chapter *Fear and Loathing in the British Press* in Hammond et al CULTURAL DIFFERENCE MEDIA MEMORIES, *Orientalism* is far more blatant in England than in America, where such moralistic generalization would create tremendous controversy. Unlike Hammond and Stirner, however, I am sympathetic to the crude but emotionally honest English press, for I feel Japan does largely deserve the censure, even if the English reasoning is ridiculous. (I want to put my letter to the *Japan Times* "A real confession is overdue" in the appendix but have misplaced it. Maybe in a later edition!)

4. Returnees My description of the way returnees are treated may be a bit old. Shortly before I left Japan, I saw many articles about the need to discriminate *in favor* of the returnees, to take advantage of their polyglot skills in an increasingly cosmopolitan world. I do not know what the situation is today.

5. Japanese Inferiority Complex. In the 1970's and early 1980's, even as *nihonjinron* boasts of Japanese cultural superiority to the West reached their zenith – you might say there was a cultural bubble that coincided with the economic one – almost all of these books claimed that Japanese should overcome their inferiority complex vis-à-vis the West and should act more brashly, as befits their new global stature. Physically, the Japanese still felt inferior and still do today. Westerners *are* on the whole more muscular and more shapely. **(i)** Overall "superiority" and "inferiority" ratings are a different matter altogether. In 1953, more Japanese felt they were "inferior" to Westerners than "superior." But by 1963, almost twice as many Japanese felt themselves to be "superior" to Westerners than "inferior." And by 1983, almost five times as many felt "superior" (Over 50% versus less than 10% "inferior" and about 40% "can't say in a word"). In *NIHONJINRON-TANKEN,* I speculate as to the reasons why the writers' consciousness is decades behind the surveys, **(ii)** as they insist that they are trying to help Japanese over an inferiority complex.

---

i. Physical inferiority complex. The complex held by Japanese toward Western whites bears some resemblance to that held by American whites versus blacks. Physique is part of it. So is sex. Merle Haggard had a certain brutally honest song about why some whites (the men, that is) hate blacks, and Japanese male magazines and cartoons credit all foreigners with porn star-class equipment. You can bring in bell curve distributions to show a certain percentage of "large" Japanese and "small" foreigners; but, when you think about it, the "we are small" rhetoric is *kinder,* for it lessens consciousness of individual differences *within* Japan. Penis-size envy is shifted from the individual to the group. Obvious compensation on the physical plane ("but we are harder;" "but ours have fatter heads;" "they come faster," etc.) is common and, if it helps, why not? It is when the compensation unconsciously jumps to a different level, such as "but we are smart!" that we all run into trouble.

ii. The surveys. The surveys were carried out by the Statistical Mathematics Research Center (Tôkeisûri-kenkyûsho) of the Ministry of Education (Mombusho). The "superior" or "inferior" question was discontinued after 1983. (see graph 1) Another question about who the respondent considered "superior nationalities" gave similar results. (see graph 2).

---

6. Number of Americans working for Japanese and vice versa I googled all around but could find nothing. Either no one keeps track of these things or whoever does fails to publicize it. When Japan had the huge trade surplus and was buying into Hollywood and Time Square and God knows what and plopping plants down in all the low-cost labor states, etcetera, I suspect what I wrote. Readers who know these things please write me at http://www.paraverse.org and I will see to it that things are put straight for the 2nd edition.

7. Gum as an American invention Americans from countries that are not between the United States of Mexico of America and Canada may protest credit being given to the "gringos" for a native-American invention. It is, however, incontestable that the Usanians made gum into big business and spread it around the world.

8. If it's not clear it's not French? Sebastian Roch Nicholas Chamfort once wrote "Our language is said to love clarity. That is, as M___ observes, because one loves what one needs most. For if it is not very adroitly handled, it is always on the point of falling into obscurity." (*Maxims and Thoughts / Products of the perfected Civilization.*) Whether any language is intrinsically more or less clear or ambiguous is a matter for debate. What is a fact is that some nationalities like to boast of being *clear* and others – Japanese for one – seem to take pride in being *ambiguous*. And, if Professor Lee is correct, Koreans, too, despite their propensity for primary colors and strongly expressed emotion. In his earlier book IN THIS EARTH AND IN THAT WIND, Lee tells the story of a famous Korean official who told two quarreling men separately that each was right and sends them merrily on their way, after which a bystander says one "if one must be right, why do you say both are right?" and he tells him "you, too, are right!" **(i)** Lee used the story to support his claim that Koreans, unlike Westerners, didn't insist upon black and white judgment, but were "tolerant enough to hold contradictory emotions" and were great ones to compromise. Playing the devil's advocate – and remembering arguments that I witnessed while living in Korea for a half year – I would claim just the opposite. Koreans have an all-or-nothing argument style that sees compromise as loss and that is why a third party such as the proverbial judge is necessary.

---

i. Have you heard the story? I came across the following version in Paul Plass's WIT AND THE WRITING OF HISTORY:

> . . . a special brand of pure wit, illustrated by a joke about subtle rabbinic modes of reasoning. "Two litigants . . . come before the rabbi. After hearing the first testimony, the rabbi says, 'It seems to me that you are right.' But after the second man speaks, the rabbi says, 'It seems to me that *you* are right, too.' 'How can this be?' says the rabbi's wife, who has been listening to the argument. 'How can both of these men be right?" 'H'm,' says the rabbi, '*You're* right, too.'"

I was delighted to see such a story told about a rabbi because it so delightfully belies the *Occidentalist* stereotype of a dualistic desert religion psychology. Had Ben Dasan (Yamamoto Shichihei) told the story, he would have made it symbolic of Japanese logic beyond logic and beyond the understanding of the hyper-rational Jew. Be that as it may, the stories are too alike for chance to get the credit. The grammar of the punch-line doesn't quite fit the interrogative style of the comment by the bystander/wife, who might more logically say "Both men can't be right!" I wrote the Seoul National University Library for a date on the story and they sent me a photo copy of a centuries-old version written in pure Chinese and credited to a book of miscellany by Yi Ki (1522-1600). I wrote Paul Plass and he told me a colleague in Hebrew Studies said it was "a floating joke with no apparent origin or special history in the rabbinic tradition," and that another colleague "heard it applied to Franklin Roosevelt."

---

9. Nature, the East and the West. Despite my iconoclasm with respect to antithetical East-West stereotypes, and my heart-felt defense of the rationale behind our once differing seasonal schemes, I do see the tremendous difference between the incredibly anthropocentric paintings and poetry of the Classical and Classic-inheriting West on the one hand, and the nature-centric Sino-sphere on the other. Lafcadio Hearn noted the lack of an Eternal Feminine in a culture where Nature was the muse. He forgot to mention the Muse's companion, the hyper-masculine image, or idol (in the Far East, rippling muscles are reserved for guardian demons). We don't notice our muscle worship, our making a fetish of the human body, where the very arts become mere *humanities*, for, to us. it is the normal state of affairs!

But when the novelist and amateur haiku writer Natsume Sôseki wrote about GULLIVER'S TRAVELS in his BUNGAKU-HYOURON (literary criticism: 1901), he could not help observing what was *not* in the imaginative work: *nature*. Sôseki admits the work is overflowing with satire and stimulating, but faults it on one count that Western critics would not even notice: "it lacks something: an element to evoke the aesthetic sense!"

> Here he [Gulliver] was drifting about from place to place. You'd think he would show some appreciation for, and note the color of the sea, the sound of the waves, birds flying, the condition of the sky, not to mention mountain, river and field scenery, but he is completely dead to all of this.

One can find some counter-examples showing Western attentiveness toward nature in works such as THE ANATOMY OF MELANCHOLY and THE COMPLEATE ANGLER, but until the late 18th century (when nature-appreciation became *the* mark of refined feminine sensibility) judged by Sino-Japanese standards, we were, on the whole, wrapped up in our own beauty, pretty much oblivious of the natural world. (An interesting corollary to this is found in the title of Sôseki's chapter: "Swift and Misanthropic Literature" because in the Japanese, "misanthropic" is "hate-world!") My argument is only with Japanese and Korean writers who crudely extrapolate from this to put down Occidentals as undiscriminating dolts.

10. Monster in all of us While my work explains why stereotypes are *largely* false, I believe that there is something to be said for most stereotypes, whether they are Orientalist or Occidentalist and that we should not just laugh them off. They are useful for self-reflection. At the same time, however, I do not like for them to be used to puff up oneself or criticize others. (Add. I note that, thanks to 9/11 and fear of terrorism, the importance of image is no longer academic.

IX

In Defense of Japanese

(lest we over-react)

It bothers me to think that some of what I have written may give those who need no excuse yet another excuse to bash the Japanese; so please bear with me as I turn my guns about and fire my last salvos home.

For a start, I would argue that far too much has been made of Japanese "racism." Yes, the Japanese do associate cultures, languages and ethnic identity (which often coincides with appearance) more closely – even obstinately – than Americans do. I have had Japanese ignore me (a white) and speak to a Japanese-American companion despite the fact that she could not speak Japanese and I was having to translate everything for her.[1] Moreover, many Japanese will speak in a natural manner to Japanese-Americans but only in a stilted, artificial manner to me. Thanks to a growing number of fluent Caucasians on TV, I am treated to more natural Japanese than I was, say, ten years ago, but the tendency is still there. Appearances dictate the response of most Japanese so, in a sense, they are "racists;" but it is more a matter of treating different cultures in different ways than of discrimination in the usual sense of disparagement.

On numerous occasions, I have run across snide criticism of Dr. Tsunoda's "racist" theory about THE JAPANESE BRAIN. Yes, he wrote about different hemispheric functions on the part of Japanese and other brains. He also used naive circulatory arguments to relate his findings to the usual antithetical stereotypes. Since the Japanese brain mixes emotion and logic in the same left hemisphere, we can never be absolutely rational like Westerners who handle logic on the left and emotion on the right, he tells us, conveniently forgetting that, by the same coin, he could say that Japanese can never be entirely emotional! *Typical stuff.* But, let's be fair. His theory is not "unabashedly racist" as one leading American linguist has charged (and many have echoed).[2] The Doctor states clearly that the differences develop after birth. Though you be white, black, red or beige, if Japanese is your mother tongue up to the age of seven or eight, you will perceive things with a "Japanese Brain." On the other hand, you can be 101% genetically Japanese yet not develop such a brain should you speak, say, English, as your mother tongue. Moreover, Tsunoda acknowledged that speakers of some other Polynesian tongues share the Japanese pattern of perception.

I found it amusing that the Japanese publisher subtitled Tsunoda's book "The Workings of the Brain and East-West Culture" despite the Doctor's claim that Korean and Chinese brains show the same pattern of perception as the West. The misleading words reflect the opportunism of cross-cultural comparison in Japan, where authors will jump back and forth between assertions of Japanese uniqueness and Japan as the embodiment of Asia. But I do not find it amusing that Americans could unfairly malign this man, and the culture that made THE JAPANESE BRAIN a best seller, for being "racist" over a decade. Dr. Tsunoda's primary findings (not his naive cultural musings) deserved a hearing *as science*; not a jeering by people too lazy to check the source of their information. [3]

We are going to see many more knee-jerk charges of racism against Asians in the future. Remember the outcry against Singapore's President Lee a few years ago when he suggested that university graduates (most Chinese by ethnicity) having fewer children than their less learned sisters (mostly non-Chinese) was a socially undesirable trend as it stood to lower the nation's intellectual standards in the long run? He may have been wrong to stress genetic factors, but that does not invalidate the gist of his argument. There *are* family and cultural traditions conducive to high levels of educational achievement. If education matters, it stands to reason that a dilution of this tradition through differential birth rates also matters. The wealthiest nations can make up for some of the loss through compensatory education for the "educationally deprived," but this is a luxury others cannot afford and may – let us be honest, we don't know – be a losing proposition in the long run. Lee offered us a good opportunity to consider where the world is going, and we, or, at least the editorials I remember reading, chose to close our eyes and kick him for reviving the specter of Nazi eugenics. It is so much easier to be correct than to think.

I expect a lot from the Chinese-oriented cultures in years to come. While the "little dragons" are not as thoroughly versed in Occidentalism as the Japanese – which is one reason, their crude pronouncements stand out all the more – one already finds a surprisingly large number of cautionary articles in their press. Reporters, almost invariably of Chinese surname, question the logic of their leader's "East-West rhetoric" (what *Occidentalism* is beginning to be called in the Orient). The Chinese have always had a strong rational, or skeptic, tendency in their letters – if Westerners cannot kill the monster of *Occidentalism*, the Chinese might eventually have to do it for us. [4] Then again, their leaders might find it too valuable a scapegoat to sacrifice.

Though not as serious a charge as racism, the claims some Westerners make about the difficulty and irrationality of Japan's mixed syllabic and Chinese character (*kanji*) system of writing is, to my mind, just plain dumb. An American linguist – the same one most responsible for the misinformation with respect to Dr. Tsunoda – writes,

> This continued use of the Chinese script within the Japanese writing system, remains the height of orthographic folly, a major foolishness not to be observed in any other modem industrialized society. (Roy Andrew Miller: JAPAN'S MODERN MYTH)

And another more objective scholar tells us it is a big waste of effort and will handicap Japan in the computer age. [5] I should think we could use any handicap the Japanese are kind enough to spot us – but, in the long run it probably doesn't matter anyway. Broaden the highway, get more cars. Speed up the script, get more writing. The traffic jam remains, so do the larger problems of the proper role for cars and computers. And, if personal testimony counts, let me say that despite shaky grammar and a limited vocabulary I write better in Japanese than in English precisely because it slows me down enough to better control my horses. In Japanese, I write in a more mature, if less fluent, vein.

The Japanese writing system may well be the most wonderful in the world. I cannot imagine one more satisfying. The Chinese characters provide a bank of basic meanings. Sure it takes a while to get the basics down. Two thousand or so kanji are not learned overnight. But learning them is good for you – I have a theory it might even reduce crime [6] – and there is an aesthetic satisfaction which far exceeds what mere letters give us. And once you've learned them, you can make sense out of almost every word you run across, even if you might not be certain how to pronounce it. *Etymology. Etiology. Ethology. Entomology.* Most English speakers – perhaps even some of my readers – a may have difficulty remembering what these words mean. In Japanese, they are all a cinch. *Word-source-study, sick-cause-study,* etc... If you are basically literate, you are scientifically literate, superficially speaking, anyway. [7]

What I have said so far is, of course, true for Chinese too. The best thing about Japanese is that it *also* uses a phonetic syllabary. This script is generally used for the grammatical details that tie together the sentence, but it is also printed alongside Chinese characters the reader might not know how to pronounce. This latter use is what makes Japan a paradise for punsters. [8]

No, even before Japanese made up their syllabets, [9] they used kanji as Joyce might have. The very first song in the MANYOSHU (oldest collection of Japanese poetry) is a study in punning of a type I call "stereo." The characters *pronounced* as arranged mean

> pretty basket, pretty basket carrier
> pretty scoop, pretty scoop carrier

but their literal denotation (*visual* reading) is:

> basket-hair-excite,
> pretty-basket-mother-breast
> cloth-awhile-think-hair-excite,
> *pretty-husband-you-want-have.*

So you have the ancient Emperor rapping about baskets and scoops, while the transcription (especially the italicized part = 美夫君志持) scoops his intent! [10] And if that isn't enough, some claim another pronunciation of the characters shows the song was really a covert political declaration. Maybe it was. Maybe it was all of those things!

Modern Japanese is hardly as confusing as the MANYOSHU but it does offer a lot of choice. Remember *wakaru* ((I) know)? I said it is usually written with a character meaning "to part"(分る). Well, it can also be written with a character meaning "to judge" (判る), or another meaning "to take to pieces" or "solve" (解る). It may also be written phonetically with no characters (わかる). In other words, you are free to nuance, or not to nuance, a single pronunciation – a single word – in any number of ways.

As linguist Suzuki Takeo has astutely noted, Japanese *proves* that writing is not necessarily reducible to being a mere copy of the spoken tongue (as many Occidental linguists have claimed). Japanese shows us that the eyes are capable of taking in more information than the ears, if only we have a writing system where this is allowed. As China simplifies – much in poor taste, if you ask me – its own characters, [11] and Korea denies them for primarily nationalist reasons, [12] I believe that we who value beauty and the potential for more than one kind of intellectual excellence owe the Japanese a vote of thanks for their steadfast defense of *kanji* in the face of a largely unappreciative world.

I am not saying everything with Japanese is going well. Besides the structural limitations mentioned in my earlier discussion of *diced* and *stuffed* translation, which cannot be helped, there is an unfortunate aesthetic trend which can be. While combinations are unbeatable for scholarly vocabulary, these words, called *kango*, are being overused at the expense of the more euphonious native expressions. (*Dakkyo* rather than *ayumiyori*. *Sokushin-suru* rather than *unagasu*. *Zetsumetsu-suru* rather than *horobiru*) Although the tendency over the past decade has been to use less *kanji* to make sentences *look softer*, [13] the native vocabulary is still losing out to these *kango*. Japanese is not *sounding* good. But this problem is not inherent to the writing system.

And finally, I would caution writers on the subject of *Occidentalism*, not to be too quick to ascribe it to nationalistic plotting, bargaining tactics or pathological psychology. The *Occidentalist* worldview makes sense on its own terms, and those who accept it are no more fools than are Americans who consider themselves especially individualistic even though they may utter scarcely an original thought in their lifetime and lack the discipline needed to do anything "my way." [14]

It goes without saying, all cultures are different. But it is not at all clear whether people are different. Japanese are said to be more dependent than Americans. Well, they *are* with respect to their companies. But Americans are with respect to their next door neighbors. Japanese are with respect to their parents. Americans are with respect to their spouse. The parts differ, but the overall level of independence and dependence probably varies little if any. Japanese are also said to be more group-oriented.[15] As Rodney Clark points out in THE JAPANESE COMPANY (1979), a Japanese manager may stress group participation in a decision where an English manager might emphasize his own role, *despite the fact that an objective study of the decision-making process shows remarkably little difference in the proportion of individual and group contribution* for companies in both cultures. While we may not admit it, people need people wherever they live.

A bit of knowledge makes the East "East" and the West "West." A bit more, I think, can put them back together again.[16]

ch.9 notes

1. Appearance and Language. While my ability to learn Japanese suffered by my not being treated to natural Japanese, I do not feel as bitter about it as some. **(i)** After all, I once listened to a rock-opera for ten or twenty minutes before I realized it was being sung in English and not Italian as I had expected. I can even remember saying, "I caught that phrase because it sounds like Spanish!" (It was "Jesus Christ Super-Star;" and I was sitting in the front row with a priest who treated me to a ticket after I sold him a proof etching of the crucifixion – many etchers destroy proofs, but I wrote "proof" on them and sold them cheaply so that people on a low budget could have my art.)

---

i. Why bitter? When you go all the way to a foreign country to learn a language only to find few people will let you hear it, you have a right to be upset, especially when you run across letters to the editor by Japanese or other Asians, whose faces get them all the Japanese practice they need – and some they do not want, as they are chided for *not* speaking *better* – with the gall to say more Westerners should try to speak in Japanese! This is a recipe for frustration. Still, one must remember that many of the Japanese are just trying to use the language they studied for years or trying to be friendly. The only people I cannot stand are those who push English on me to show off – but these are usually completely seen through by their families and neighbors, who may even compensate for the jerk's behavior by treating me to natural Japanese more quickly than is usually the case!

---

2. Dr. Tsunoda, racist? The man who unfairly brought *race* into the picture while discussing Tsunoda's work is Professor Miller (JAPAN'S MODERN MYTH):

> "the brain of any other racial group;"
> "on one side of his racial fence are . . .;"
> "the racist thrust of such a thesis;"
> "rarely in modern times has anyone dared to put forth as unabashedly racist an approach. . .;"
> "doctors who stand ready to put science and medicine at the beck and call of racism."

Miller makes these charges despite writing "nor does he even suggest that this difference in function is the result of heredity." (But Miller also speaks of "the kind of unique Japanese linguistic feature that triggered the distinctive evolutionary process responsible for the development of the Japanese brain." **(i)** Miller recognizes that the Japanese language is supposed to be at the root of the difference, but mistakenly takes this as culturally phylogenetic ("determined long ago in the history of the Japanese race") rather than culturally ontogenetic (the result of learning Japanese at an early age, i.e. nurture, not nature!). He is right that Tsunoda's argument is "a vicious cycle of interconnected illogicality," where the language is unique because of the brain and vice versa. Tsunoda naively connects this or that linguistic trait popularly considered Japanese to the particular pattern of cerebral dominance for verbal and natural sounds he claims to observe. But this is secondary to his basic claim to have found changes in the functioning of the brain (what is unconsciously perceived by the respective hemispheres) due to language acquisition. While much of Tsunoda's research was apparently poorly done – otherwise, it should have been replicated by now **(ii)** – he wrote nothing that warrants Miller's charges, unless researching difference alone (and some procedural mistakes) is a crime. I, who have spent twenty years of my life deconstructing stereotypes of difference, don't think it is.

---

i. Unique Japanese linguistic feature. Tsunoda hypothesized that vowellyness – if you'll excuse my ugly neologism – of Japanese and some Polynesian tongues accounted for the different cerebral dominance. If vowels by themselves could be words, then vowel-like sounds without consonants to define them would, theoretically, go to the left hemisphere rather than the right as with most language. My *guess* is that the Polynesian sample was too small and that the nature of Japanese writing, with its complex kanji-meaning-sound relationship might be a better explanation. Children encounter this early enough for it to have an effect on their brain functioning. But, until/unless Tsunoda's cerebral dominance test results can be duplicated, *any* explanation is moot.

ii. Poor research? Since difference is usually a more interesting and significant finding than no difference, there is a tendency to pay more attention to – and, presumably publish – research that finds it. This bias is, obviously, something that must be kept in mind lest we lose balance of the total picture. But the offhand dismissal of findings of difference involving different genders, races or cultures by Americans as "unscientific" *by definition* is now so common (that is my impression, correct me if I'm wrong) that they – you, if you are an American scientist – can hardly be trusted to objectively check experiments such as that of Tsunoda. Japanese scientists are a different matter. Since they are not so hypersensitive about difference as Americans, their failure to confirm his results is a strong indication that *something* was wrong with his method of testing. But, Tsunoda was an outsider (His eight page summation of his work and thoughts "Logos and Pathos: Difference in the Mechanism of Vowel Sound and Natural Sound Perception in Japanese and Westerners, and in Regard to Mental Structure" was published in the *"Journal of Dental Health"* (Vol. 28 No. 2 July 1978) of the Medical Research Institute, Tokyo Medical and Dental University.) and his research in later years has gone off in even stranger directions, so it is at least possible (not probable) that he was not taken seriously (by scientists) in Japan, too, no one has done *proper* testing of his findings.

3.The Japanese Brain: a mine for science? Even findings that are not yet confirmed are worth thinking about. Some of Tsunoda's observations *are* fascinating. He found cigarettes altered the pattern of perception in a different way with the Japanese language type brains and the others. Certainly, we find Japanese medical doctors exceptionally poor at quitting compared to their Western colleagues. But he gave no good reason why this might happen. I wondered (in a letter to molecular biologist Shibatani Atsuhiro **(i)** written in 1980) whether it might be because the large amount of natural noises (insect and frog and instruments with a voice-like timbre) allegedly going into the verbal (left) hemisphere of the Japanese type brain – rather than the right, as with other language type brains – would mean its owners would *have to* learn to filter out noise (information overload) more than people with other types of brains. (Tsunoda jumped so rapidly to connect his findings to Japanese and Western cultural and linguistic stereotypes that he failed to consider many of the secondary implications of his own findings!) If so, I hypothesized, perhaps smoking helped to strengthen this filter. In 1997, I read that nicotine is said to do just that for schizophrenics! ("Scientists locate gene linked to schizophrenia, chain smoking" (AP 97-1-22 Japan Times)

---

i. Shibatani Atsuhiro. I wrote Shibatani, an internationally highly-published scientist who was later to become the dean of Nara Woman's College in Kyoto, when he was at a university in Australia (forgive me for forgetting which) about renaming the insulting scientific nomenclature *Didus Ineptus* (Dodo) and the possibility of an downside-up map for his part of the world. He sent me strong sympathy but little hope for the good name of the Dodo (evidently names are harder to get rid of than species), a copy of an already extant and extremely exuberant map of Australia on top of the world, and, because I'd mentioned my work on cultural stereotyping, a copy of his review of Tsunoda's work that was carried by the British Journal of Socio-biological something-or-other. I sent him a long hand-written rebuttal of many points made in his largely favorable review, which he kindly thought they should print but that was impossible, of course, for I write in an utterly unacademic vein and have no credentials (as if ideas need credentials!).

---

4. *Occidentalism* for the Chinese leaders. In retrospect, my remarks on China and Occidentalism lack balance, for, as the note on pgs 52-3 points out, Occidentalism is used against the Chinese establishment, too. Even as negative Occidental images are used to raise antipathy against the West on trade issues, or to convince people why social controls are necessary, etc., positive ones are used to push reform and fuel revolution. Occidentalism can be useful to both sides.

5. Another scholar's *kanji* handicap. I refer to Professor James Unger's THE FIFTH GENERATION FALLACY (Oxford UP 1987) where he argues that because whatever advances in artificial intelligence made to cope with Japan's mixed *kanji-kana* writing system can be applied to other writing systems as well, the efficiency gap or *kanji* handicap will remain and a phonetic alphabet or syllabary will always be the more efficient way to input data. That, I think is incontestable, but it does not follow that using characters is, therefore, less efficient for the smooth operation of the *society as a whole* or for the retention of a high level of culture. (To take a parallel example from Europe, I note that in 1574, "Tycho Brahe referred enviously to the precocious mathematical knowledge of his classical forebears, 'while we unfortunately, have to spend the best years of our youth on the study of [their] language and grammar, which they acquired in infancy without trouble." (in John Hale: *The Civilization of Europe in the Renaissance*: 1993/4). But I think we might remonstrate that such pain might well have something to do with the launching of modern science.)

6. Kanji learning and crime. I would guess that time spent studying by young men is inverse to time spent doing criminal acts. Assuming that even your bad eggs want to be able to read comic books and the horse-race pages in the newspaper if nothing more, they *must* spend many disciplined hours in memorizing *kanji.* They cannot get away with doing practically nothing as they can in an alphabet culture which has lost its ability to make students study for one reason or another. And, while doing this, they learn to forego instant gratification. Not a few students dislike *kanji.* But, they do not necessarily know what benefits it brings them. For a start, they learn that one must work to get something, and they learn manual dexterity and aesthetic balance (from the placement of the parts of the character) in the bargain.

7. Superficial literacy and *kanji.* Suzuki Takao has repeatedly argued that difficult words in English are *opaque* while those in Japanese, constructed of *kanji* with meanings understandable to the literate layman, are clear, or, to use his term, *transparent.* He has also used the metaphor of *television versus radio.* Japanese is like television, where you can turn off the sound and still have a chance to guess what's going on where English is like the radio, you either know the word (have it *on*) or you do not (it is *off*).

Miller (and in his wake, Dale, Unger **(i)** and many others) say "No!" etymology can *not* be relied upon for meaning. Just because you can "read" a word from its *kanji* parts doesn't really mean you can understand it! Strictly speaking this is right. But they are wrong to think it invalidates Suzuki's claim, for he nowhere claims it always brings 100% understanding of a word. Suzuki only states what is obvious, and what I have experienced countless times since learning Japanese: It is usually easier to guess specialized terms written in *kanji* in Japanese than it is to guess our Grecian and Latinate English. Unger is correct to say that there is no intrinsic ideographic property of *kanji* that makes it better for transmitting meaning than the alphabet. But this does not change the reality Suzuki and I *know*. **(ii)**

---

i. Etymology can be misleading? Miller used the example of *jinruigaku: human-type-study* for "anthropology" to show that the denotation of a word is not enough to grasp its connotation. Unger seconds him, quipping "if etymology were meaning, we would have no need for textbooks, only dictionaries." Moreover, Miller "could have gone farther: etymology can be misleading." Take *anti-Semitic*. "Arabic is a Semitic language, but this word definitely has no connotation of Arab." (Unger: 87.). I get it! "A little learning is . . . ." – so better to know nothing, then, professor? I joke, but a less sophisticated scholar, Wm. C. Hannas, claims "there is a tendency among literate East Asians" to confuse recognition of character components

> with understanding the word itself, when in fact no such understanding has been achieved. The user literally does not know when he or she does not know the word . . . the other harmful side effect of overanalyzing a compound is that one tends to see less, more or something other than the meaning of the word itself. (ASIA'S ORTHOGRAPHIC DILEMMA: University of Hawaii Press 1997)

I find this demeaning to East Asians, for it makes them out to be children who take symbol – or parts of symbols – for reality. A hundred pages after this warning about the dangers of *over*analyzing, Hannas turns about and writes "there is nothing in the mechanism of character-based literacy to encourage the analytical mindset." Indeed, "East Asians are not splitting up sounds at the root level [unlike the alphabet, characters are "concrete" in their "treatment of sound"], and hence may have less predisposition to analysis." And that is why, he hypothesizes, their scholars write so poorly. **(a)** You have to admire Hannas' chutzpah! There are many who credit the alphabet for far more than it deserves credit for, but few would have the guts to put down the Chinese character and, with it, the character of those who use it, like this! **(b)**

---

a. Poor writing in Asia? It seems Hannas has the most bad experience with "abysmal 'informative' writing" in Japanese. In his discussion of sloppy writing, he is so busy blaming the Chinese character that he neglects to mention the phonetic syllabary. Earlier in the book, he regrets that *kana* didn't evolve into an alphabet. He holds the existence of characters with a syllable-like aspect responsible for this stymied evolution, so, if the syllabary can not develop the analytical capacity of its user, the fault belongs ultimately to the character. So Chinese characters are doubly nefarious. Did I get that right, professor? To be fair to Hannas, he admits East Asians have fine imaginative literature written by "professional writers," but I think he is wrong here, too, for supposing it is because the literature is closer to the spoken word. Much of my favorite Japanese literature is far from it.

b. "Characters steal character" I may not care for it, but Hannas's bold book was eaten up by writer, playwright and movie critic Donald Richie, who reviewed it under the above headline in his *Japan Times* column "The Asian Bookshelf."(98/3/11) .

---

ii Ideograph or not! Or, *why reality stands.* Professor Unger is right that there is nothing intrinsically meaningful about Chinese characters as compared to English roots. The only problem is that most of us do not know the roots that are used by science. Why not? I think it is because we do not *need* to learn Latin and Greek to read the newspaper. (And even if you do learn them – I mastered a fair amount of Latin – you usually forget most of what you learn because you get no reinforcement from your general reading.) We don't need to know "ornitho" for anything but "ornithology." Japanese, on the other hand, *do* need to learn the characters for "bird" and "study/lore" simply to be literate, so they have no trouble with the Japanese equivalent of *ornithology*. Of course, this also speaks to a problem with English, about our bifurcated vocabulary, but, practically speaking, things work out pretty much *just like Suzuki says they do.* (For a more nuanced treatment, see my EXOTIC TONGUES if/when it is published.)

---

8. Punning in Japanese. I give plentiful examples in the book-to-be mentioned above. These puns, on the whole, classier than English language puns because they are literate: it is hard to groan at a pun that may only be caught with the eye. As such, they also constitute proof of the fact that writing need not be just a way of putting spoken words on paper. If you know the world of written Japanese, you need not stretch out to include mathematics, musical notation and "the new super-alphabet of the computer keyboard" to recognize "writing as a mode of communication *sui generis*." (Roy Harris: SIGNS OF WRITING. Routledge 1995) Just as important, the existence of plentiful *good* puns gives lie to the following assumption long held by more Western intellectuals than Japanese. After a short "history of the pun" Addison concludes that the pun is not included in the company of *bona fide* wit.

> The only way therefore to try a piece of wit, is to translate it into a different language: if it bears the test, you may pronounce it true; but if it vanishes in the experiment, you may conclude it to have been a pun. (No.61)

Natsume Sôseki found this misleading. He wrote that Addison's idea of translation as a measure of the universality of a work's value made sense, but it by no means followed that a translatable work was superior literature.

> Universality only means that anyone can read and take interest in something; it indicates the breadth of interest, but has nothing to do with a work's depth. Translatability or untranslatability ought not to become the litmus test of a literary work. Strictly speaking, there are any number of things which are of the highest literary value yet hard [virtually impossible] to translate. And that does not only go for puns. (BUNGAKU-HYÔRON: 1901)

I doubt if we have any major literary figures who

could read an exotic tongue as well as Sôseki could English. If they could, their literary theories would surely be different.

9. Japanese Syllabets Japanese first used Chinese characters to represent their sounds, but within a few hundred years invented and used a syllabary together with the characters. Because the syllables are the minimum unit and, like the Greek *mora* relatively short, I call them "syllabets."

10. MANYOSHU punning. I am not giving the ordinary Japanese understanding here. Most contemporary Japanese know that Chinese characters were used for phonetic purposes – as *syllabets*, to use my term – that had nothing to do with their meanings. They also know there were some clever punning uses. But they do not have any idea of how many. I have not found a single Japanese aware that the first poem/song in the anthology includes a clear request for marriage written in the Chinese characters (ostensibly only used as meaningless syllabets for the Japanese), and even commentators who note that in ancient times a man asking a woman's name was asking for her hand fail to provide this additional piece of information. Since most books no longer provide the original Chinese characters, but give a version written in an easily readable manner (*yomikudashi),* students have no way of knowing about this. My favorite MANYOSHU "stereo" is the word *koi* (love/longing) written by some poets with two Chinese characters meaning respectively "lone" and "sad!" (For a more complex analysis and more examples, see EXOTIC TONGUES when/if I write it.)

11. Character simplification. Unger's research on literacy in Japan (The 5th Generation Fallacy:1987) suggests some simplification – not abandonment as he hints would be best – might be a good idea. But, I feel that the authorities all too often do not make the right decision with respect to *what* characters to simplify and what characters to include on or drop from the list of characters suitable for mass media use. There is a big difference between what characters are hard to *write* and what characters are hard to *read* (i.e. hard to remember), and this is not reflected in the choices. In a debate published in Asahi Shinbun's weekly magazine *Aera,* I used the example of "mouse./rat." This character (see below) may be a bit complex, but it is both unique – less liable to be confused with another character – and looks very much like a nervously scampering mouse. Such a character, I argue, ought to be on the list. Some say I am being elitist about this – not all have time to learn many *kanji* we are told – but I cannot help noting that the blue-collar crowd singing their karaoke, enjoy reading songs with lyrics including any number of rare old Chinese characters (usually used for romantic places or names) far more difficult to read than my example!

鼠

12. Koreans and Chinese characters When I lived in Korea, there were almost no Chinese characters used and I was continually treated to boasting about the incredible scientific qualities of the Korean alphabetic-syllabary (aspects of both are combined in syllabet clusters). When the Far East seemed to be outperforming the West in the 1980's and 1990's, there was a movement to restore the study of Chinese characters as the visual Lingua Franca (?) of the region.

13. Hard and soft looking sentences. A high percentage of *kanji* makes a sentence look hard because it suggests bureaucratic writing or scientific writing full of specialized terms and because it packs space and *actually looks heavier* than the *kana* syllabets. The native words (*yamato kotoba)* often may be expressed with a single Chinese character (acting more in a symbolic rather than phonemic capacity), but they are strongly identified with a historical tradition where women wrote poetry with delicate sentiments in delicately penned *hiragana* (the soft, curved syllabary), while the *kango* Chinese character combinations with which men have written history are written with more deliberately penned *kanji* often supplemented with the extremely stiff-looking *katakana* syllabary. The percent of native words is high in children's books – especially folk tales – and the link with *hiragana* is reinforced by the fact that Japanese children begin to read using that syllabary alone (Syllabets are far easier to read than our alphabet, so they are off and reading in no time flat!) **(i)** So, the least glance at a sentence in Japanese can give one an impression of "hard" or "soft." **(ii)**

i Easy reading. Pronouncing words a syllabet at a time makes them easier to understand in Japanese while pronouncing them a letter at a time makes them harder to understand in English. That is why so many of our children are slow to catch on.

ii. *Yamato-kotoba* (native words) versus *kango* (kanji combinations). I write the above in defense of Watanabe Shoichi **(a)**, who listed the different feeling given by these two types of words. Dale gives a table of six differences and then tells us that

> his [Watanabe's] antithesis between *kango* and *yamato kotoba* in effect disclose a series of psycholinguistic contrasts between mature, adult usage and the child's chatter, explicitly associated with a rejected paternal image (*kango* ["Hard, like the brawny muscles of the father"]) on the one hand, and a yearned for maternal image (*yamato kotoba*, ["Soft, like the tender feel of a mother's skin"]) on the other. To recognize one's unique identity in the character of the latter points once more to an underlying regression to narcissism, . . . (Dale: 1986)

I can feel the hard/soft difference between these words/styles and I did not learn Japanese until I became an adult. As I hope you may gather from my previous note, Dale is using *real differences* to prove the person who wrote them down – and other Japanese who feel the same way – suffers from a couple of Herr Doctor Freud's psychological complexes. *Phooey*!

---

a. Watanabe Shôichi is a sort of Japanese George F. Will, but a bit broader-minded for knowing a foreign language, English (and a fine translator of one of my favorite conservatives, Chesterton). If he waxes overly lyrical on *Yamato kotoba*, let it be known that he also has a thing for English one-syllable words, which, he notes, dominate strong and simple poems that speak to our heart. Dale is wonderfully erudite – his knowledge of German scholarship (important for understanding the development of pre-World War II Japanese intellectual trends) is outstanding – but his treatment of Watanabe hardly does him justice!

---

14. Individualism =American self-Occidentalizing. Many Westerners, from scholars to humorists have commented on a Japanese tendency to Orientalize themselves. **(i)** Far fewer, if any, have commented upon our tendency to Occidentalize ourselves, no doubt because the concept of Occidentalization didn't exist. We tend to exaggerate our individualism and forget how much our character has changed over time. Are not the Japanese today far more diverse in clothing and hairstyle than supposedly individualistic Americans were in the 1940's and 1950's? Or, taking corporate relations, were the men in the gray flannel suit, the organization men of the same era really more independent than their colleagues in Japan? Or, what if we go back to the turn of the Century, the days of rugged individualism? Here is "a model factory" in New York:

> ". . . the work here was harder, and the day, with only a half hour for lunch, seemed endless. The iron discipline forbid free movement (one could not even go to the toilet without permission), and the constant surveillance of the foreman weighed like a stone on my heart."

Back in St. Petersburg, Emma Goldman and the other workers "were allowed sufficient time for our noon meal and twice a day for tea. We could talk and sing at work; we were not driven or harassed." In old Russia, even the working class had lives. In the USA? If you were not rugged – or rich – you were practically forbidden to be *human*, much less an individual. In MEAT-EATERS THOUGHTS, RICE EATERS THOUGHTS (1966) Sabata Toyoshi wrote that it was not the Judaic-Christian tradition or Classic philosophy, but the extremely harsh collectivism of early modern Europe (whereas Japanese cooked their staple rice or gruel at home, the Europeans were obliged to have their wheat milled and their bread cooked communally and so forth) – not to mention the religious-moral pressures which allowed almost no privacy ! – that gave birth to modern individualism *as a reaction*. (More discussion in my *Topsy-Turvy 1585* (Paraverse Press: Summer 2004) To a lesser degree, we even see this in the United States today. We need our individual rights because we have so many fundamentalist types who would dictate our lives right down to what we do in bed if given half a chance. But I am straying too close to the world we live in, where I prefer to dwell in ideas. If our history is bad, our political science (?) is a joke. Here is the joker himself, the irrepressible Professor Bloom!

> It is now fashionable to deny that there ever was a state of nature. We are like aristocrats who do not care to know that our ancestors were once savages who, motivated only by fear of death and scarcity, killed one another in quarrels over acorns. (THE CLOSING OF THE AMERICAN MIND)

If I am not mistaken, Professor Bloom is convinced that only belief in the Hobbesian badness of man makes us work to cultivate virtue. **(i)** That may be why he takes care not to point out that from what we now know about socio-biology and anthropology the idea of unconnected individuals as primitive or natural is *absolutely ridiculous* (He seems to me both the same and the reverse of the Grand Inquisitor in Dostoevsky's novel). More remarkably, this fictional *individual who never was* not only became the kernel of, but *remains* the kernel of our political science instruction. **(ii), (iii),** This is a dead-horse who is fed more than he is flogged. **(iv)**

---

i. The badness of man: a bad idea. The Biblical understanding of man is much more deeply embedded in our psycho-sociological worldview than we realize. Not only laymen, but cultural anthropologists easily conflate the entirely different matters of *conscience* and *sin.* Ever since Benedict, **(a)** our "sin culture" has been contrasted to Japan's "shame culture," with the implication – sometimes stated, sometimes not – being that ours is a deep inner morality, while theirs is a shallow outer one. Some Japanese protest, *no, shame is deeper than sin, it is primal*: the guilt associated with shame, with letting down the group is deeper than that felt by someone who has sinned, as sinning is a more superficial thing based on a fiction of deity and rules written in a book and may even be eased through the rite of confession. What they are actually talking about (whether they realize it or not) is the fact that the sense of shame – as opposed to embarrassment – is born of and can hurt the conscience. **(b)** Because more Japanese are given tender loving care when small, I believe more Japanese than Americans have a conscience. (This may be why Japanese have many times more people in mental institutions than in the USA: people with consciences tend to harm themselves rather than others. **(c)** The idea of *sin,* i.e., a crime that God will punish, is only needed when people lack a *conscience.* For the good, the Golden Rule suffices; and even it goes without saying: *it is not a "rule" but a description of what comes naturally.* Belief in the "badness of man" is one way out of a bad society – the other being to stress the goodness of man hoping people will live up to what they think is natural. But such badness was hardly intrinsic to human or any other nature.

---

a. Ruth Benedict. THE CHRYSANTHEMUM AND THE SWORD. Her PATTERNS OF CULTURE should still be required reading. I was amazed to find undergraduates in a course on comparative culture reading a book written in a wretched academic style – would they start by deconstructing their bloated vocabulary! – about Orientalism, prejudice and whatnot, when they had not yet read this basic book and other much more readable texts of cultural anthropology. At this rate, we will have a society full of people who know what is politically correct but little else!

b. Sin and guilt conflated in translation. Benedict used both "sin" and "guilt" in her book. But in translation, both tend to become the single term *tsumi[ishiki].* This term has a broad connotation that does indeed cover both of these English terms, but it is weighted on the side of "sin" and can even mean "crime." And, this in translation, suggests, in effect, that the West might be the more superficial culture. (NIHONJINRON-TANKEN) The translator might have been a bit more careful – Japanese has an exclusive term for conscience: *ryôshin* (良心:literally "good heart) – and Benedict, of course, does not use the terms interchangeably. But, still, I feel Benedict is partly responsible for the misreading, for not taking the space to define more clearly the difference between "sin" and "guilt." Then, again, to have done so, would have meant going into the natural development of a conscience and clearly discrediting the Judeo-Christian claim to be the font of morality for the West. My guess is she was not prepared to do so. (Dale, who is a little bit too quick to absolve Benedict of all responsibility, correctly points out that Benedict herself qualified: "they [the

Japanese] are also overcome by guilt when other people know nothing of their misstep." (see the chapter "The Shame of a Shame Culture" in Dale's *The Myth of Uniqueness*: 1986)

c. Mental Institutions in Japan and the USA. "Japan has 330,000 people in mental institutions, of whom about 80% have been compulsorily committed (compared with 44,870 confined in prisons). The immensity of the Japanese figure may be understood when it is compared with the figure of 120,000 in the United States, despite the fact that the population of the latter is nearly double Japan's." ("introduction" to Gavan McCormack and Yoshio Sugimoto ed. DEMOCRACY IN JAPAN Hale and Iremonger (Australia) 1986). Our number of prisoners are, of course, a factor of ten above the Japanese figures. This high crime rate is often attributed to individualism, but that only makes sense if you forget most criminals do bad things to be more highly regarded by their peers, to have stuff to show off, or to pay for drug addiction caused by lack of the self-control that is the *sine qua non* for a real individual.

---

ii. The individual who never was. There is a book called JOHN RINGO – *The Gunman Who Never Was*. The author argues the main reason for his legendary fame, besides the nice ring of his name, was the fact so little was known about him – he did exist, but did absolutely nothing of note – that the Western writers could flesh him as they would! The fiction of the sole-man, or individual of Locke, Rousseau, Hobbs *et al* is just such a fiction.

iii. Our political instruction. I found the textbook and readings at my political science 101 course at Georgetown absolutely ridiculous and set about on my own trying to get a scientific (rather than historical/philosophical) angle on the subject. The best thing I found was a book by the great geneticist C.H. Waddington: THE ETHICAL ANIMAL.

iv. A prolific dead horse? The dead horse of unnatural individual autonomy has been flogged by gestalt and transpersonal psychology in the West even as it is immediately resurrected with talk of empowerment and self-realization (Goethe is the only one who ever wrote an entertaining line on that subject (a))! In Japan, the "individual" is flogged, partly for being fiction, partly for being used as a measure to put down Japanese, and partly for being Western, rather than human. Not surprisingly, Japanese declare the concept inapplicable to their society – as if it was applicable to Western society! – and create "emic" (making sense to a culture from the inside out: i.e. from the Japanese viewpoint) theory using the "human nexus," "holon," "relatum" and other such building blocks all made of pretty much the same anti-autonomy paradigm of "among-man" (*kanjin*) – the context as primary – replacing "lone-man" (kojin) – i.e., the individual as the basic unit. Personally, I do not like this *emic* business, because I'd prefer to see claims made about Western society and Japanese society reassessed. New terms allow an easy way out: for most of the differences=stereotypes are allowed to stay and are simply revalorized.

---

a. Goethe's idea. Well, actually, I read it in DEAR BERTAND RUSSELL (Allen & Unwin 1969). Russell "nicely pointed out" that "Goette in *Wilhem Meister* sets forth the view that each individual's end should be self-realization, and that this end is best promoted by a combination of masonic mysticism and affairs with housemaids."

---

15. "Group-oriented," you say? Sugimoto and Mouer make this question moot with the observation that we are *all* group animals, but the Western the Japanese groups are of different types (Perhaps "herd" vs "union," but I do not have the books here to check.) This concept bears some resemblance to Nakane Chie's observations that Americans are masters of the ad hoc group, while Japanese do well with hierarchically structured groups.

16. Cultural difference. It would seem that nine-tenths of it is in the mind. There is a need to think about differences that are not readily apparent (see E. Hall's classic SILENT LANGUAGE, a must-read for all monolingual Americans!) and – my point – similarities that are even less so.

X

Songs from Xanadu

(a professor tells it like it is)

On reflection, perhaps I was too hasty letting Western translators off the hook that Professor Eto baited. There is at least one area – not one mentioned by him to be sure – where a post-modern convention has indeed imposed itself upon translations from an Eastern tongue. The victimized language is, however, not Japanese. I am talking about Chinese poetry. Pound did it right. So did I. T. Headland, whose CHINESE MOTHER GOOSE RHYMES charms today as it did in 1900. These folk had rhythm and rhyme. Just like the authors of the originals.

Professor Crump pulls no punches in his introduction to SONGS FROM XANADU, a collection of Mongol Dynasty Chinese verse:

> Kenneth Rexroth and other contemporary poets are much in favor of turning originals in another language of whatever age into *modern* idiom .... He is doubtless right as a poet, though I must confess that some of the modem idiom efforts he would probably approve of sound like so many trendy bumper stickers to me.

I think the Professor is too generous. Many of the bumper stickers do, after all, rhyme and the Professor, like me, enjoys good old-fashioned English verse. Syllabic we are not – haiku is, stylistically speaking, Greek to us [1] – but rhyme, by God, we can. And, if we don't do what we can, what *can* we do?

> But my tastes aside, I made a rational decision to turn Mongol Dynasty song-poetry into English rhymed verse for two simple reasons: Chinese verse has always rhymed (as has much of English verse in the past). Furthermore these Mongol Dynasty *ch'u* were, after all, the popular songs of their times, and in both English and Chinese, popular songs have leaned more heavily and for the longest time on rhyme.

The professor cites two scholars who decided not to rhyme for fear of what rhyming six or seven lines with the same endings would do to the meaning of their translation:

> Of course they could not end six or seven lines in a row with the same rhyme! . . . but their statement is a straw-man. There is of course, a middle ground . . . Is not the restrained, or merely occasional use of rhyme in translations (and it need not be the same rhyme throughout) more descriptive for a reader in that it would at least indicate the Chinese original was rhymed? I was saddened not long ago when a young sophomore came up to me after a class in Chinese literature in translation with an excited sparkle in her eye and confided she had read translations of Chinese verse with pleasure since her first year in high school and was now delighted to find out that Chinese poetry also rhymed.

The professor then notes another translator excusing himself for not rhyming because "rhymes are much more abundant in the Chinese language than they are in English."

I cannot help chuckling because the same school of translation when faced with Japanese poetry excuses itself for not rhyming in English because rhymes in Japanese are too *few*. [2] As to the translator's claim that "any attempt to apply rhyme in the translations would have seemed forced and unnatural," the professor is refreshingly blunt:

> I protest again that the judicious use of rhyme need not wrench one's translations to an unacceptable degree at all. It strikes me that the real reason these translators used no rhyme is that they did not want to be bothered by the added difficulties. Then why not tell us so instead of positing dubious universal truths? (Ibid.)

Amen.

We began our survey of *Orientalism*, *Occidentalism*. and translation with a piece of *Orientalist* doggerel. The little Japanese children depicted were paragons of angelic behavior, and yet we found within the quaint language unmistakable prejudice with respect to the Far East. I'd like to finish with a couple of stanzas from a verse in Professor Crump's anthology showing just the opposite of the "frightfully polite" Easterner. Chinese authorities are embarrassed about such poems – the "Country Cousin at the Theatre" is considered to poke fun at the working class – but it is precisely such revealing work (Consider Duerr's Country Wedding) that magically cuts through time and distance allowing us to feel our common humanity.[3]

Despite the substantial progress made against obvious *Orientalism* and discrimination in recent years, many Westerners still appear to consider Far Eastern people to be less fully human than they themselves. When a Korean shopkeeper killed a black teenager in Los Angeles in 1992, many articles and letters to the editor accused her of shooting the girl "in cold blood" or "over pennies" or "a $1.79 bottle of orange juice." Whether or not the girl really intended to shoplift or the woman really intended to pull the trigger; the fact is the Korean woman had her face whacked but good. Being human, she *must* have been seething with anger. It is a tragedy that the girl was killed; but it is a shame so many people black and white could dehumanize the woman with loose talk about "cold blood." I would submit that this proves we still have a tendency to deny Asians their emotions, our human emotions.

Exchanges of *haute culture* do little to correct such a tendency. We need a broader exchange, within the country and between countries. In his entertaining survey LEARNED PIGS AND FIREPROOF WOMEN (1987), the sleight of hand artist Ricky Jay ventured that the scatological antics of a modern day Japanese Le Petomane, performed on the Osaka TV show 11 PM and partially aired in Chicago one night did more good for the Japanese image than years of the usual high-brow cultural exchange.[4] *Exactly.* A Roman once wrote "Nothing human is strange to me." I believe that for most people this only holds true for the vulgar. Vulgarity, whether you admit to liking it or not, is never completely foreign to us.

We are now ready for Professor J. I. Crump's translation. The stanzas describe what a country bumpkin saw in a play when he came to town and what saved his life:

> Squire Chang backs up `cause
> forward won't do
> And with his right foot in the air he
> hoists his left one too!
> Poor Chang is whip-sawed fro and to
> Til he's so hotted up he don't know
> what to do,
> So he
> Bangs his meat-club on the ground and
> snaps it right in half
> And I nearly bust my side while I
> double up and laugh.
> I keep hangin' on and hangin' around
> to see the thing through
> Just to listen to them talk and
> to see what they would do
> But my bladder is achin' so I can't

catch my breath –
Those crazy pizzles *made* me leave
Else I'd have laughed myself to death!
(Ibid.)

Versified slap-stick – or should we say *snap*-stick in this case? – does not *itself* convey deep emotion. But that is beside the point. Emotions are not so much conveyed as *granted* to others on the basis of an assumption of common humanity. It is this common humanity that such a verse confirms which makes it possible for us to overcome our prejudice with good faith. [5]

ch.10 notes

1. Haiku and Greek. English tried to match syllable-counting Greek poetry for centuries with little success. We cannot really match haiku for the same reason: the Greek *mora* and the Japanese syllabet (i) are short and relatively uniform while our syllables are far too varied in length to work right. If the only way we can get the same snap into our poems is through rhyme, then it is more faithful to the original to rhyme, even if it is *not* rhymed. *Call this the structural equivalent of figurative translation.* But most modern intellectuals detest rhyme too much to seriously consider this possibility. English professor and translator Lawrence Venuti lambastes an 1858 *London Quarterly Review* of Newman's unrhymed Horace, for claiming Newman's foreignizing version appeared "somewhat quaint and harsh", whereas "the rhymed versions of Lord Ravensworth and Mr. Theodore Martin" possessed "the qualities of easy elegance, of sweetness of cadence." And, further, after giving examples of Newman's translation, for truthfully writing "This is hard to read, while the Latin is as pleasant to the ear as the fountain which it brings before us to the imagination." Venuti fumes:

> This reviewers' negative evaluations rested on a contradiction that revealed quite clearly the domestic cultural values they privileged. In calling for a rhymed version, they inscribed the *unrhymed* Latin text with the verse form that dominated current English poetry while insisting that rhyme made the translation closer to Horace. The reviewers were articulating a hegemonic position in English literary culture, definitely slanted toward an academic elite: Horace's text can be pleasant to the ear only for readers of Latin. (THE TRANSLATOR'S INVISIBILITY)

While I appreciate Venuti's defense of the original, I feel that his interpretation is unfair. The reviewers are only being honest to their ears. Since popular culture then (as now) loved rhyme, it is ridiculous to accuse *them* of an elitist position. They only say this: *those who cannot read the original should be able to enjoy something equally delightful in translation.* Venuti has it completely backwards. Unfortunately, without seeing Ravensworth and Martin's rhymes, as well as Horace's original, we can not say whether we share the taste of the reviewers.

2. Rhyme in Japanese. While end-rhyme is rare, there is an awful lot mid-line, so that an AAB scheme (mostly Dickinsonian weak rhyme) haiku might be a more fair approximation of the original Japanese single-line form than no rhyme at all. Popular songs are also full of assonance that works like end-rhyme when the breaks in the melody serve to accent it. Most Japanese are not very aware of this, but the poets know. See EXOTIC TONGUES if/when it is published for a more thorough treatment. Rhyme is a favorite hobby-horse of mine.

3. Vulgarity for understanding, a qualification. On second thought, vulgarity is called for only when it happens to balance an image of the other as prissy and proper. When the other is already stereotyped as vulgar, the effect might be counterproductive. The Peasant Wedding picture of brutal-looking folk would be useful to show to someone who thinks vulgarity is new to the world and born of upper-class decadence. It would not be so eye-opening for someone who already thinks of the vulgaris as vulgar. Since many Asians already think of Americans as vulgar, we do not need to advertise *our* vulgarity.

4. Japanese vulgarity. The English not only picked up on it but started their own show based on the grossest of the Japanese shows. The late "people's princess" was a big fan of the show. She would have loved to have known Mr. Vulgarity himself, the man whose television show was the model for Mr Hill's show, Beat Takeshi, whose movies have brought him great fame in the West in recent years.

5. Such a Verse. My mother did not want me to print this poem. The last paragraph, perhaps the best in the essay was added in order to save it!

6. Additional note Douglas R. Hofstadter's *Le Ton beau de Marot* (1997) – read too late to mention elsewhere – raises some of the same issues I do, usually coming to the same conclusion but in a more mathematical(?) manner, but sometimes coming to a different conclusion, as when he expresses great amazement and ultimately disapproval of vernacular translations of Chinese. He notes (correctly) that "spiciness" in English tends to come at the expense of universality but is unfair to translators when he complains about one using "arse-licking" or "screw 'em," et cetera as "reeking of English" and "stripping Mr. Average of his Chineseness" and about others of putting words like "clout," "kids," or "hick" into Chinese mouths. I believe this argument is wrong on two levels.

First, it overlooks the fact that the Chinese – or, at least Chinese in many parts of China – are known for using particularly colorful invective (in that sense they are the opposite of the Japanese, who are remarkable for using little of it). True, the words aren't necessarily the same as those used in English. For example, the Chinese are far more into farts and constantly speak of people as "fart-crotches" and I doubt if one would want to English *all* such terms. Yet, disallowing colorful terms and ungrammatical sentences would be to turn all non-English speakers into a singular boring fiction.

Second, while Hofstadter notes the translators have no choice because it is English's singular misfortune to lack unlocalized exclamations – indeed, even if the translator were to write "damned" rather than "screwed," peculiar Western notions of sexuality would simply be replaced by peculiar notions of theology (this, unlike the case in Japanese, where powerful emotions can be expressed by culturally neutral grammatical changes) – I wonder how he can call colorful language in translation "ludicrous," "grotesque," and "jarring," without suggesting what, then, we *should* do to convey the vulgarity of the original. To my mind, a cheap novel or mass-market non-fiction might best do just what Studs Terkel did and Hofstadter pooh-poohs. And a book for the thinking reader should, I think, do *more*. It should expand the reader's horizon by introducing common Chinese expressions such as "fart-crotch." At the same time, the translator should be clearly present in the notes, making certain that such novelty is properly qualified.

I think such an approach might actually be more in line with Hofstadter's own taste, which is playful and allows, to give but one example, that the opacity of English words made of foreign roots – he gives the example of *dinosaur names*, obvious in Chinese but mysterious and therefore magical in English – may actually be a plus.

appendix

1

(*Japan Times* "Guest Forum" July13, 1986)

Ecology, Buddhism and Christianity Reconsidered

Mirror, mirror on the wall, who is the most ecological of all?

In the prewar years [shortly before World War II], most Japanese schools of thought and religious sects vied with each other to be accepted as "the most Japanese of all," even to the extent of distorting their own moral doctrines – a point tellingly criticized by two brave academics, Kyoshi Miki and Jun Tosaka, both of whom died in jail as a result of their thought-crimes.

While Tosaka, a brilliant left-wing rhetorician's rhetorician didn't balk at taking on Kyoto's intellectual wizard of the East, Kitaro Nishida, insultingly arguing that his philosophy of *mu* (nothingness) did indeed boil down to *nothing* of worth, Miki, like Nishida, was eager to formulate a philosophy capable of conquering the West.

And, like Nishida, he believed the best chance lay in Buddhism, which was, after all, originally an imported religion bearing the requisite stamp of universality – as opposed to inherently Japanese philosophy such as neo-Shintoism and national organicism (*kokutaishugi*) being pushed by the government of the time.

Be that as it may, the first Japanese to launch a successful challenge to the Judeo-Christian worldview was probably Daisetsu Suzuki – whom the irrepressible Reginald Blyth lauded as "the only man who can write about Zen without making me loathe it." If the late Rene Dubos (THE WOOING OF THE EARTH:1980) is correct, Lynn White's seminal article ("The Historical Roots of the Ecological Crisis," *Science:*1967) pinning the blame for environmental problems on the teachings of Christianity was merely a rehash of the ideas first expressed by Suzuki in an article entitled "The Role of Nature in Zen Buddhism" (*Eranos-Jahrbuch 22:1953*)

Today, in Japan, as in the rest of the "developed" world, this *something*, which may be called "ecological validity," is fast becoming the litmus test for all philosophical and ethical systems of thought with aspirations of universality, and a convenient tool to grade otherwise "relative" cultural lifestyles. [1]

Commandments Compared

One of Tohoku-bred, Kyoto-schooled Umehara Takeshi's many books, *Tetsugaku-no Fukkyo* (the revival of philosophy: 1972) agrees with Toynbee's The-Future-is-East (the-West-is-dying) hypothesis, and specifies just where Western philosophy/morality is inferior to that of Buddhism and Animism.

While I hold no truck with much of Western philosophy, and am largely sympathetic to the so-called "New-Age" criticism of Baconian-Cartesian-Kantian thinking (I also think Bacon *et al* have something to be said for them: see, for example, Loren Eiseley's THE MAN WHO SAW THROUGH TIME), Umehara is a wee bit too full of Eastern hubris for me.

For example, he points out that in Buddhism "No killing" is the *First* Commandment, whereas in Christianity it is way down in the number *five* position and covers only humans at that – *if that,* considering the bloody pages of the Old Testament.

There is no contesting the blood in the Bible. If Mark Twain were here today, he would certainly compare it to a spaghetti Western or samurai drama. But, the Commandments are open to other interpretations. The first four concern the relationship of man to deity and child to parent. Follow the first four, and the rest follow naturally. To use the Tao-like phrase of Saint Augustine, "Love God and do as you please." In this sense, "Thou shall not kill" *is* the *first* of what might be called the secondary group of Commandments.

Moreover, one may cite Ecclesiastes iii 19: "That which befalleth the sons of men befalleth beasts; . . . as one dieth so dieth the other; yea they have all one breath; so that man hath no preeminence above a beast." and conclude that the 5th Commandment means we can no more kill a beast without due cause (self-defense, food, clothing) than a man. Indeed, a 15th century manuscript, "Dives and Pauper," argues just that (see Keith Thomas's masterful MAN AND THE NATURAL WORLD).

To economize the limited space remaining, I am going to minimize my citations of persons and books and present a grossly generalized summary of anti-Western/Christian standpoints often encountered in writing by Japanese intellectuals, and hypothetical counter-arguments.

Criticism 1 – Whereas Christianity clearly sanctions the taking of non-human life, Buddhism teaches that the life of a fly is as valuable as the world.

Reply – While, in a sense, the life of a fly is equal to that of a human, this equality, vulgarly understood, can rationalize the total disregard of human life as being "nothing more of worth than an insect (*mushikera dôzen*)," as indeed happened not long ago. [2]

Criticism 2 – Whereas Christianity sets apart human and other life, Buddhism teaches non-discrimination.

Reply – Theoretically, there is some truth to this; but when it comes to popular Buddhism, i.e., reincarnation, with souls working their way up from rung to rung to Buddhahood, Buddhism can indeed serve to validate and even encourage discrimination between men of different ranks (*mibun*) and other animals, as suggested by Etsuko Sugimoto in her long-selling classic DAUGHTER OF A SAMURAI. [3]

Criticism 3 – Whereas the Judeo-Christian mentality, originating in a harsh desert environment, considers Nature as an enemy to be fought, Buddhism teaches harmony with Nature.

Reply – The opposite hypothesis is possible: Namely, that the spare desert environment fostered a sense of appreciation for the miracle of life, [4] which explains why the Judeo-Christian God called his creation "good," while Hindu-Buddhist thought, being born of a luxuriant jungle culture, was unappreciative, or sated, enough to blame the sensual-material world for human suffering and dismiss it as *maya.*

Criticism 4 – Whereas the Christian God gives humans "dominion" over Nature, Buddhism doesn't support the exploitation of the natural world.

Reply – As Jeremy Riftkin argues convincingly in THE EMERGING MAJORITY, dominion need not be interpreted as tyranny, but rather the duty to be a responsible steward for a world which, like it or not, is fully in our charge today. [5]

Criticism 5 – Whereas the Christian worldview is linear and progress-oriented, the Buddhist one is cyclical like Nature. [6]

Reply – Pre-modern Christians could not conceive of "progress," a concept born in the 18th century, and there is much in the Bible of a seasonal and cyclic nature going on and on, *world without end . . . amen.*" This isn't to say all Nature is cyclical, since there is some linearity, if one accepts the second law of thermodynamics.

Criticism 6 – Christianity teaches man to despise Nature as a symbol of the Fall. [7]

Reply – Perhaps. But one can find Christian authorities who have taught that it is the special duty of humans to care for the rest of Nature precisely because it was we who caused Nature's Fall.

In a similar vein, it is noteworthy that one of the intellectual roots for the movement to prevent cruelty to animals in the West is the Christian argument that since only humans go to heaven – a belief not likely to be shared by most modern Christians in the West, who could hardly countenance leaving their pets behind – it behooves us to see that other animals enjoy their one and only life!

A Real Problem

In other words, Christianity or Buddhism can be construed to say just about anything we wish or allow them to, which is why comparison of their relative ecological worth is a silly proposition to begin with.

Perhaps the only anti-intellectual, downright dangerous "Christian" sentiment I've ever had the misfortune to run into came not from the Bible but the mouth of ex-American Secretary of the Interior James Watt, who justified his extreme laissez faire attitude toward natural resource exploitation at congressional hearing several years ago by saying something to the effect that, *Hey, Christ will return soon and this world will be over, so we might as well enjoy its riches now, as God surely intended us to.*

Remembering the classic Western stereotype of Buddhist (Asian) passivity and Christian (European) activity, one can't help chuckling at the irony of this all. But this Panglossian worldview is no laugh. Combining the medieval fatalism of the "Born Again Christian" with modern consumption patterns *a la* American Dream is a surefire way to ensure that the Christian myth of the Apocalypse *does* become the reality of the end.

In the final account, the desire to be in the ecological avant-garde – note Prime Minister Nakasone's U.N. address of last fall – is not necessarily a bad trend. If, as Toynbee believed, Russia and China took up Marxism with a vengeance in order to assert their superiority over Western civilization by vaulting ahead into what was perceived as the Way of the Future, Japan may well choose to play the role of a Deep Ecology State as a means of self-assertion.

Should such be the case, I suppose one could still say that this is just another version of *out-Westing the West;* but look at it this way: There are many worse questions that could be asked to the Mirror.

app.1 notes

1. The end of cultural relativity? Relativity was an improvement on subjectivity, but when the world's ecological and cultural diversity, as well as the base upon which it stands is in danger, different lifestyles are no longer relative. If – to give but one example – the United States keeps gasoline prices low to guard its wasteful culture of unlimited mobility, it commits a crime against the future and deserves the censure of other more responsible societies. If, on the other hand, the Muria of Northwestern India wish to arrange the sleeping schedules of their young in the interest of equality – so that ugly teens get to sexually experience beautiful members of the opposite sex – that is their option and outside cultures have no right to criticize it a a violation of "human rights.". Only parts of culture that impinge on the interests of the whole world are what is no longer "relative." Yet, because diversity has ecological value of its own, small groups can and should be allowed some freedom to do things that should not be permitted in the case of large societies. (There are exceptions to this rule. But the matter of whether to permit cruelty against individuals, such as genital mutilation, is too complex to take up here)

2. The life of a fly. In this world, on a common sense level, all life is *not* equal. Ordinary Japanese worked together to try to save the life of Hana the elephant during the war. They would not work so hard to save a fly, no matter what Zen may say about equality of souls. Higher life is, if nothing else, more valuable for being rare and, let's be honest, for being like us. Likewise, no unborn or newly born infant is worth my life or yours. They may be worth the world to their parents if they want them, but this value is not absolute. **(i)** It is contingent on that love. There are lives and there are lives. This difference was naturally felt by people over the ages around the world, and that is why abortion and infanticide were traditionally accepted where manslaughter was not. Some say admitting difference in life is Nazi; I say that murder was made easier (in Japan, at least) by misguided extrapolation from ideals of spiritual, or soul equality. **(ii)** Now, the Japanese know better; but there are Americans who still talk loosely about "life" and would kill – or condone killing – doctors for practicing abortion.

i The newly born. The same thing goes for pets. We now make a big deal out of culling. Well, kittens smittens! The life of a kitten's mother is worth a million times more than *its* is. That is *not* because the kitten physically depends on the mother, but because of *all the loving, caring and suffering that go into an adult animal's life.* Likewise for wild animals. I mourn every *adult* seal that dies before its time infinitely more than I mourn a baby seal that is clubbed to death. We have a Cult of the Infant that has weakened our ability to recognize what matters in life. (See Nancy Schieper-Hughes: DEATH WITHOUT WEEPING for a mature and insightful study of a culture that must prioritize the actual lives of older children and adults over the mere potential of babies and young children.) I see the extrapolation of the literal infantilism our ignorant culture permits back to the even less valuable life of the fetus, icon of the so-called Right-to-Life movement, as a moral tragedy. Our culture no longer knows what is truly precious.

ii Soul equality. The Tibetans have taken this farther than any one I know – unless, we allow Pythagorean beans a say – for they strive to reduce the numbers of lives=souls they take by eating only the *largest* animals available. Had they lived by the sea, the blue whale would have been their only diet, but living on land, they settled on oxen. Kill one life=soul and feed a village of 300 souls for a week. The South-eastern Asian and Japanese practice of eating tiny fish or shrimp with a hundred lives=souls to the spoonful and thousands per meal would horrify them! It would knock their karma back to the Stone Age. See Rin Chem Lha-Mo's WE TIBETANS (1926). I think someone has reprinted it.

3. Buddhist nondiscrimination. Etsuko's puppy caught a cold, but was not allowed to sleep wrapped up in a blanket inside because it was "improper to its station and might even harm its karma," according to her parents. The puppy died and Etsuko grew up to blame Buddhism for making Japanese immune to the suffering of other people and animals beneath their station in life. The earliest rationalization of what otherwise might be considered cruel behavior by the doctrine of Pythagoras – as Europeans once called all belief in reincarnation – that I have read in English appeared in *THE WORLD* of Adam Fitz-

Adams' on Thursday, February 12, 1756. I hope the readers will forgive me for choosing a particularly humorous paragraph:

> Never can the delicious repast of roasted lobsters excite my appetite, whilst the ideas of the tortures, in which those innocent creatures have expired, present themselves to my imagination. But when I consider that they must have once probably been Spaniards at Mexico, or Dutchmen at Amboyna, I fall to, both with a good stomach and a good conscience, and please myself with the thoughts, that I am thus offering up a sacrifice acceptable to the names of many millions of massacred Indians.

I should like to think that in my case the lobster was Andrew Jackson for his role in forcing a highly literate people to walk the Trail of Tears. He should have been impeached for not following the dictates of the Supreme Court and at the very least we should petition to remove him from the $20. bill. He could be replaced with Mark Twain (As England has Dickens and Japan has Soseki).

4. Harsh desert environment. A culture drying up its natural environment and, with it, the niches for the myriad gods of a poli- or omni-theistic animism to survive, so that it might eventually be doomed to wander the barren globe like a tumbleweed! The world reduced to a bare horizon, an above and below, God and a no-God, right and a wrong . . . . As an idea, this Occidentalist scenario for the birth-of-the-West does have a certain intellectual attraction. The concept has even been given a positive reading by Thomas Cahill, an apparent believer:

> If God – the Real God, the One God – was to speak to human beings and if their was any possibility of their hearing him, it could happen only in a place stripped of all cultural reference points, where even nature (which was so imbued with contrary god-inhabited forces) seemed absent. Only amid inhuman rock and dust could this fallible collection of human beings imagine becoming human in a new way. Only under a sun without pity, on a mountain devoid of life, could the living God break through the cultural filters that normally protect us from him.
> (THE GIFTS OF THE JEWS:1998)

Or as someone who doubts the worth of monotheism might put it, natural and cultural deprivation is filled by awful fantasy. But reality is more complex. In the 19th century, desert Bedouin were reportedly animists who found plentiful Gods in the innumerable heavenly bodies. (I believe Lady Anne Blunt's inspired writing was one of my sources) More recently, Leslie Marmon Silko has written movingly about the way the stark and, to outsiders, barren land of the Arizona Hopi has worked to foster a deep appreciation for what little life there is – so much so that the elders claim to be spiritually *blessed* by such scarcity. But, far from reducing all value down to a thundering Singularity on High, they find the sacred in the small things around them. Not only the lizard and rare plant, but the very stones are treated with (or, supposed to be so treated, for the Hopi are human) reverence (article by Silko in D. Halpern ed. IN NATURE) It would appear that a God beyond Nature and the attendant ecological short-comings, if any, intrinsic to Middle-East= Western Religion can not be simply reduced to the desert.

5. THE EMERGING MAJORITY. Riftkin noted hopefully that fundamentalist Christians are the only people with the organization and the gumption to get off their asses and really save the world. If they were to turn radically green, the environmental movement might get serious. Unfortunately, this very big IF has yet to pan out.

6. Cyclic versus linear time. Actually, the difference between the modern West and the rest of the world is not so clear-cut. The Chinese have their own linear calendar dating back to a certain "First Emperor." And the Japanese, even if they do have their short *gengo* eras going back to year one every couple decades, also have a sense of linear time, of things building up from a small pebble to a moss-covered boulder (perhaps a coral-influenced idea) an idea found in an old poem now part of the national anthem. How can it be otherwise for any *civilization*, any culture with true writing? When you have literary figures with strong personalities like Tabito, (i) Okura, (ii) Murasaki, (iii) Shonagon, (iv) and Saigyo, (v) whose writing has lasted a thousand years, how can you possibly be lost in some vague world of endless repetition? Linear time, like many things, is not as uniquely Western as many think.

---

i. Otomo Tabito. His thirteen poems in praise of drink in the MANYOSHU long precede Omar Khayyam. The first says a cup of raw *sake* beats worrying. Good clarified sake is clear and would not work as well as cloudy=raw (*nigori) sake* to blank out one's memory. Unfortunately, Japanese poetry has no Fitzgerald. **(a)** All of the translations I've seen are *boring as hell.* I hope I can improve the situation. Here are a few:

don't think,
drink: cloudy sake
will fix you

prohibition

ancient sages
called wine "sage"
what the hell's
the matter
with our age?

moderation, you say?

rather than be
a half-hearted lug
let me
soak in wine,
a jug!

a red-faced riposte

teetotalers
how they raise
their brows
looking smart
as apes!

karma be damned!

this
is my life
my time for fun
let me be
a bird or bug
next time

Japanese monkeys (macaques) have bright red faces and many, if not most, Japanese turn bright red when they drink, so I added considerable information to the title of the penultimate poem. Then, again, *none* of the poems had titles to begin with. As for the last poem, Buddhism doesn't forbid drink as such; but drink has always been identified with a worldly life, and Buddhism didn't think much of *that.* A bonze who was beyond worldly concerns, on the other hand, could walk about drunk and be none the worse for it.

(a) Omar Khayyám and Fitzgerald No note was needed or intended here, but a neighbor with Alzheimer's was institutionalized and his books ended up in the trash where I found a translation of Khayyam with a yellowed clipping of an undated article from the San Francisco Chronicle (from the era of Prohibition, perhaps?) that is too much fun not to share. After introducing the Fitzgerald translation

> *For 'is' and 'is not' though with rules and line,*
> *And 'up-and-down' by logic i define,*
> *Of all that one should care to fathom, I*
> *Was never deep in anything – but wine.*

the article gives another version of the same poem by Mirza Ali Kuli Khan, Imperial Consul from Persia, which read as follows: *"For although I have studied everything there is to know, and feel capable of giving an opinion upon the subjects, yet I never was deep in anything but the intoxication one feels in contemplating the profundity, the mystery, of life, and the unknowable things of the infinite."* Then, the article continued as follows:

> Omar Khayyam's reputation was cleared yesterday before San Francisco's exclusive society. The blot that had existed on the old "Tent-Maker's" memory since Edward Fitzgerald translated his quatrains into English verse was wiped out by Mirza Ali Kuli Kahn at the St. Francis Hotel, and the audience breathed a sigh of relief. They never believed all of those awful things about Omar, anyhow.

The "wine" was only a metaphor, he claimed, for spiritual intoxication. Perhaps, but the use of such a metaphor suggests a positive view of drinking. And what do we do with the taverns and jugs and whatnot in other verses? I suspect the truth lies closer to E.F. than the Consul. Then again, I also think Solomon really did adore the voluptuous female body he sang and was not only exploiting it as a metaphor for religious buildings or I forget what.

ii. Yamanoue Okura. This poet of the MANYOSHU made a poem to excuse himself from an official banquette because his crying child and wife who holds him await at home. Some years later, his child died and he wrote a poem that is the first real tear-jerker – as opposed to lament, of which there are many in Japanese classical poetry, as elsewhere – I know of. A few lines from the middle of MANYOSHU poem #904 in Ian Hideo Levy's translation show why:

> When dusk came / with the evening star, /he would say, / "Let's go to sleep," / and take us by our hands / and urge us in his lovely way, / "Mother and father, / never leave my side. / Let me sleep between you / like the middle branch / of the lily's three."
>
> (THE TEN THOUSAND LEAVES: vol.1)

iii. Murasaki Shikibu. Her TALE OF GENJI is often called the world's first true novel. I particularly enjoyed her character's comments about how it was only right that a woman of good character believed every thing she read; about the way a step-mother carefully made certain that her daughter did not see story-books about stepmothers, because they always made stepmothers mean, even though most are not; and the chapter deliberately left blank in mid-book. The world's first novel was also the first "post-modern novel," a meta-novel sometimes reminding the us of "our" first, Laurence Sterne's TRISTAM SHANDY.

iv. Sei Shonagon. This woman (born c. 965) is *outrageous*. Read THE PILLOW BOOK OF SEI SHONAGON (trans. Ivan Morris) and see if you don't agree that Oscar Wilde was her reincarnation. A good example of her outrageous style:

> A preacher ought to be good-looking. For, if we are properly to understand his worthy sentiments, we must keep our eyes on him when he speaks; should we look away, we may forget to listen. Accordingly, an ugly preacher may well be the source of sin . . . (Ibid.)

She also did the most interesting *mono-wa-tsukushi*, or listing of things (e.g. – opening a page at random – "*Squalid Things:* The back of a piece of embroidery / The inside of a cat's ear / . . . A rather unattractive woman who looks after a large brood of children / . . .") – in Japanese history.

v. Saigyo. This twelfth century Buddhist priest and poet was Basho's favorite. His *uta* (5-7-5-7-7) claiming a snipe rising from the Marsh in the fall dusk moves anyone with a sense of melancholy is, thematically speaking, a proto-haiku. (Later than Basho, Issa has the snipe stare at him as if to ask, *do you have that sensibility?)* I am most impressed with something Saigyo did that the high-brows never mention. He developed metaphors of the heart further than anyone. To mention but two of dozens, he wishes to drown himself in a heart-pool full of tears (early *haikai* (the linked-verse of *Inokoshuu)* parodies this with a man yearning for a bucket of the beloved's piss to drown himself in (*mi-o nage-shinde omoide-ni sen / kimi-sama-no shoben-mizu-no-fuchi mogana!)*, the experts entirely miss the connection) and he calls his own love-sick heart a wailing new-born baby within!

7. Despising nature. Japanese, like Chinese – and perhaps, like all people? – tend to call bad people "beastly" or "a beast wearing a human mask" etc.. A Japanese acquaintance who heads an animal rights group wrote letters to Buddhist and Shinto (as animists) leaders criticizing the metaphors they used (in public statements) as denigrating to non-human life and contradictory to the tenets of their religion! Ah, but it is hard to praise one thing without putting down another inadvertently. A letter to *Asashi Shinbun* criticizing the loose way journalists referred to single human lives as "more valuable than the world." (*chikyu yori omoi*: literally, "more weighty than the earth"), puts it like this:

> "No words express human arrogance as well as this term. It's just as if the earth were our possession to do with as we like." (1988-6-30)

It is also a false statement about the value of a life. Shortly after the US took Iraq, I wrote the Ombudsman of NPR to complain that so little attention had been given to the Museum of Antiquities and to express my dismay that we thought the life of a single serviceman worth more than the treasures of all time, treasures, that I might point out, many have died to make and to defend. *Is living all we care about anymore?* If I had wanted to multiply myself, my life, I would have gotten married and made lots of children rather than books, like this one. When my remarks were broadcast around the nation, I noted they were followed by a young woman at Harvard, who spouted the pc commonplace that *all history was not worth the risk of losing a single human life.* My jaw dropped. If that is how she feels, why waste her life at Harvard! Our lives are worth what we make of them. Does she have any idea how many people have died making and collecting such artifacts, such history? I hate to preach, but, lady, mark my words: *if no one feels that culture is worth dying for, we will end up with nothing worth living for.*

GLOSS for APPENDIX 1 from Lee Gurga, editor of *Modern Haiku* (a) –

I have only had a chance to glance at it (in the bathtub), but I will share a few observations if you are interested. I was particularly struck by appendix 1, "Ecology Buddhism and Christianity Reconsidered." I thought much was right on, but would like to correct one misconception. You have equated, as almost everyone does, Christianity with Western Christianity. The positions of Eastern (i.e., Orthodoxy) Christianity are quite different. Orthodoxy views man as the *priest* rather than *ruler* of nature. In addition, the Orthodox view of time is cyclical rather than linear. (See, for example, "Man the Priest of Creation: A Response to the Ecological Problem" in *Living Orthodoxy in the Modern World.*) A famous story tells of a priest on the Island of Patmos (where John wrote the book of Revelation) who said that there is another commandment that is not in the Bible: "Love the trees." Here is a quote from another chapter in the book, "Orthodoxy and Modern Depth Psychology," which also has bearing on the issue of ecology: "Yet for those in the Church, the danger is of the false notion of 'salvation' that has disfigured all Western traditions, high church, low church, middle of the road, conservative or radical . . . *From an Orthodox perspective, the spirit of 'we are saved from the world' is not holy, but Satanic.*" Perhaps you get the idea. [My italics.]

a) ***Modern Haiku*** is the oldest and most prestigious haiku magazine in America. Like a good key lime from which you may squeeze out more juice than it could possibly hold, this compact magazine holds riches beyond its size, as may be imagined from the editor's FAQ:

"Please be assured that submissions are never rejected because of lack of space." (beautiful!)

appendix

2

How to Make a Difference

I had thought to add this list of *sixteen ways to falsify or exaggerate cultural difference* to the long version of my annotated translation of Padre Luis Frois's 1585 treatise listing 611 contrasts between "us" (Europeans) and "them" (the Japanese), in case my qualifications were insufficient to prevent the flood of difference from overwhelming the reader and serve only to reinforce the old saw that *"East is East and West is West"* (which, in Kipling's poem, soon continues *"But there is neither East nor West when . . ."*).

I thought it might be good atonement for the exuberant excess, exaggerated contrast found not only in Frois, himself, but in my notes.[1] For, though my main concern as a responsible writer was to explain away difference which might be misconstrued, I simply could not resist introducing curiosities (collecting anything – even ideas – is contagious) I knew would delight readers because they delighted me – how unfair for scholars to keep the good stuff to themselves for moral reasons! – even though I knew they threaten to exoticize what I would prefer to make familiar.

On second thought, I decided my notes probably had enough qualifications scattered throughout to do without this exercise, and the tremendous length of the annotation, which turns the book into a twenty-first century THINGS JAPANESE, decided the matter. Besides, it is more appropriate for *this* book, dealing directly with mistranslation of culture and antithetical stereotype. So let us get on with what is, as far as I know, the longest list of the pitfalls of comparative studies yet published. I apologize that many if not examples repeat information given in the main body of the book. This will reframe them in an overall perspective I think useful to students of comparative culture.

Comparing incommensurables – Apples and pears. E.g., Lafcadio Hearn's contrast[2] of complex and enormous Gothic Shrines of the West with simple wooden Shinto shrines in Japan, when he might better have mentioned North Europe's stav churches, or the large and ornate Buddhist architecture in Japan! (See Steadman: THE MYTH OF ASIA 1969)

Comparing the real to the ideal – E.g., decision making in smoke-filled rooms in Japan versus public democracy in the West. It is fine for Japanese writers to browbeat sleazy Japanese politicians, but haven't they heard of Huey Long? Mayor Daley? (Compare Nakane Chie: JAPANESE SOCIETY and Mike Royko: THE BOSS)

Claims reflecting personal bias – E.g., the Western executive claims the decision was all his own, while the Japanese claims it was made by consensus. Research shows, however, the decision process was, in reality, not all that different. The CEO only made different claims about it (See Rodney Clark: THE JAPANESE COMPANY 1979).

Offering partial truths – Japanese conservatives use their soldiers' low desertion rates in WWII as proof of high social cohesiveness Western soldiers lacked, but fail to mention the higher suicide rate of Japanese recruits, resulting partly from the greater difficulty of desertion.

One-sided generalization – A respected professor of geography claims that Japanese, being a "forest civilization" don't like to be clear-cut, and therefore often say *"wakaranai,"* meaning "[I] don't know" or, literally "don't cut." He neglects to say that the positive form of the same verb proves Japanese "understand" by "cutting." Likewise, in THE JAPANESE BRAIN, the otorhinologist author claims Japanese can not be entirely rational, while forgetting that by the same token they couldn't be entirely emotional either!

Simplification – Christianity is said to separate man from the rest of nature, while Buddhism does not. But what about the karmic cycle incorporated by Buddhism that has man at the top of the chain? Isn't this also anthropocentric? (Gill: "Ecology, Buddhism and Christianity Reconsidered" *Japan Times*, 1986/7/13)

Naive interpretation of actual difference – An American boasts of having the "greatest wife in the world" while Japanese, "not wanting to hurt others feelings (i.e., make them jealous)" prefer to complain. The fact that Americans assume the other will be worried if one complains and is pleased at the other's good fortune is missed by the Japanese in search of the anticipated contrast of boastful Americans who care only about themselves and Japanese who care for others.

Bias in data available for comparison – Japanese contrast jolly "dry" American country music with their own melancholy "wet" *enka*. In translation, *"Green, Green Grass of Home"* has no hanging and becomes pure nostalgia, as does the *"Tennessee Waltz,"* where nothing is said about losing one's sweetheart to another while dancing the same! Cognitive dissonance is relieved by the translators before it even happens.

Selected examples – What, ask Sugimoto and Mouer in a number of books published in the 1980's, if we were to contrast the traditional Japanese sports like sumo, judo and kendo (sword-fighting) with the traditional Western sports of baseball, rugby and cricket? Which would *then* come out the more individualistic and the more collective people? But who makes *that* contrast? (Actually Michael Novak did point out the individual values inherent to baseball and made the Japan connection in his JOY OF SPORTS, but the Japanese were not the focus of the book.) Their point is that cultural comparison often relies upon arbitrary choice of evidence.

Prejudicial claims – E.g., a Japanese woman has her girl crawl through a milk-delivery hole to help a woman without a key open her apartment door, and commented that an American would *never* do such a thing because if that person were ever robbed they would fear being accused. Or the musicologist that claimed a Westerner could not comprehend an *enka* (similar to Dolly Parton's *"I'll Always Love You"*) where a woman gave up the man she loved because she thought it better for him, "because Western people either love someone or hate them." Perhaps we should call this "imagined evidence based on a fact."

Mistaken logic – A book claiming to teach Japanese to be better cosmopolitans by "knowing how we and the Westerners differ" showed a Western man taking a coin to call the vending company rather than kicking the vending machine as a Japanese would – because, according to the authors, Japanese are basically animistic so they react emotionally to a machine, while the Christian Westerner treats it rationally as a soulless object. Logically, this makes sense, but, as a matter of fact, there are more shoe and knuckle marks on the American vending machines I've seen than on the Japanese ones!

Absolute contrast – We are short/small; they are tall/big. Lifting differences to a whole-culture level may take the onus off the individual who is short/small and feeling inferior to his countrymen, but the bell curve of natural difference says absolute contrasts only exist in fiction.

Anachronistic comparison – Japanese scholars in the 1970s and 80s often contrasted blood-thirsty eye-for-eye Western justice with Japanese mercy, not uncommonly citing the Heian era with its 300 years of no capital punishment. What if they instead wrote of the draconian justice recorded by Westerners in 16th and 17th century Japan? It continued up to the twentieth century. Likewise, Westerners tend to contrast the modern fiction of an individualistic West with traditional Japan, forgetting their ancestors were only recently sleeping ten to a room, and have a long history of restricting individual liberties such as freedom of religion and freedom to drink, which were long enjoyed by the Japanese.

A-geographic comparison – To compare the farm culture of old Japan to the industrial West, forgetting about the fact that urban Japan boasts a long tradition of watch-making and playing with automata, not to mention pure science such as mathematics was to make Japan's miracle far more miraculous than it was. Contrasting the animal protein consumption of Japan with America won't lead to the same conclusion a comparison with the people of a mountainous land surrounded with water like, say Italy, would. Overlooking place is akin to, but less obvious than, overlooking time.

Incomplete comparison – It is true that we use the first-person pronoun over ten times as much as the Japanese do. But to attribute this to our pushiness and lack of humility is to forget that Japanese syntax makes the impact of the pronoun ten times greater, so that the psychological impact of the whole conversation is about the same. Likewise for the alleged Japanese tendency to *dependence* versus our independence, as argued by a Japanese psychiatrist Doi Takeo. True, Japanese depend on their companies more. But we borrow more from our neighbors, and depend more – some say too much – on our spouses. Meaningful comparison requires a culture-wide perspective?

Difference as inevitable – Japan's leading theorist of environmental influence on culture/civilization, Watsuji Tetsuro (1935) hypothesized the English, living in their damp and dark country were attracted to Christianity because it offered them something different, the dry light of the desert; but Japanese writers in the 1970s and 1980s typically explained the lack of success on the part of Christianity in Japan to the "wet" nature of their "monsoon climate" and heart of the Japanese being a mismatch for the "dry" religion. Both explanations are reductionist and must be taken with a grain of salt, but the latter is less so, for if opposites attract, difference is not permanent, whereas the attraction of likes (and correlative repulsion of opposites), would freeze cultures into opposite molds forever.

app.2 notes

1. ***How Fair Frois?*** Not a few of the sixteen logical faults, the bulk of which can be summed more simply in a single word, *exaggeration*, can be found among Frois's 611 contrasts. But, aside from those which touch upon religion – *"our monks fight for the purity of their hearts; the bonzes keep their temple and its garden grounds immaculate while their souls are filthy"* – most of his contrasts were relatively benign. Written before stereotype set in, the distiches neither make value judgments nor invite them. They are, as you can see in ***Topsy Turvy 1585*** (summer 2004) simply observations, and the lack of interpretation leaves little ground for prejudice to root. When we read, for example, that "We pick our noses with the thumb or index finger," while "The Japanese pick their noses with their pinkie because they have small nostrils," we cannot find fault in either party, even if we can be disgusted with both!

2. ***Hearn on Big and Small.*** Lafcadio Hearn did not so much belittle the small as to adore it and feared his Lilliputian paradise would be destroyed by the Brobdingnagian onslaught. At the same time, however, he realized that *living large* (if I may requisition a contemporary term from Black English) was no guarantee of living *long*.

> "Just as we have exterminated feebler races by merely *overliving* them, by monopolizing and absorbing, almost without conscious effort, everything necessary to their happiness, – so may we ourselves be exterminated at last by races capable of *underliving* us, of monopolizing all our necessities; races more patient, more self-denying, more fertile, and much less expensive for nature to support. These would doubtless inherit our wisdom, adopt our more useful inventions, continue the best of our industries, – perhaps even perpetuate what is most worthy to endure in our sciences and our arts. But they would scarcely regret our disappearance any more than we ourselves regret the extinction of the dinotherium or the ichthyosaurus." (*Out of the East* 1895 (found in Rudofsky: *The Kimono Mind*) – but, if I am not mistaken, first penned in a letter.)

As Rudofsky correctly noted, Hearn is not a mere sentimentalist. I would add that what Hearn had was *taste*. Anyone who has it and is honest cannot help but take sides. *Rise, Ye Sea Slugs!*

appendix

3

Picking on the Outsider?

Peter Dale's "THE MYTH OF JAPANESE UNIQUENESS REVISITED," and the work of Robin Gill.

i
the odd beachcomber?

While I have a reputation as a writer in Japan, I am totally unknown in the English world of letters.[1] So, when someone at Ohio State University told me early in 1998 that he believed my work had been cited in a book by Peter Dale, I told myself *I'll believe it when I see it!* and promptly forgot all about it. [2] Then, on March 22, 1999, to be precise, I discovered that I was indeed mentioned in THE MYTH OF JAPANESE UNIQUENESS REVISITED (1988).[3]

My specialty – in the words of Japanese reviewers – is putting noted academics on the chopping board (*manaita-no-ue),*where I dissect them with a scalpel (*mesu-o irete),* although one reviewer (a translator of Gregory Bateson) wrote, instead, that I thrust academic powers right out of the ring like Konishiki, the Hawaiian sumo-wrestler, (before he got too heavy).[4] It was purely incidental. I prefer arguing pure ideas, but often found people claiming they were not ideas held by anyone who was anyone, so I was forced to add a man (or woman) to each idea. My intentions were never to be mean, much less *ad hominem.* I just want to be convincing, fun and fair.[5] The last desire, being *fair,* was the reason I had to see Dale's book: I borrowed it via Worldcat (interlibrary loan) because I wanted to be certain he had a chance to correct himself on any points mentioned in his previous book [6] which I planned to criticize in this book and another I am still writing.[7]

As it turned out, Dale's new book was a short speech and had nothing in it concerning specific claims made in THE MYTH OF JAPANESE UNIQUENESS. My debut was only four pages into the book, near the end of a paragraph which began with praise for "the solitary figure of R.A. Miller" and "his valiant efforts to stem the [*nihonjinron*] tide . . . in the sphere of philology." (*Nihonjinron,* again, is an interpretation of what is Japanese resting upon an inverse interpretation of what is Occidental, which tends toward stereotype, caricature on both sides of the equation, and is mostly written and read by Japanese.)

> By the end of the seventies, however, a critical backlash began to emerge and . . . the deluge of *nihonjinron,* once triumphant in their surging cascades over undefended shores, now met with an increasing variety of practical breakwaters, moles and weirs, thrown up both by the odd beachcombers on the fringe of Japanology like Robin Gill or myself, and also by sturdy cultivators from its reed plains in the hinterland.

I was amazed to find myself cited; and with no citation! Did the absence of a footnote here indicate I was too well-known to even need one? I was also *delighted* with the metaphor. I don't know about Dale, but I grew up a hundred yards from the beach!

ii
the teasing cat?

The body of Dale's brief work is a summary of what he considers the six main lines of resistance against mainstream *nihonjinron.* On page fourteen, he gives me a long paragraph. The first sentence is almost right:

> The third line is illustrated by the essayistic volumes of Robin Gill, written in Japanese, which play a teasing cat-and-mouse game with the numerous oddities he manages to fish out of that widow's cruse of conceptual curiosities constituted by the *nihonjinron.*

The three books published by that time, which Dale cites in his footnotes, are outgrowths of what began as a single manuscript.[8] *Omoshiro Bunka-ko* (later reprinted as *Eigo wa Konna ni Nippongo*) concentrates on language-related myths of difference, on introducing and debunking the anti-stereotypes of "Japanese" and "English;" *Han-nihonjinron* deconstructs and/or complicates stereotypes linking culture and the natural world or reducing culture to climate; and *Nihonjinron Tanken*, more generally, introduces and tries to heal what might be called Japan's "uniqueness syndrome." [9] That is to say, my books are a bit more thematic – i.e. organized – than Dale's words suggest. As far as teasing goes, I do not deny my play, but I seriously doubt I tease for the sake of teasing as much as Dale himself does (see THE MYTH OF JAPANESE UNIQUENESS); and my "oddities" are, for the most part, examples chosen to convince *and* entertain the reader.

If I fished for material, it was for the most part not in the nature of a raccoon groping blindly about, but in the more deliberate manner of a spear-fisherman. Still, I was pleased with what Dale wrote. The names and designs publishers forced on my books did not show their clear difference – the *eigyôbu* (sales dept.) thought more general books meant a broader readership (not true because the market must be split with thousands of other such books) – so a quick glance through them might give someone the impression of, shall we say, *frivolity*. Regardless, Dale's metaphor was, again, uncanny: I *have* written a book on cats and am fascinated with their way with mice![10] It includes some poems on the same. Here is one of mine about the paradox of "teasing" (Meg is a calico) and another on "fishing" by Issa.

a killing instinct?

meg's mouse:
the more it dies
the higher
it flies!

(*haha neko ya nani mottekite mo ko o yoburu – issa*)

come, kittens, come!

mother cat
anything she brings back
is advertised

I have laughed myself to tears over the commotion made by a mother cat bringing back *a single lima bean* (I wrote a haiku on this, punning on the name of the bean in Japanese, before I knew Issa haikued the same absurdity: *soramame mo ôgoe de tsugeru neko no oya* (or, was it *neko-no baka?*) I hope I didn't bring back too many lima beans . . .

At this point, the reader might believe I am over-reacting to Dale's description of my work. Not, really, for even as I read this much, I could see where he was heading.

iii
the assiduous iconoclast?

Dale's next sentence concludes with a *direct* criticism that is absolutely true yet completely misses the point.

> Gill's otherwise assiduous iconoclasm, though successfully and often wittily pulling the rug from under the feet of innumerable Japanese commonplaces about cultural uniqueness, fails to construct a coherent interpretative strategy to account for the phenomena of *nihonjinron* production.

"Fails" is a value-laden word; but, unlike Dale with his Freudian interpretation, I did not *pretend* to account for the phenomenon. I decided from the start to write books that would *free* Japanese from their uniqueness-mongering and fixation on difference. To do so did not require a complete understanding of the psycho-historical roots or nature of the pathology. I concentrated on the claims *themselves* because they usually contain *enough* truth that a psychoanalytical approach (there must be something wrong with you if you believe this rot!) would do little good for the reader, and, remember, the Japanese layman (not the Western academic) was my target. Many, if not most of the claims had to be taken at face-value and either *disproved* or reinterpreted.[11]

Furthermore, the fact that some lines of *Nihonjinron* argument were borrowed from pre-World-War II Germany – and the details traced by Miller, Dale and others more scholarly and fluent in Western languages than me – neither proves they are bad nor proves they are wrong. In my humble opinion, guilt by association does not change minds. Unless beliefs are factually disproved – something Japanese reviewers credited me with doing.[12] – Japanese readers will feel embarrassed, perhaps even ashamed, about their "prejudice" and try to conceal it from themselves and others by making a big deal out of superficial cultural similarities and human brotherhood, all the while believing in their gut that "we" and *gaijin* [Western aliens like Dale and I] are hopelessly different. [13]

While it is true that I barely touch upon the deeper causes, the *why*'s of "*nihonjinron*" production,[14] on a shallow, more practical level, I did more than anyone I know of to demonstrate *how* difference is exaggerated to produce stereotypes. [15] I wanted to make this explicit by using subtitles for chapters in the second part of my TBS Britannica book: "chronological incommensurability", "selective data", "generalizing about differences of degree", "prejudicial interpretation," "contrasting the ideal and the real" etc., but the editor was afraid of "making the book look difficult" – it was intended for a popular audience – so I was unable to reveal the, admittedly jerry-built structure into which I fit the "oddities." [16]

I ask the academic: Why do we write? Is it writing to change minds any less important than accounting for things? Bad naming and book-designs (here, too, the publishers did not follow my advice: I am so happy to have my own press now!) prevented me from publishing a best seller – although the language book, with a new name reflecting its content was reprinted in a mass market pocketbook (*bunko)*[17] – so, *in retrospect*, I might have done better for myself, for my reputation, by building a structure *kudoi* (boringly obvious) enough to satisfy English readers of scholarly pretension. In that sense, yes, I *failed.* I did not, however, *fail* to account for phenomena. I just *didn't.* That *was* my strategy.

iv
the blind ecologist?

Dale's next sentence finally reveals *his* intent (not necessarily conscious) – distancing this odd beachcomber on the shores of Japanology from the more competent scholar, . . . himself (?). Or, at least that is how I read it. He is welcome to do so, but I fear he did not have time to read my books closely enough to understand them, though he does come close:

> His overriding concern indeed to marry his ecological outlook to a certain vein of nature-worship in Japanese tradition often blinds him, and his refutations often show him working within the assumptions whose validity he would deny to the Japanese, inverting a *nihonjinron* thesis to obtain a kind of *seiyôron.*

All of my books do, indeed, reflect my environmental concerns.[18] One of the main reasons I sought to heal *the uniqueness syndrome* was because I felt the Japanese fixation on difference was hurting their ability to create a new relationship with the natural world. After all, the impact of humans upon natural diversity – not only biodiversity, but what might be called geo-diversity – i.e. the destruction of the biosphere is now *the* absolute value by which cultural difference may be judged. Culture may be relative, but only with respect to this over-riding concern.[19] Today, *cultural anthropology should and must be judgmental.*

But I question Dale's *details*. Perhaps there is a tendency toward "nature-worship" in me, but I did not neglect to bring out the complexity of the relationship between nature and culture in Japan and the West. I did indeed show there were parallels in the West to some of the nature-loving aspects of the Japanese culture. But I criticized much in both cultures as I did so. In some cases, the parallels I draw are not quite perfect. But I fail to see how my ecological outlook – my being "Thoreau-like," as one Japanese reviewer put it [20] – and my effort to make the West meaningful by comparison to Japanese tradition, *blind* me, and wish Dale had provided examples!

Yes, I *do* often work within the assumptions I criticize. In *Han-nihonjinron*, I tentatively accept Dr. Tsunoda's claim that Japanese brains can't keep emotion and rationality separate; but ask, how he can claim Japanese are not completely *rational* without considering the opposite possibility: they can not be completely *emotional*! Pointing out contradictions by first granting the other's assumptions is a particularly effective form of argument, and I resent the implication that it is a short-coming. The game could get complex and to a reader too busy to examine it slowly, it might seem absurd. To give one of the craziest examples, I also posit that *if* bug calls and other natural sounds are processed in the dominant (verbal/left) hemisphere of the Japanese brain as Tsunoda claims, a filter might develop to tune this out and that might help explain why so many Japanese could do intellectual work needing concentration in incredibly noisy offices, tuning out the world so completely they often jumped and uttered an exclamation when spoken to. My aim, in that case, was to demonstrate that the Dr. wasted so much energy tying his findings to *nihonjinron* stereotypes that he (and his reviewers) failed to properly develop even the simplest ramifications of his own findings! [21] I was showing the reader how *nihonjinron* kills the development of my favorite creatures, ideas.

Yes, *seiyôjinron* (Westernology – I put in the *jin*="person" to keep it symmetrical with *nihonjinron*) spoofs were one of my tactics. Most commonly, I invented what a Westerner with a *nihonjinronka* (a *nihonjinron* writer) mentality and style might write. The idea was to be to offset and cancel out. To pervert by inversion. I didn't think careful intellectual readers would have any trouble with this. But remembering that Carlyle's German professor of clothing – an obvious fiction to me – managed to fool a number of reviewers of SARTOR RESARTUS,[22] I did not forget to write the following disclaimer in the foreword of *Han-nihonjinron* just to be safe:

> . . . please be careful not to take my hypotheses, paradoxes, odd ideas [in Japanese, this is more poetic: *kasetsu, gyakusetsu* and *chinsetsu*] and whatnot created versus established stereotypes of *nihonjinron* and ethnography, and make new *nihonjinron* of them. My hypotheses are supposed to be tools for thought, not the gospel truth [*seikai* = correct interpretation or answer]. Not wanting to write a book that drags, I do not weigh down my hypotheses and statements with qualifications, but there is not a page in the book where I do not qualify what I wrote within my heart.

v
the baffling fool?

The misevaluation of my work up to this point was irksome but forgivable. I imagined that Dale was either too busy to give me a careful reading, less than fluent in Japanese, or relying upon second-hand information. But what about this?

> If the Japanese are told their language is animistic, they are wrong, retorts Gill: to the contrary, and his judgment will baffle not only *nihonjinron* writers but also English linguists.
>
> "English differs from many Far Eastern Languages including Japanese in having a character (*seikaku*) that readily lends itself to pantheism or primitive animism."

Baffling, indeed! It baffles me that a scholar as good as Dale should take a single sentence, that makes perfect sense *in context* and misuse it in this way. Let's see the context. The very next sentence, which Dale fails to provide (the above quote is his final word on me, after which he proceeds to "the fourth current of development" Sugimoto and Mouer[23]) immediately begins to answer the riddle posed by my "baffling" assertion:

> Which is to say (*to iu-no-wa*) that, first, there is no need to differentiate live and dead things by expressions like "*iru*" and "*aru.*" [basic forms of the verb "to be" used respectively for sentient and insentient beings in Japanese]. "Here *is* a rock" and "Here *is* a man" use the same verb "is."[24]

After this, I mention that wholesale anthropomorphism (*gijinho*) only entered Japanese through translated literature,[25] that even today Japanese don't write things like a typhoon "killed many people," (*hito-o koroshita*) but that people "die because of a typhoon" (*taifu-ni yotte*), and that this close relationship with nature was a two-way street because human things and action could be *naturalized* as well (I gave dozens of examples of animals who became verbs and, in a side-track, the elemental descriptions of man – the opposite of anthropomorphism – found in the Celtic *Ossian*). I concluded by agreeing with Reginald Blyth that *personification* is not a pathetic fallacy – no one is that naive – but poetic.[26]

My ostensible aim was not to make silly claims about more or less animistic languages, but to explain the mushy anthropomorphism in a passage John Muir wrote about Yosemite boulders in an 1873 letter[27] that I had just quoted at length. A Japanese friend I asked to translate it wrote in the margin that she really hated his style (*dai-kirai)* and found it horribly *affected* (*sugoku kiza*).[28] I put her remarks into the text as a gloss and addressed them. My unstated, but primary aim was to counter the usual claims about the separation of man and nature in English, as a Christian and Cartesian Western language, for were an *iru/aru* type of distinction=discrimination made by the English "to be," instead of the Japanese, I knew damn well how the information would be plugged into *nihonjinron,* or naive *Occidentalists* East or West.

After quoting Blyth on personification and moving to the next sub-chapter heading ("Caring for Rattlesnakes!"), I admit that Muir's style may seem childish – especially compared to the self-consciously natural style of post-Bashô haiku – but argue this does not nullify the genuine depth of his feelings for boulders, which the reader could only imagine by knowing more about the man and his relationship with nature, which I then explain in considerable depth. My style may be organic, less organized than scholars who outline before they write, but readers who take the time to wander *with me* find the essays go somewhere – *they* may sometimes disagree with my conclusions, but they do not scratch their heads and wonder about my judgment in the manner readers might from reading Dale's misleadingly short snippet of my work! [29]

vi
the expat writer?

How I hate introducing – i.e. talking up – my own work. It is *humiliating*, a waste of time and one reason I have avoided academia like the plague. But the English language press, for reasons only they know, failed to report what I was up to in Japan. Since none of my family back in the USA spoke any Japanese, this meant that I could not share the fruits of my intellectual labor with them. In 1986, against my better judgment, I wrote an article for the *Japan Times* "Guest Forum" titled *"Beating 'We Japanese' Syndrome"* in which I included an introduction to my three published books (and that of two of the other five lines of attack mentioned in Dale 1989).[30] Here is the outline of *Han-nihonjinron*:

> *Han-nihonjinron* (anti-Nihonjinron) takes on stereotypes related to Mother Nature while trying to unobtrusively show the underlying similarities in human nature.
>
> The first part of this 400-page-plus book disproves much of what is known as *fudoron,* i.e., the attribution of certain types of ethnic or national character to certain types of environment.
>
> The middle part questions whether Japanese culture is really so close to Nature and Western culture so opposed to it as is commonly written.
>
> The last part attempts to go beyond the Japanese (*wa-fu*) versus Western (*yo-fu*) framework to consider the meaning of living naturally. For example, robes for

> menswear would be more suitable for [smuggy] Tokyo summers than either trousers or stiff kimonos. Bow shooting by feel (a la Roger Ascham [31]) beats both modern Western target archery with its technical gimmickry and Zen archery (*Kyudo*) with its troublesome conventions.

Had I more space, I would have expanded the outline to include the fact that the subtitle of the book, written in English, was "a touch of nature" [makes all men kin= the Bard] and the *obi* (book-belt) blurb by the well-known playwright and novelist Inoue Hisashi said: "an interesting book written from the standpoint that humans are one creature!" (*hitotsu-no seibutsu*). (*Since everyone knows, or is supposed to know that humans share a common nature, it is hard for the reader unfamiliar with the Japanese mindscape to see how such a book could be interesting! Indeed, for an English language reader, I might take a different approach, emphasizing difference – for we tend to belittle it, with the result being that we do not realize how much others have to offer us.*)

I also might have elaborated upon *fudoron*, a subject treated at length by Dale, too. Dale analyzes the German influences on Watsuji. I – all too aware of the German influences in Watsuji's phenomenal, or rather philologic-phenomenological fifty pages of sophistry about the respective nature of "coldness" in Japanese and Western languages – instead, concentrate on the *significance* which Watsuji and contemporary intellectuals gave to climate and environment-related cultural differences, the *homo* (like) versus *hetero* (different) attraction hypotheses outlined in the body of *Orientalism & Occidentalism*.

The last part of the book is my favorite. I have always been more interested in the World of *Why not?* than the World of *Why!* (A book on men and open-ended clothing entitled *Re-dressing the World*, has been underway for about 30 years!)

How sad that the only introduction to my work in English other than my own is Dale's! English-speaking readers who missed the *Japan Times* article (or comments on a couple of my articles published in *Chuokoron* [32] – a top monthly that also published a chapter of Dale's MYTH OF JAPANESE UNIQUENESS in translation – by Amano Yosei in his "From Japanese Magazines" column in the *Mainichi Daily News*) would not even know I exist. And reading Dale, Japanologists who might have heard *rumors* of my existence, will shake their heads and emphatically not miss me. A Japanese phrase comes to mind: *tabezu girai* – being soured on something you haven't even eaten. (*Sorry for being morose, but it is lonely when one is not recognized at home.*)

vii
the undiscovered theorist

To me, my observation about opposite possibilities for interpreting the assumptions of *fudoron,* as mentioned above, was a *major* discovery. As far as I know, no one had (and, no one *has*, as of this writing!) pointed out such a tendency, which, I believe, bears many implications for a subject of interest to Western scholars, *the nature of cultural borrowing.* One cannot simply talk about carefully selecting foreign items because they match your culture – many claim Japanese to be good at this – without stopping and asking, do these things fit the importing culture *because they share something?* Or do they complement it because *they do not*?

There are many such *ideas* scattered about my books. I am not an intellectual miser. I would like for people to see and use these ideas. In Japan, reviewers were too busy waxing enthusiastic about my *general* endeavor of "forcing an opening in nihonjinron" (*nihonjinron-no kaikoku-o semaru,* where *kaikoku*, "open-nation," was the expression used to describe what Perry's black ships did to break Japan from isolation) or "splendidly deconstructing" (*migoto-ni kaitai shite-shimatta*) the same,[33] or naming the big-shots, unlucky enough to be put up on the chopping board, to pat attention to my more positive would-be contributions to the world of ideas.

I am the first to admit that I contributed little to research on the history of *nihonjinron* and less to creating theory useful to academia. My aim was simply to gain the perspective needed to kill prejudice based on the perception of difference. As Inoue Hisashi was astute enough to notice, my perspective *is* my strategy. It is: *To assume that people are at heart alike.* That is, indeed all of it. But, from that, it follows that any given difference between cultures should be offset by another difference. This you must find, study, and, finally, use to explain the relationship between the two. If this is done in a convincing manner, the unfamiliar (or worse) may be turned into something that makes sense. In a word, *apparent difference understood demonstrates similarity.*

There is no need to repeat here the examples given in this book. I trust the reader gets what I am driving at by now.

In NAVEN, Gregory Bateson explains sex-reversal carnivals as a balancing mechanism for *cultures with strongly divergent gender roles.* [34] To my mind, *all* cultures are unique bodies incorporating unnatural traits (in the sense that culture is not nature) offset by *other* unnatural traits to create a totality that is natural in the sense that it suits human nature. Some offsetting may be done in sequence, that is, chronologically one after another, as with NAVEN, but typically it is done more or less simultaneously, in parallel: *the carnival never stops.* Doubtless, the parts of the cultural bodies correlate in a way bearing some resemblance to the "implicational universal" idea of linguistics. [35] But, if such theory is applied, I would hope that the mind of "universal grammar" could be exchanged for the heart of common sense.

viii
peter dale's reply

Am I unfair to Peter Dale when I say he is unfair to me? I would be delighted if he would do me the honor of responding to my criticism and leave him this space, or more if he should want it.

If I receive it prior to preparing the second edition, I will post it at my website, http://www.paraverse.org/.

app.3 note

1. *My reputation*. With seven books published from good publishers, many good reviews and scores of articles or columns published in many leading magazines, I was well-known in Japan. In the USA, where I have published nothing but letters to the editor, I was unknown when Dale wrote. Only Worldcat notes I have five books at the Library of Congress (all donated by the author) and a dozen or two more at some University libraries. (I am just getting started publishing in English in 2003 with *Rise, Ye Sea Slugs!* See the reviews at my website!)

2. *Discovering Dale wrote about me*. I thought I was alerted by Professor Unger, whose publisher, Oxford University, once wrote me in Japan for a blurb for his FIFTH GENERATION FALLACY. It was the first and last request I have had from the English language world for a blurb. As it turns out, his Japanese wife had happened to read one of my books. Later, I happened to be in Columbus because one of my sisters lives there and . . . It must have been someone else I talked to at OSU, because the professor, who beat me at Go several times in a row (I am practicing for revenge), says it was *not* him, and his memory is probably better than mine. *Whoever it was,* I *thank you.*

3. Peter Dale: THE MYTH OF JAPANESE UNIQUENESS REVISITED (Nissan Occasional Paper Series No9, 1988)

4. The reviewer's name is Sato Yoshiaki. The words *"nippon akademizumu-ni konishiki-no-gotoki tsuppari-o kamashita"*. (The book reviewed was GOYAKU TENGOKU (Mistranslation Paradise) which Hakusuisha published in 1987. In that book, I connected Occidentalist prejudices on the part of the Japanese with *patterns of mistranslation.* The most common description of my books was *"tsukai"* (painful pleasure) and Dale, as a Freudian, might especially appreciate the common corollary expression of "sticking in a painful pole," (e.g. title of a review of *Han-nihonjinron* in *Ohara Ikebana* (July 1985): *jiminzoku-chushinshugi-e-no tsubo.*)

5. By *fair*, I do not mean only fair to certain scholars, but something broader. Ex-Harvard University Japan literature scholar Itasaka Gen, reviewing *Han-nihonjinron* and another of my books together in *"Honnyaku-no Sekai"* (translation world) magazine, put it this way:

> these books feel good to read because they are not obsessed with Japan and open up into a singular culturology (*bunkaron*) **. . .** they're marked by a lack of prejudice favorable or unfavorable with respect to the old generation. (*furui sedai*)

Note, that Itasaka did not feel I was simply hitting out at random, but grasped my overall strategy. I hate translating reviews to blow my own trumpet like this, but the English-speaking world has treated me as if I never existed.

6. **Peter Dale: THE MYTH OF JAPANESE UNIQUENESS** (Routledge and Nissan Institute for Japanese Studies: 1986)

7. The books in which Dale will be mentioned are this one and EXOTIC TONGUES (2006?)

8. A fourth book, on mistranslation, is mentioned in note 4, above, and a fifth book named *Koramu!* (hakusuisha) which developed the concept of Occidentalism in one essay followed a few years later. Dale made a couple mistakes in his bibliography. For the record, not "Togen Shoten," but Kirihara Shoten is the correct way to pronounce the publisher of *Omoshiro Hikaku-bunka-ko.* Not *Nihonjinron Tankyu,* but ~ *Tanken,* for the TBS Britannica book. (And, I might add, not Rob Mouer but Ross Mouer, for the citation following mine!)

9. I also called this "'We Japanese' Syndrome" and as noted already, I always make clear the fact that E.O. Reischauer, who is usually attacked as a myth-maker, was the first person I know to seriously address the problem. .

10. HAN-CHAN'S DREAM includes many colored illustrations (mostly cats sleeping), so I must wait until I find a publisher willing to bet on a large enough run to keep the price down.

11. Taking claims at face value means respecting the mind-life of others. It is normal to like and dislike – life without discrimination would be a poor thing indeed! Given some of the assumptions Japanese have concerning the West and its languages, I argue that only a tasteless idiot would *not* be prejudiced against us. (See ORIENTALISM AND OCCIDENTALISM ch 3) *Someone who hopes to free people of prejudice must first respect them.*

12. A local paper, the *Tokushima Shinbun*, gave the most compressed description of my approach's practical success: this book [Omoshiro Hikaku Bunkaron] packs dynamite power for destroying stereotypical *nihonjinron=gaikokujinron.* It is mainly [done through] comparative demonstration (*hikakuronsho*) of philology (*kotoba-kurabe).*

The effect of this "explosion" was described by the common – but interesting – idiom *me-kara uroko,* like "scales [falling] off [the reader's] eyes." Sato Yoshiaki, in a more complex analysis of what makes my books *work,* wrote that demonstration alone wasn't enough to beat *nihonjinron*, for a Japanese reader could still find refuge from barbarian logic (*keto-teki-riron*) in Japanese sentiment (*nihonteki-shinjo*) and keep the stereotype game alive. He credits me with going further, going above the superficial differences of our respective languages and making Japanese readers *feel* the similarity through my use of a primary language – then, his analysis gets too difficult for the subject (me) to follow! (Remember, this man translated Bateson!).

13. Dale's Style of Criticism. One might even be harder on the guilt-by-association style of criticism. *To make people ashamed of their "prejudice" without curing them of it is to force them to be hypocrites.*

14. I do give some *why's* of *nihonjinron* production in *Nihonjinron Tanken.* (The mistake in the title made by Dale suggests to me he might not have read it). See the fourth chapter of Part One which translates (badly) as "the source of the stereotypical *nihonjinron* and superiority complex" and the fifth chapter of the same: which translates as, "What lurks behind the uniqueness syndrome?" In the former, I develop the concept of a singular mixed inferiority-superiority complex and relate this to *nihonjinron..* I do not develop a coherent system but in retrospect, it is an ontogenetic and Adlerian sketch versus Dale's phylogenetic and Freudian tour de force. In the latter, I show a tendency toward boasting about the nation's uniqueness, especially superiority versus China and Korea goes back at least until the first Europeans (who reported it) visited, and discuss why I think Motoori Norinaga's uniqueness mongering won out over Ichikawa 匡麻呂 (kyômaro?)'s broad-minded humanism ("whatever the country, people are people"). I also prove by long quotes from the diary of the captain of Caroline E. Foote (H. F. Zandt: *Pioneer American Merchants in Japan*) that even with this strong ethnocentric current, common Japanese experienced no difficulty in interacting with Europeans, so long as they were confident the authorities were not around. That is to say, the fully developed *Uniqueness Syndrome* was not intrinsic to Japanese as an insular people (I also take issue with the very concept of *insularity* in this book and others) or as a "primitive" Asian people (I quote a cosmologist-anthropologist, Iwada Kenji – whose books, I think, supply more stimulating intellectual fare than our icon, Joseph Campbell). The *nihonjinron* as we know it developed after this time. And I argue that it stays in place out of momentum more than anything else (of course, I mention the utility to the leaders and trade negotiation, etc.). I quote the expansionist minister Gilmore Simm's response to a survey sent to him by the New York Historical Society about the possibility of adopting a National Name for the United States of America (a mere description, as Washington Irving, the instigator of the survey, observed). Simms said he'd go for the *Republic of Washington* – not Irving's *U.S. of Allegania* – but the cause was a lost one, *for even if the nation's name were "Squash" people would be too timid to change it.* (I introduce almost as many Western oddities as Japanese ones, because the West is the half of *nihonjinron* I know most about). But I put all this into a footnote because I could take or leave the *whys.* My books were first and foremost prescription, de-brainwashing, not dissertation.

15. I hope my list of 16 ways difference is exaggerated (Appendix 2) is passed around and added to. I believe that teaching students the *hows* of cultural misunderstanding helps them to become wary, to become more critical thinkers, where simply jumping on the *Orientalism-is-bad* pc bandwagon teaches them nothing. It grieves me that I have yet to find a citation of the first book to make any serious effort to explain *how* difference is exaggerated, John Steadman's THE MYTH OF ASIA (published about the same time as Said's less readable classic) in any book on Orientalism, Occidentalism or *nihonjinron* (other than my own).

16. A writer trying to get published does not always have control over his books! I wanted a tiny pointing hand saying "☞ Beware of comparing incommensurables!" "☞ Beware of generalizing about . . ." etc.. But, then, if I had my way, the TBS Britannica book would have been called what Dale was to name *his* book or, as a second choice, "the uniqueness syndrome." The editors did use the latter for the title of one part of the book and almost used it for the subtitle, which they insisted upon modifying to "uniqueness sickness" (*unikusa-byô*). I think they were wrong. I am delighted to be publishing myself, now, for it is much more satisfying to be responsible for one's own fortune!

17. The name *Omoshiro Hikaku-bunka-ko* ("interesting comparative culture thoughts") is *nauseating!* (My mother, a writer, taught me never to *say* something is interesting, but make it speak for itself). The publisher did an excellent job of editing; trusting them to pick a good title from a list I supplied, I visited the States and . . (!) The pocketbook version, eventually published by Chikuma bunko, has a much better title: EIGO-WA KONNANI NIPPONGO – English is *this* Japanese! Still, Chikuma insisted upon writing "Nippongo" in *katakana*, rather than Chinese characters as I wished! (Thereby, scaring off readers who might have been more interested in Japanese than English.) The new version contains 10% added material instantly recognizable because of the different margin – this method allows books to be improved upon without losing their original authenticity. I am grateful to the publisher for allowing it and hope others adopt it.

18. In most of my books the environmental theme is not too obvious, for I dislike preaching. Dale seems to be writing about *Han-nihonjinron*, alone.

19. The overriding importance of cultural diversity should allow small cultures leeway for error, but large cultures cannot be granted such immunity. Americans, for example, by their failure to raise the gas tax and rein in their obscenely wasteful cars, and by allowing air-travelers to be *rewarded* for flying more (rather than less), prove their culture is an unabashedly *bad* one, bent on the destruction of the world.

20. Matsuoka Seigow, the Japanese avant-garde's favorite intellectual in the 1970s, put it this way (speaking of *Han-nihonjinron*): "the author's Henry Thoreau-esque (*soro-bari*) naturalistic perspective is a splendid one . . . it feels far better (*yori zutto kibun-ga ii*) than reading ten volumes of the popular JAPAN AS NUMBER ONE [E. Vogel's best-seller] type of book." These remarks were published in a book published by NTT (Japan's major telephone company)! Matsuoka was the head of Kousakusha when I began working there in 1980, but left the following year and had no part in the editing of my book.

21. From a logical point of view, the strangest thing about Doctor Tsunoda's best-seller was its subtitle: "the workings of the brain and East-West culture" (*no-no hataraki to tozai-no bunka*). For as noted in *Orientalism & Occidentalism*, the Korean and Chinese speakers did *not* share the Japanese pattern of brain function (they are the same as the West). The *orientalism=occidentalism* bias in *nihonjinron* is so strong that the fact Asia is not one often throws it for a loop.

22. See the Norton critical edition of Carlyle's best known work for the ridiculous reviews. I see I mentioned Herr Teufelsdrockh earlier. But it's worth a second mention. Norton should make more of an effort to market their wonderful critical editions. It upset me to find Oxford's less interesting classics in all the large bookstores in Japan and nothing by Norton. In the US, too, the excellent line is not pushed. It is hard to find at the Norton Website when it should be the company's pride and joy. *I just do not get it.* Am I the only one to appreciate this sort of thing?

23. In *Nipponjin-wa 'Nippon-teki' ka*, are Japanese Japanese-like? (the last word is much better in the original Japanese!), Sugimoto Yoshio and Ross Mouer sometimes do the same thing I do: show the arbitrary nature of *nihonjinron* by creating counter-examples. E.g.: pointing out Japanese traditional sports are mostly *man against man*, unlike the team sports of the West, so that using that data to jump to a conclusion in typical *nihonjinron* style, it is the Japanese who become the more individual and Westerners the more collectivist. Dale's introduction of their work in REVISITED is excellent, so I need write no more.

24. The bracketed "sentient" and "insentient" are the more accurate. It is trees and natural phenomena other than animals that really are left in the cold. In another one of my books – I can't remember which – I also discuss the fact that Japanese inherit from Chinese a tendency to use different terms for human and non-human things. The fact that there is no generic "male" and "female," but different terms used for humans (*dansei/jousei*) and other animals (*osu/mesu*) is only the most common example of language dividing humans from the rest of the world.

Donald Keene has a sentence somewhat like my remarks on "is" in a paragraph lamenting the loss of distinctions in translation.

> The translator who has before him a text employing the fourteen commonly distinguished levels of politeness in Korean will run up against the deadly democracy of the English language, where we use the same verb and level of politeness for "God is," "water is," and "that dirty dog is." ("The translation of Japanese culture" in APPRECIATIONS OF JAPANESE CULTURE)

Since we have a tendency to value equality over all, Keene's "deadly" modification is a fine expression! Perhaps I should have spoken of "ecological democracy" rather than "pantheism" or "animism!"

25. My current understanding – that I am still working on – is that there was far more anthropomorphism than usually admitted in Japanese, but that it took different forms from Western anthropomorphism. I find a lot in early haiku (*haikai*).

26. See Blyth's ZEN AND ZEN CLASSICS (vol.5) and, for that matter, *anything* of Blyth's. He is *always* fun to read and always will be.

27. *Han-nihonjinron,* as a popular work, had no notes. I do not have more precise information on Muir's letter. Let me just say the boulders were throbbing with blood and engaged in active communion with Muir. Muir, too, is worth reading. What a shame to stop with *Stickeen!*

28. My friend is translator Kataoka Shinobu. While I like to write in Japanese, I do not like to translate myself or others into Japanese if I can help it. When correcting Japanese translations from English, I often must venture translations in order to open up Japanese translators to possible improvements (usually ways to cut and combine boring sentences). But, my translation into Japanese would then be proofed by a Japanese editor.

29. The first edition of *Han-nihonjinron* did, however, contain a dozen or so sentences which baffled even the author, for the publisher was undergoing a crisis which had the editors – including me – working around the clock and the editor of my book, who was a bit erratic when well-rested, made some *bad* decisions while sleepy. He misread my messy writing, failing to understand the intent of my long-sentences which he changed when cutting them up, and failed to repress his urge to use intellectual expressions deriving from French. The only critical – as in questioning the correctness of my judgment – line I ever got in a Japanese review took up a line from which he removed an important qualification when he rewriting. Most of these problematic lines are repaired by the third edition of the book. Be that as it may, the passage quoted by Dale is not one of them. I do grant to Dale that the statement *taken by itself* is outrageous. There is nothing like an outrageous claim to catch the reader's attention, and I do it a lot. Sato Yoshiaki, in his review, also notes my outrageous (*tondemonai setsu*) that "English, basically, is all onomatopoeia." But, since Sato actually read my book through, he was not baffled by it. Instead, he marveled that I could make such a claim extremely convincing (*kare-ni kakaru to jiwa to iu settokuryoku o motte-shimau)* and explains how he thinks I manage it. Dale might better have let a Japanese friend read my book and see if he or she was baffled!

30. I find the date Jan. 12 followed by a question mark next to a copy of the *Japan Times* article. Sorry, I cannot be more certain. There is one idea in the article that is worth repeating. I have already repeated it in the body of *Orientalism & Occidentalism,* but will repeat it once again, here. I opined the low quality of *nihonjinron* was partly caused by *cultural relativism.*

> "The cultural relativist may emphatically deny having likes and dislikes for the objects of his study, but the reader *will* form opinions good and bad about the

> peoples being compared. Worse yet, the premise that one's work is harmless permits, or even encourages the scholar to make irresponsible generalizations, and publish mass-market books full of shallow intercultural comparisons."

This is one *why* no one else has given for the proliferation of low quality *nihonjinron* by people who should have known better in the 1970's. I think it is important that our teachers understand *why relativism can be a double-edged sword* if they are going to teach it to students with limited information and experience with other cultures.

31. Roger Ascham's sixteenth century *Toxiphilious* suggests practice shooting at lanterns in the dark to cure one of sighting! He is for truly natural *shooting by feel*. The book also reveals an attitude that reminds one of Zen, which is why I quoted it at length in my book *Han=nihonjinron*.

32. June 1986 for my article on whaling (there is some (anti) *nihonjinron* in it and this is expanded upon in my 1989 book *Kora!mu:* Hakusuisha) and in June 1990 for my article criticizing the way Professor Lee's naive but good three-way cultural comparison of the West, Korea and Japan evolved into a post-modern East versus West equation, with Japan and Korea together. The title of the latter essay is *"Professor Lee, Cultural Imperialism is a No, No!"* (*i-sensei, bunka-teikoku-shugi-wa komari-masu*). I had wanted to use the word "Occidentalism" in the title but had to be satisfied with using it within the article. The article's title – made by the editors – notwithstanding, Lee O-Young, as his name was Englished for IN THAT WIND AND IN THAT LAND, is one of my favorite essayists, and I was only using him to illustrate a trend. It may sound personal but I do not mean it to be so. The only thing that can match Young's style in English is Krownhauser's *Amerikajinron*. THE BEER CAN BY THE HIGHWAY (1961). Lee O-Young's best selling book in Japan has been translated into English as: *The Compact Culture: The Japanese Tradition of Smaller is Better*.

33. These expressions all come from the same Kyodo News Service review of *Han-nihonjinron*. As far as I know, the review was not translated into English.

34. Gregory Bateson's NAVEN is of regrettably narrow scope. I would like to see the ideas of offsetting balance taken beyond male/female carnival=sacred-time/normal-time and other such dramatic themes into culture as a whole. If some-one has done this, I would appreciate a gloss to add to the second edition.

35. Implicational Universal of Culture. I have heard of correlations between, say, *harsh treatment in childhood* and *homicide rate*. I would like to know what other correlations have been studied already and are being studied. There are so many possibilities! For example, I think there might be a link between a *peaceful culture* and *abortion* on the one hand, and *war-making* and *control over women's bodies* (denial of the right to abort) on the other, for failure to control one's own population would have necessitated killing; but this sort of thing could be objectively tested by having different people ignorant of the correlations under investi-gation measuring the respective traits in a large list of cultures.

So, after 9/11, POSTSCRIPT

what does this Orientalism-Occidentalism stuff mean?

To almost everyone but me, "Orientalism & Occidentalism" was a purely academic issue when I wrote this book. Now, with Occidentalism held responsible for inflaming the hearts of Jihadists and Orientalism one reason for our failure to take the threat seriously enough, this little book would seem to be both *more* and *less* important than it would have been.

It is less important if we agree with Buruma and Margalit when they write that "A distaste for, or even hatred of, the West is in itself not a serious issue. Occidentalism becomes dangerous when it is harnessed to political power." (*Occidentalism: The West in the Eyes of Its Enemies:* 2004)

But it is more important, if we acknowledge the fact that, as Buruma and Margalit also show, *ideas move around.* Why wait for prejudice to be "harnessed" before treating it seriously? Moreover, even if Jihadists may not espouse rationalism, the Islamic world has always respected good argument. I think, a strong awareness of how differences that create and justify prejudice are invented (see *Appendix 2*) will prove a very useful tool for the debates and deconstruction (minus the jargon!) needed if we are to overcome prejudice.

It also might help to *complicate matters*, to break up the conventional East-West polarity by pointing out the fact that the Islamic world is linguistically and intellectually *cognate*, not *exotic* to us, at least in comparison to the more removed Sinosphere and, as such, very much a part of the larger Occidental world. (And, could we not, perhaps add the *Medient* and *Mediental* world to cover the in-between cultures of India and Africa?)

Of course, argument alone will not get us far without the clincher: *example.* If "we" cannot restrain our insane lust for money and irresponsible, if not criminal, consumption (reflected in "Flier Miles" and huge air-conditioned houses as much as SUV's) of the last quarter century and create a kinder society at home and a more giving one abroad, we and our world are doomed. (*Sorry.* I don't mean to be dramatic. *That is how I feel.* We were going to hell in a bucket before 9/11, and nothing has changed except our velocity.)

ACKNOWLEDGMENTS

I regret to say I got damned little input for this one. Some people read the original manuscript as mentioned in the foreword and I thank them, but only my mother and, possibly, Jeanie who typed the first draft mailed home from Japan shortly before I got a computer and learned to type provided any detailed input. No one but I have read all the notes. I pray this will not be the case for the second edition and beg everyone who feels he or she has something to contribute to *please* send me your opinions, refutations, additions and corrections.

(**Addition to second printing**: The first printing was so full of typos and my postscript so wild that I have been forced, in retrospect, to consider it a reading copy, which I have now redone. There is one gloss (I hope the first of many!) from *Modern Haiku* editor Lee Gurga and a page-long addition prompted by fine criticism from William J. Higginson, author of the classic *Haiku World.* – An International Poetry Almanac.

More glosses are not only welcome but desired. The book is 180 pages now. Why not make it 200 or so for the next edition? I have a new policy, or rather, idea to encourage glosses. *Anyone who writes a gloss that is accepted is welcome to add a few lines of self-advertisement.* If you think my readers will enjoy your book or article, mention it/them! – rdg (http://www.paraverse.org)

indices

names

ideas

浮け海鼠 *Also*

by robin d. gill from Paraverse Press,
a far wilder and woollier work with 1000 holothurian haiku, including the original Japanese:

Rise, Ye Sea Slugs!

blurbs

From Literature: "*Uke Namako"* [the Japanese title] is the most touching, fun, erudite, and altogether enjoyable thing I have read in ages. It is also the most intelligent approach to Japanese poetry I think I have ever seen. – Liza Dalby, anthropologist and author of *Tale of Murasaki.*

From Science: "It's amazing; I absolutely love it. I've spent many years studying my little friends and have always felt that they have been unkindly maligned or forgotten. The contrast between Japanese and European literature on cukes [sea cucumbers] couldn't be greater . . . Alas, the divide between science and literature, even in terminology much less in theory, is quite vast at points and I admire your blending of the two in a deep and satisfying way." – Dr. Alexander Kerr, evolutionary biologist, James Cook University.

reviews

This single-topic tome may be our best English-language window yet into the labyrinth of Japanese haikai culture. If you have read Yasuda, Blyth, Henderson, Ueda, and Shirane, then read Gill. He will expand your mind. If you have not read those guys yet, then read Gill first. He's more fun. – William J. Higginson (author of the classic *Haiku World* – an International Poetry Almanac) in *Modern Haiku* (winter-spring issue 2003-4)

An intriguing blend of science, lore, poetry and speculation which touches on countless points of knowledge, without being pedantic. Not for everyone, but for the intellectually adven-turous, you'll find plenty here to reward your enquiry. The Japanese for all poems is included. – Jim Kacian (editor of *Frogpond*) in the same.

(Note: the first edition is a 484 (large) pages in length, yet only $25. The second edition will probably be about 600 pages and $30. Please visit http://www.paraverse.org for news and details.)

Reviews of previous books by robin d. gill

about the identity/image of Japanese and their antithesis, the stereotypical West, published in Japan/ese only (sorry).

"I bow my head to the author's linguistic prowess." – Inoue Hisashi (on a reader's card) – a top Japanese novelist and playwright. [re. *Omoshiro hikaku bunkakô*, later republished by Chikuma bunko as *Eigo wa konna ni nippongo* = English is *This* Japanese!]

"What felt good about reading it [*Han=nihonjinron* = anti-Japanology, published by Kousakusha] was that the book doesn't get bogged down in Japan, but develops into a theory of culture *[bunkaron]* ... it is remarkable for not being prejudiced either for or against the past." – Itasaka Gen (review in *"Honyaku-no Sekai"*), a Japanese literature scholar who formerly taught at Harvard and later became the president of Tenri University.

"The author's Thoreauvian naturalism is splendid . . . and the book [*Han=nihonjinron*] leaves you feeling better than reading ten of those popular *Japan-as-Number-One* type books." – Matsuoka Seigow (review in an NTT book) – one of Japan's top editors and well-known avant-garde thinker.

"A splendid deconstruction [on Ibid] of longstanding stereotypes of Japanese national/cultural character *(nihonjinron)* that, wearing the academic guise of cultural anthropology and topographic/climatic reductionism, *(fudoron),* have titillated our pride." – Kyodo News Service (review carried nationally).

"Whether due to the flexibility and uniqueness of the perspective or the continual dissimulation of the author's Japanese writing, this book [*Nihonjinron Tanken* TBS-Britannica] is simply thrilling. Introducing example after example of things from other cultures that have been held to be unique to Japan, the author's point is that we must not allow our obsession with "Japaneseness" to stop us from facing up to the human agenda in this Age where we are capable of spoiling the earth." – TSUMURA Takashi (also Kyodo), a well-known practitioner and advocate of Eastern medicine and meditation.

(The reason I did not try to get these or my other books translated is because I tailor my books to the understanding of my imagined audience. Books that would make sense to everyone tend to be trite – or, stylistically speaking, overly plain – for they must be both redundant and general.) For the same reason, *this* book will *not* be translated into Japanese.)

Please visit *Paraverse Press* at **http://www.paraverse.org/** and check out the author, his published books and those to come. The next, **TOPSY-TURVY 1585** – *611 ways Europeans and Japanese differ, as described by Luis Frois, S.J.* will be published June 21, 2004, after which we will concentrate on the writer-publisher's main interest, haiku, for the time being. – rdg

The suggested retail price for ***Orientalism & Occidentalism*** is **$12.** Order information is at **http://www.paraverse.org**. If you like the book please publicize it, for we have no connections.

Printed in the United States
25261LVS00002B/157-158